gta papers 5

SOCIAL DISTANCE

Adam Jasper (ed.)

gta Verlag

Introduction: The Width of a Desk
Adam Jasper

Adam Jasper is a postdoctoral researcher at the Institute for the History and Theory of Architecture (gta), ETH Zurich.

It's a set-up cartoonists know well: a doctor sitting at an enormous desk (as much an attribute of the profession as coat and stethoscope), on the verge of delivering unwelcome news. The doctor's desk is drawn to appear imposing and wide. In cartoons, the width of a desk figures as a metaphor for the power of the medical profession, the social distance between omniscient doctor and the fragile patient. The joke only resonates because doctors' desks actually often are unusually wide. The wide desk helps prevent inadvertent contact between doctor and patient, thereby offering both of them a measure of protection against contagion. The doctor's desk grants social distance in a double sense: as a symbolic distance as well as a quite literal physical distance.

The historian's desk is wide but perhaps not so imposing. *gta papers* is dedicated to questions of architectural history and historiography, but this issue is a response to "the current situation"—the novel coronavirus pandemic—in recognition of the irreducibly historical disjunct that it represents. When we began gathering material for it in early 2020, one of the concerns that we had was that the crisis might be over, and half-forgotten, by the time the ink was dry. Sadly, this appears not to be the case.

What we sought, in putting together this volume, was a variety of approaches to pandemics, an alternative to enforced passivity in the face of phenomena that seemed to lurch at us out of a distant collective past. We knew that orienting ourselves via the micro-organisms would not help us much. In his 1967 essay on eighteenth-century nosology, Jean-Pierre Peter wrote of the difficulty in even naming diseases. [1] Not only do names vary from place to place and time to time but the categorization of diseases shifts depending on the ascendant medical approach. Diseases have been classified on the basis of symptoms, anatomical theories, etiology, climate, microbiology and more lately, genetic sequencing. A term as frequent in the literature as tuberculosis might cover a host of illnesses that we would now think of as wholly unrelated. To make matters more confusing, the diseases themselves change, both biologically, and, in the physical responses that they evoke. Even within a single society, the impact of a disease, its virulance and gravity and the response that it evokes, varies between social classes, races, and age groups. The study of nosology alone therefore reveals that disease and health cannot be captured solely in biological terms but must be approached through their cultural and political dimensions as well. So it has been with coronavirus, COVID-19, or SARS-CoV-2—terms that we read as synonyms but whose connotations vary.

1 Jeanne-Pierre Peter, "Disease and the Sick at the End of the Eighteenth Century," in Robert Forster and Orest Ranum, eds., *Biology of Man in History: Selections from the Annales, Économies, Sociétes, Civilisations* (Baltimore: Johns Hopkins University Press, 1975), 81–124, here 95–96.

This issue of *gta papers* therefore should not, and cannot, be read as a diagnosis of a calamity that is far from over. Rather, we gather disparate approaches that may help us to orient ourselves and our research methods. From the Plague Column of Vienna, better understood as a kind of votive offering than as a public sculpture, we leap centuries to the invention of the rapid sand filter, a technology for water filtration without which the explosive growth in urban populations would not have been possible prior to the invention of antibiotics. We study cordon systems from the Austro-Hungarian Empire and the city walls of seventeenth century London. We move from the early modern villa to the murals of Mexico City, from contemporary hospitals to nineteenth-century bedrooms. Our scales shift from isolation on household balconies to the attempted isolation of nation states, from mammalian placenta to plastic bubbles. Finally, this issue closes with a visit to the recent past, with reflections upon the first, vicious visitation upon New York City of what we, at the time of writing, still call "the current situation."

It is important to add, in this short introduction, a note of thanks to the community that made this oversized issue of *gta papers* possible. Even under normal circumstances, scholars exist as a kind of diaspora, scattered in institutions of research and education around the world. In the last year, however, that isolation has often been total. The great generosity with which our call for papers was met is proof of the deep intrinsic motivation of all of our contributors. International meetings were held between kitchen tables and guest bedrooms hastily converted into offices. The authors, designers, and editors exchanged files without ever meeting. In the face of locked offices, closed archives, and in some cases, personal tragedy, they continued to work, and—at the time of writing—continue to work via improvised means. Seen in this context, the care required in preparing such an issue takes on a new meaning—not as escapism, but as an expression of respect for the endurance of medical professionals and volunteers.

Burnacini's Cloud
Markus Wörgötter

The Plague Column in Vienna — the Pestsäule — is dedicated to the Holy Trinity. Completed in 1693, it is allegedly the monument to an answered prayer. [1] The supplicant of this particular prayer, Holy Roman Emperor Leopold I, was not in Vienna at the time of his petition, however. The emperor and his court had left the city in July 1679 when the epidemic surged and chaos erupted. In Vienna, the plague claimed at least twelve thousand lives within the first few months, and the ruler, powerless in the face of an enigmatic and inexorable calamity, invoked the grace of God as a last resort. The answering of Leopold's prayer was as incomprehensible as the plague itself.

Can one find encrypted in the Plague Column analogies between the miraculous nature of salvation and the mysterious nature of infection? Until the second half of the nineteenth century, the chief mode of transmission was believed to be the miasmas that were emitted by decomposing bodies and spread invisibly by the wind, known as *Pesthauch* (plague breath). However, deadly outbreaks of plague followed all too closely the panicked emperor's movements, spreading from Vienna to the Kahlenberg, Heiligenkreuz, Mariazell, Prague, Brandýs, Pardubice, Kladruby, and Linz. Little did Leopold know that he brought the plague with him in his luggage.

The itinerary of the emperor's flight outlined the territorial map of Habsburg absolutism, which

opposed the declining Holy Roman Empire with a new Austro-Hungarian-Bohemian ruling entity that legitimized itself through the concept of the Trinity of the Catholic God. In the 1680s, Johann Bernhard Fischer von Erlach designed the Plague Column based on the iconographic program of the Jesuit

Franciscus Menegatti. Fischer von Erlach ingeniously transferred the principle of the Trinity from Heaven to Earth: not only is the Christian God tripartite but also the Habsburg Empire. The Trinity is repetitively depicted on all parts of the monument: a three-sided pedestal bears a three-sided obelisk, three bronze prayer scrolls, three coats of arms of the crown lands, and three sets of four-stone reliefs. The camouflage for this profanation of transcendence is provided by a fantastic cloud structure, for the realization of which Lodovico Ottavio Burnacini, a theatrical architect and master of stage design, was employed. As a theater architect, Burnacini had achieved fame for his spectacular stage designs. In 1668, for Antonio Cesti's opera *Il pomo d'oro*, he developed entire cloud structures in which actors dressed as gods floated down suspended from ropes, and he created room-filling cloud monsters with gaping mouths, inside whose maws entire landscapes and panoramas of burning cities appeared.

Burnacini's contribution was primarily concerned with the transmission of Grace, with media in both the literal and symbolic sense. Spatially, Fischer von Erlach's three-part division of the column was arranged vertically: at the bottom the pedestal; in the middle the cloud; at the top the glittering, gilded representation of the Trinity. Temporally, the emperor's prayer, "ascending like incense," makes its way upward via the cloud. [2] In the opposite direction, Divine Grace radiates down and—so history would have it—ends the epidemic. Burnacini's cloudscape, however, has so far received little attention in the literature, which is primarily concerned with the symbolism of the pedestal. Such clouds have their origin in the "intermedium" of baroque theater. While the actors occupied the expanse of the stage in its width and depth, the intermedium used the vertical. During scene changes in performances, this space was handed over to the wild ideas and mechanical effects of the scenographer. Was not the plague also, at least metaphorically, a scene change—an interruption of the great theater of the world—and, at the same time, as Michel Foucault argued, an experimental laboratory for disciplinary power? "It is a segmented, immobile, frozen space. Each individual is fixed in his place. And, if he moves, he does so at the risk of his life, contagion or punishment." [3]

The carved form of Burnacini's cloud famously metastasizes into an enormous mass teeming with bodies. It towers unsteadily above the symbol-laden pedestal and almost engulfs Fischer von Erlach's obelisk. The architect's division of the spheres assigns the emperor his place on this side of the line between Heaven and Earth. The Habsburg, with all the insignia of his absolute power, knells—quite unlike his ancestor Charles V, who in Titian's 1554-painting *La Gloria* is depicted in penitential robes and surrounded by squadrons of angels—in almost intimate proximity to the Holy Trinity. A first draft by Burnacini shows Leopold, like Charles V, integrated into the salvation event, but it was never realized.

The division between Heaven and Earth in the final execution emphasizes the autonomy of the column of cloud, evoking associations that reach beyond the orthodox interpretation of the baroque column. Stanislaw Lem, in his legendary 1968 science fiction novel *Solaris*, describes similarly strange entities called mimoids. They are products of the *res cogitans* of the ocean of an alien planet. This plasma ocean, "a sort of gigantic entity, a fluid cell, unique and monstrous," [4] is capable of producing a gelatinous substance that solidifies into recogniz-able shapes that slowly disintegrate again. The logic and sense of these formations is inaccessible to human reason; the intelligence presumed behind them appears indifferent to the terrestrial visitors. Lem's description of the abortive birth of a mimoid in an alien ocean — "the observer now becomes a spectator at what looks like a fight to the death, as massed ranks of waves converge from all directions like contorted, fleshy mouths which snap greedily around the tattered, fluttering leaf, then plunge into the depths. As each ring of waves breaks and sinks, the fall of this mass of hundreds of thousands of tons is accompanied for an instant by a viscous rumbling, an immense thunderclap" [5] — is nothing but a grotesque fantasy in the spirit of the literary scholarMikhail Bakhtin, who conceives of the gro-tesque body as a colossus that exceeds the possi-bilities of individuals:

"it swallows and generates, gives and takes. Such a body, composed of fertile depths and procrea-tive convexities is never clearly differentiated from the world but is transferred, merged, and fused with it. ... It acquires cosmic dimensions while the cos-mos acquires a bodily nature." [6]

My imposed reading of Burnacini's cloud as a grotesque body frees it of its servitude as a medium. The cherubs' bellies, fat limbs, and chubby faces belong to the same substance as the shimmering gray cloud substrate from which they wriggle, and with which they are simultaneously fused. Unlike Titian's *La Gloria*, where the transition between countless angel heads and celestial architecture is fluid and where radiant clouds and putti merge into one another, the Plague Column's cloud's optical effect, which conveys the density of an aerosol frozen into stone, is based on fleeting, often ghostly phenomena caused by the incidental light. The intended overwhelming of the eye derives its effectiveness from the contradiction between the expectation of translucence, the reality of opacity, and the fragmentation of appearances, as Wölfflin explains: "the eye always remains in a certain restlessness in the face of the incomprehensible." [7]

The numerous drawings handed down to us from Burnacini prove that he was considered a master of the grotesque. Perhaps it was also his affinity with vulgar physical theater that was seamlessly combined on the seventeenth-century stage with an elevated style of declamatory rhetoric. In the structure of the Plague Column on the Graben, the affectively overloaded but symbolically undetermined, grotesque body becomes a point of reference for the question raised at the beginning regarding the place of convergence of different forces.

Bakhtin's treatise, written during Stalin's Great Terror and only published in 1965, celebrates the grotesque body as an anarchic symbol for overcoming eschatological fear experienced in the face of human catastrophes, which at the time of the late

Renaissance clearly included the plague. The humorous culture of the common people triumphed over cosmic fear by designing a body that, according to Bakhtin, was itself wrought from the flesh of the cosmos, and understood the death of the individual as part of a great renewal. Grotesque travesties and the speech of the common people sharpen awareness, for "natural catastrophes, like other catastrophes, usually also awaken historical criticism and lead to a revision of all dogmatic positions." [8]

Markus Wörgötter is an artist and independent curator.

1 Gerolf Coudenhove, *Die Wiener Pestsäule: Versuch einer Deutung* (Vienna: Herold, 1958), 12.

2 Coudenhove, *Die Wiener Pestsäule*, 15.

3 Michel Foucault, *Discipline and Punish: The Birth of the Prison*, trans. Alan Sheridan (New York: Vintage Books, 1977), 195.

4 Stanislaw Lem, *Solaris*, trans. Joanna Kilmartin and Steve Cox (London: Arrow, 1973), 26.

5 Lem, *Solaris*, 118.

6 Mikhail Bakhtin, *Rabelais and His World*, trans. Hélène Iswolsky (Bloomington: Indiana University Press, 1984 [1968]), 339.

7 "Das Auge bleibt angesichts des Unfassbaren immer in einer gewissen Unruhe." Heinrich Wölfflin, *Renaissance und Barock* (Basel: Koehler & Amelang, 1986 [1888]), 70–71. Note that the Kathrin Simon translation of this sentence runs, "in the face of this intangibility the eye remains perpetually in a state of unrest." Heinrich Wölfflin, *Renaissance and Baroque*, trans. Kathrin Simon (London: Collins, 1964), 64.

8 Bakhtin, *Rabelais and His World*, 340.

fig.1 The Pestsäule
Source: Markus Wörgötter (2021)

fig.2 Matthäus Küsel, after Lodovico Ottavio Burnacini, *Höllenschlund* (Hell Mouth) from Act II, Scene 6 of the opera *Il pomo d'oro* (1668). Copperplate 29.2 × 43 cm
Source: Vienna, Theatermuseum, Inv.-Nr. GS GFeS3330 ©2021 KHM-Museumsverband

The Prophylactic Landscape: Sand and Typhoid on the Merrimack River
Laila Seewang

Prologue: Sand

Laila Seewang is Assistant Professor in Architecture at Portland State University.

1 George Johnson, "Rapid Sand Filtration," *Journal of the New England Water Works Association* 31 (1917), 390–473, here 390. Johnson continues, "from its very inception it established its popularity over all other hitherto attempted methods of purifying water, and has steadfastly held that position throughout the thirty-two years which have since elapsed." He quotes statistics that in 1890, the death rate from typhoid was forty-eight per hundred thousand, and in 1917, thirteen per hundred thousand, and attributes this change almost entirely to water filtration of municipal supplies (391–92).

fig.1 The patented Warren rapid sand filter Source: Allen Hazen, *The Filtration of Public Water-Supplies* (New York: Wiley, 1910), 176

2 By the turn of the century, Berlin had implemented the largest network of sand filters in the world to process the entire city's waste and had a municipal water supply system based on the extraction of ground-water passing through the naturally occurring sandy soil. But in 1885, only a handful of US cities had any kind of filtration at all—slow or rapid.

3 Johnson, "Rapid Sand Filtration," 395.

"The first municipal water filter of the rapid sand type was built at Somerville, NJ, and thus began its wonderful history." 1 By 1917 the rapid sand filter was the standard defense against typhoid epidemics in the United States. fig.1 The intrinsic qualities of sand provide a plausible explanation for its success. Sand naturally filters impurities out of polluted water by trapping foreign particles between granules. Sand filters rely on a biofilm that develops on top of the sand to trap inorganic material and adsorb soluble organic particles. The main variable is the size of the grains of sand, which in turn determines the speed of water filtration. The larger the spaces between granules, the faster the water passes through, the result being that more impurities evade adhesion by the biofilm. By 1885, when the Somerville filter began operating, what would soon become known as "slow" sand filters had been operating for over half a century in Europe, as part of the new municipal water and sewage networks constructed to combat cholera. 2 In the United States, patented rapid filters developed to deliver purified water for manufacturing purposes—powering water and steam engines and processes such as dying or bleaching. Using larger sand and processing water up to forty times as fast as a slow filter meant that filter beds could be smaller, reducing the land requirements that made the European systems so costly. 3

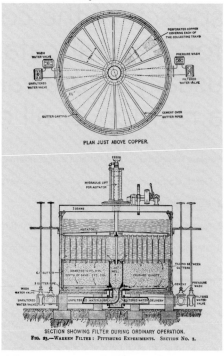

PLAN JUST ABOVE COPPER.

SECTION SHOWING FILTER DURING ORDINARY OPERATION.
FIG. 23.—WARREN FILTER: PITTSBURG EXPERIMENTS. SECTION NO. 1.

In 1917, the rapid sand filter was lauded as an object of technology, ensuring public health in the face of large-scale urban growth—indeed, even making it possible. But it was less clear in 1885 that this would be the case. To understand its significance, it is illuminating to consider the sand filter as the end result of a large design project that assembled a network of public health officers, scientists, mill companies, municipal governments, and typhoid bacteria—to ask how the project was synthesized into this specific form. From this perspective, the development of the rapid sand filter becomes a design process that pitched a clear motivation against an uncoordinated set of methods.

Inland Waters

As the United States economy transitioned from seafaring mercantilism to inland manufacturing, settlements along rivers increased in both number and density. **4** The mill towns established along Merrimack River in the nineteenth century best exemplify this post-Revolutionary landscape. **figs. 2 and 3** In 1828, the Boston Associates, a group of merchants-turned-industrialists, established Lowell, Massachusetts, as an industrial town, scaling up the textile mill technology from Manchester, England, to include both spinning and manufacturing. **5** By the 1850s the Merrimack River,

with its dams and canals, was the pre-coal engine that drove US textile manufacturing. Lawrence, downstream from Lowell, began in 1845 as a speculative follow-up project. The undertaking paired the construction of the United States' largest dam with the leasing of plots to mills driven by mechanical hydraulic power. Almost one hundred thousand people were crammed into the valley, producing a vast array of commodities: not only textiles but also paper, timber, leather, combs, tools, pianos, buttons, cigars, and mattresses. **6**

Lowell and Lawrence were planned as healthy working towns, with attention paid to boarding houses for female workers, churches, and schools. But water was perceived primarily as a source of power for factories, not human consumption, and the

4 Robert Dalzell details this transition from mercantilism to manufacturing in *The Enterprising Elite: The Boston Associates and the World They Made* (Cambridge, MA: Harvard University Press, 1987), 7–12. Sven Beckert describes this moment as a transition from war capitalism to industrial capitalism in *Empire of Cotton: A Global History* (New York: Penguin Vintage, 2015 [2014]), 29–55. The essay at hand is concerned with the geographical and technical changes in urban relationships with water associated with this moment.

fig. 2 The Merrimack Manufacturing Company (also known as Merrimack Mills) in Lowell, Massachusetts, ca. 1850 Photographer: unknown/Source: Lowell Historical Society

5 Lowell was named after Francis Cabot Lowell (1775–1817) of the Boston Associates, who traveled to England and Scotland in 1810 to learn about cotton textile manufacturing, primarily the power loom which, at that point, was heavily guarded technology. While cotton spinning was established in the United States as early as 1790, manufacturing with a power loom was still a British industry. Dalzell, *Enterprising Elite*, 5–6.

6 Theodore Steinberg, *Nature Incorporated: Industrialization and the Waters of New England* (Cambridge: Cambridge University Press, 1991), 205.

fig. 3 The Merrimack River at Lowell, Massachusetts, ca. 1900–1910 Photographer: unknown/Source: Library of Congress Prints and Photographs Division Washington, DC, reproduction number LC-D4–34904

towns produced typical environmental problems; unlike cities on the coast that could flush waste out to sea, the waste generated by inland mill cities had nowhere else to go but into the same river from which drinking water was extracted. Lowell and Lawrence were consistently at the top of the list for typhoid-related deaths in Massachusetts. Combined, the towns had a quarter of the population of Boston, yet also a significantly higher mortality rate: "These two cities had sixty-nine more deaths from this disease (in the twelve months) than the city of Boston with four times the population." [7] The mill towns were typhoid ground zero.

Ellen Swallow Richards (1842–1911), a scientist based at the then-newly established Massachusetts Institute of Technology, would become deeply involved in the design project. She was the first woman admitted to the institute and indefatigably championed a vision of environmental and social reform through science. She articulated the need for strategies to protect American society from invisible enemies that drew on the language of the frontier:

"Only through a belief strong enough to ride over unbelief and inertia, a belief in the value of science for personal life strong enough to make a wise choice possible, can the will to obtain a better environment be developed ... Today, belief is much more difficult than ever before because the dangers are unseen and insidious, and our enemies do not generally make an appeal through the senses of sight and hearing. But the dangers to modern life are no less than in the days of the pioneers, when a stockade was built as a defense from the Indians. We have no standards for safety. Our enemies are no longer Indians and wild animals. Those were the days of big things. Today is the day of the infinitely little. To see our cruelest enemies, we must use the microscope. Of all our dangers, that of uncleanness leads — uncleanness of food and water and air." [8]

If public health had been a religious matter governed by charity in the early part of the century, it became an economic strategy during industrialization. [9] The first committee on public health in Massachusetts convened in 1849, and the resulting report was described by their successors, over half a century later, with a touch of the characteristic boosterism of US rhetoric of the time, as "the best public document ever written in Massachusetts, and one of the great documents of the world." [10] The enthusiasm of the language speaks more of the progressive reputation that the Massachusetts Board of Health would later acquire but obscures the slowness of that progress. People — human density, poor living conditions, and individual morality — were seen as the site for intervention, rather than the environment at large.

7 Hiram Mills, "Typhoid Fever in Relation to Water Supplies," *Twenty-Second Annual Report of the State Board of Health of Massachusetts* (Boston, MA: Wright & Potter, 1891), 525–47, here 528.

8 Ellen Richards, *Euthenics: The Science of Controllable Environment. A Plea for Better Conditions as a First Step Toward Higher Human Efficiency* (Boston, MA: Whitcomb and Barrows, 1910), 28.

9 Dorothy Porter, *Health, Civilization and the State: A History of Public Health from Ancient to Modern Times* (New York: Routledge, 1999), 46–61, 109, and see 148-155 on the development specific to the United States in this period; Barbara Gutman Rosenkrantz, *Public Health and the State: Changing Views in Massachusetts, 1842–1936* (Cambridge, MA: Harvard University Press, 1972), 113–14.

10 Massachusetts Department of Public Health, *The State Board of Massachusetts: A Brief History of its Organization and Its Work* (Boston, MA: Wright & Potter, 1912), 7. In 1930, Massachusetts's key role in the development of US public health policy was still legendary. One article closes with the statement, "it may truly be said that Massachusetts was the cradle of public-health engineering." Harrison P. Eddy, "Massachusetts: The Cradle of Public-Health Engineering," *Sewage Works Journal* 2, no. 3 (July, 1930), 403.

It was not until 1869 that a Board of Health was established and, reflecting the prevailing conception of health as a moral and philanthropic concern, within the decade it had been merged to become the Department of Health, Lunacy, and Charity. It was not until 1886 that the Massachusetts Board of Health was reorganized as an independent body under the guidance, for the first time, of a physician, signaling "the substitution of scientific for ethical objectives." [11] The new board was charged with advising "towns, corporations and individuals in regard to the most appropriate source of supply for their drinking water and the best method of assuring the purity thereof and disposing of their sewage." [12] In addition, it embarked upon two investigative projects: a map and an experimental station, both closely involving Ellen Swallow Richards.

The board contracted the laboratory for sanitary science at the Massachusetts Institute of Technology, the first in the world, to conduct a two-year sanitary survey of the Commonwealth's waters, performing chemical analysis on each source. Richards was in charge of the work, under the direction of Dr. Thomas Drown, and spent two years supervising the collection and analysis of approximately forty thousand water samples from across the state. [13] The results were compiled as a map, the Normal Chlorine Map, for the state of Massachusetts—a project that would later be replicated by other states. fig. 4 The map was a stock-take of the health of water resources that fell within the state's jurisdiction. The map

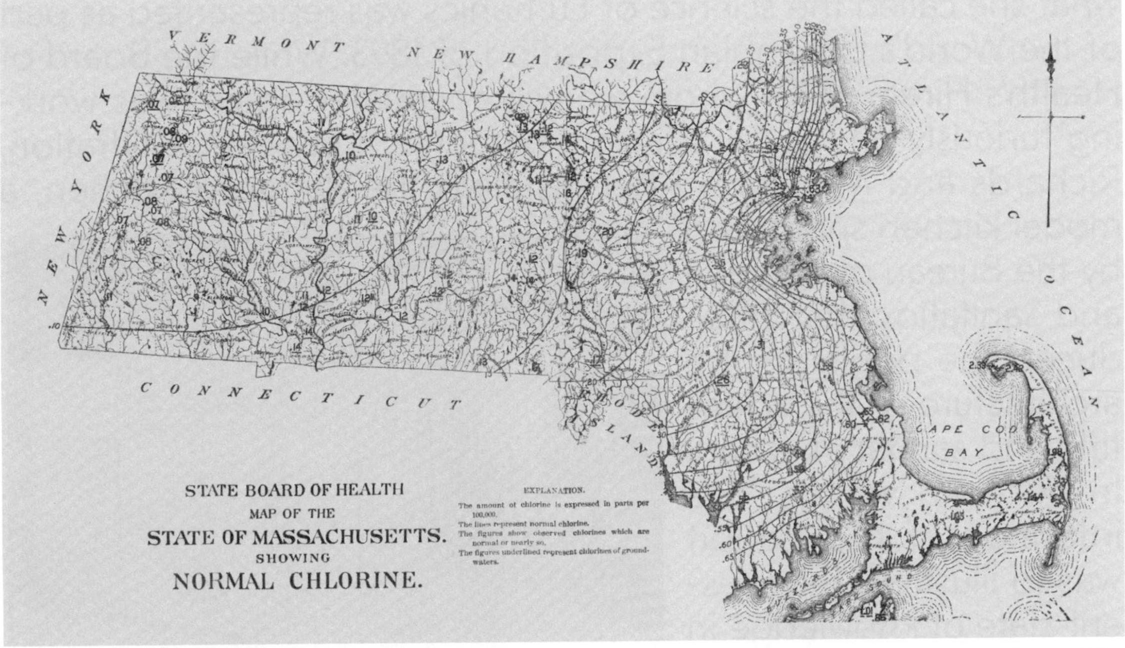

11 Rosenkrantz, Public Health and the State, 178.

12 "1886 Chap. 0274. An Act to Protect the Purity of Inland Waters," Special acts and resolves passed by the General Court of Massachusetts (Boston: Secretary of the Commonwealth, 1886).

13 The findings were published in the Twenty-Second Annual Report of the Massachusetts Board of Health (Boston, MA: Wright & Potter, 1891). The State of Massachusetts is still officially recognized as a commonwealth, but for the sake of clarity, "state" will be used for the remainder of this essay.

STATE BOARD OF HEALTH
MAP OF THE
STATE OF MASSACHUSETTS.
SHOWING
NORMAL CHLORINE.

EXPLANATION.
The amount of chlorine is expressed in parts per 100,000.
The lines represent normal chlorine.
The figures show observed chlorines which are normal or nearly so.
The figures underlined represent chlorines of ground-waters.

fig. 4 The Normal Chlorine Map for Massachusetts Source: Insert in Ellen Richards and Alpheus Woodman, Air, Water and Food from a Sanitary Standpoint (New York: Wiley, 1909), 60—61 [no page or plate number, bound insert]

interpreted Richards' results as a territory of aqueous risk, with isochlors, or lines of equal chlorine content in water bodies, covering the state. Any water source that contained higher amounts of chlorine than shown on this map indicated human pollution: the extra chlorine came from ingested salts in humans or animals

14 Folded insert, United States Government Planning Office, *United States Congressional Serial* Set 12 (Washington, DC: Government Printing Office, 1905). Background levels of chlorine steadily drop from a high content (due to salty sea breezes) at the coast to a much lower content inland.

fig.5 The Rumford Kitchen at the 1893 World's Columbian Exposition, exterior Source: *Report of the Massachusetts Board of World's Fair Managers* (Boston: Wright & Potter, 1894), 40–41 [no page or plate number, bound insert]

15 Rosenkrantz, *Public Health and the State*, 73

that had been passed through the body but could not be absorbed into the earth and ended up in waterways. ₁₄ Cut off at the state boundary, the map did not aid an understanding of watershed ecology—although Richard's misgivings about this are hinted at in her tentative continuation of some rivers into the void beyond state lines—but rather devised a new way of seeing the territorial background, establishing baselines that could reveal unusual levels of pollution. The map, simplified as it was, established a general field upon which specific causes could be discerned. Whereas during the

RUMFORD KITCHEN.

heyday of the mill towns, workers—especially immigrant laborers—were blamed for epidemics, increasingly "knowledge of specific agents or conditions became identified as the cause of preventable disease ... personal behavior became less important as the determinant of susceptibility." ₁₅ More than a survey, the map offered a conceptual environment that became a precondition for the development of environmental technologies that would intervene in this landscape.

Despite her pioneering research, Richards' other scientific endeavors still emphasized the responsibility of individuals to educate themselves about environmental hazards. Her work on what she called the science of Euthenics was represented as part of the World's Columbian Exposition of 1893. While the Board of Health's Hiram Mills (whom we will encounter again) was working furiously on the fair's failing experiment in sewage filtration, Richards and Mrs. John Abel installed the Rumford Kitchen, a

fig.6 The Rumford Kitchen at the 1893 World's Columbian Exposition, interior (partial) Source: *Report of the Massachusetts Board of World's Fair Managers* (Boston: Wright & Potter, 1894), 44–45 [no page or plate number, bound insert]

16 Ellen Richards, letter to the Massachusetts Board of the World's Fair Managers, December 27, 1893. Massachusetts Board of Managers, World's Fair, *Report of the Massachusetts Board of World's Fair Managers* (Boston, MA: Wright & Potter, 1894), 43.

model kitchen sponsored by the Bureau of Hygiene and Sanitation that introduced the public to the architecture of the scientific and sanitary kitchen. In her own words, "the intention of the exhibit was to illustrate the present state of knowledge in regard to the composition

RUMFORD KITCHEN INTERIOR.—A Second View.

of materials for human food, the means of making these materials most available for nutrition, and the quantity of each necessary for a working ration." ₁₆ Visitors to the kitchen could purchase, for a small fee, a healthy meal based upon one quarter of a day's rations. Accompanying the kitchen were also posters, charts, diagrams, books, and menus that educated the public on proper nutrition.

The exterior of the Rumford Kitchen resembled a homestead, but the interior had been transformed into a teaching laboratory that revealed different aspects of food preparation and consumption. One small area resembled a cramped kitchen sink that, instead of a pile of dishes, contained small glass bottles. Test tubes and pipettes lie in place of a drying rack with clean dishes. The nutritional value of different foods, or "materials," could be assessed on a nearby chart. **figs. 5 and 6** There was nothing intuitive about how the space was to be used in the scientific kitchen; it required, as displayed by the books and lessons occupying the interior, a rigorous re-education in home science. Municipalities might protect the drinking water that entered this space, but it was only with the aid "of scientifically trained women ... brought into service to work in harmony with the engineer who has already accomplished so much" that the same vigilance over the food "materials" that entered this space and the ways in which they were handled could be guaranteed. [17]

Richards transferred chemical science from the environment to the domestic realm in characteristically graphic terms:

"Instead of blaming water supplies, dusty streets, or even contagion by the breath, sanitarians are everywhere putting emphasis upon the actual contact of moist mucus with milk and other food, in preparation or in serving. It is not a supercilious notion to examine tumblers for finger marks, or to object to the habit of wetting the finger with saliva in turning leaves of books. These little unclean acts are the unconscious habits that cling to a person in spite of education from reading." [18]

In 1882 she published *The Chemistry of Cooking and Cleaning: A Manual for Housekeepers*, promoting good nutrition, "pure" foods, proper clothing, physical fitness, and especially sanitation, as efficient practices for environmental management. [19] Her work can thus be seen as an educational campaign urging people to protect their bodies in many small ways from latent environmental danger. But it did so when bacteriology in Europe was already leading to the notion that public health protection had to be offered at a larger scale by the state.

Instead of educating people, the board would need to undertake a massive environmental design project. The second project undertaken by the new board would experiment with implementing water infrastructure at the civic scale that had already been established in Europe. It addressed the third of its charges under the Inland Waters Act: "collecting information

fig. 7 Cropped image of a map of the Lawrence Experiment Station on the old Essex Company land Source: *Atlas of the City of Lawrence* (Springfield, MA: L.J. Richards, 1896), courtesy of the Lawrence History Center

17 Richards, *Euthenics*, 138. "The following pages will deal chiefly with such portions of the subject of Sanitary Chemistry as come directly under individual control, or which require the education of individuals in order to make up the mass of public opinion which shall support the city or state in carrying out sanitary measures ... The Federal Department of Labor has studied workingmen's houses, but living in the house has not been worked up. The housewife has no station to which she may carry her trials, like the experiment stations which have been provided for the farmer." Ellen Richards and Alpheus Woodman, *Air, Water and Food: From a Sanitary Standpoint* (New York: Wiley, 1909), 1.

18 Richards, *Euthenics*, 100.

19 Ellen H. Richards, *The Chemistry of Cooking and Cleaning: A Manual for Housekeepers* (Boston, MA: Estes & Lauriat, 1882)

20 „Water Supply and Sewerage", *Nineteenth Annual Report of the State Board of Health of Massachusetts* (Boston, MA: Wright and Potter, 1888), 2–66, here 66.

fig. 8 Lawrence Experiment Station, exterior, ca. 1900–1910 Source: courtesy of the Lawrence History Center

fig. 9 Lawrence Experiment Station, interior, ca. 1900–1910, Source: courtesy of the Lawrence History Center

21 John Snow's work first identified the risk of contaminated water as a potential source of contagious disease. He began publishing on the topic of cholera and its transmission through water in 1849: John Snow, *On the Mode of Communication of Cholera* (London: John Churchill, 1849). By 1854, he had identified contaminated drinking water, namely the Broad Street Pump, located next to an old cesspit, as the source of London's 1854 epidemic. John Snow, "On the Communication of Cholera by Impure Thames Water," *Medical Times and Gazette* 9 (1854), 365–66.

in regard to experiments ... made upon the purification of sewage." [20] In 1886 it established the Lawrence Experiment Station on Essex Company land, and it is here that Ellen Swallow Richards worked in a collaborative team with not only other chemists but also with a new breed of scientist: bacteriologists. The station was located on a spit of land in the Merrimack River and gradually grew from one shed and a sandpit into a seemingly haphazard collection of uninsulated weatherboard structures surrounding tanks of sand. **figs. 7, 8, and 9**  If brick was the material that defined the architecture of the industrial town, the laboratory sheds that would shape the future of industry were a kind of exercise in timber vernacular, descendants of the pioneer timber shed, the shack, the lumberman's cottage. If the Normal Chlorine Map had dovetailed with the aesthetics of the frontier landscape, the station appropriated its architecture. But now the architecture housed the most advanced sanitary laboratory in the United States. The interiors were highly organized into clear surfaces and a dizzying array of storage options. The spaces were designed around the use of glass containers: jars, test tubes, pipettes, beakers, glasses supported by smaller timber contraptions. The site at large was landscaped into holding tanks, basins, pipes, embankments, and gullies. The pioneer sheds of the station provided the studios in which the prophylactic landscape was designed.

Hiram Mills is the figure who first brought together private industry, public health, and academic science at Lawrence to activate Richard's new chlorinated territory. He had been Chief Engineer at the Essex Company, and later Chairman of the Committee on Water Supply and Sewerage at the Massachusetts Board of Health, and had been set the task of cleaning the water the Essex Company had done so much to pollute. The modest funding Mills acquired was spent on staff: initially, a chemist, a biologist, a bacteriologist, and two assistants, all from the Massachusetts Institute of Technology. By 1886, bacteriology had established itself upon the success of germ theory that was initiated with John Snow's research in London and developed by the work of Louis Pasteur and Robert Koch. [21] Taken together, this work revolutionized how the environment was conceived: environmental threat no longer resided in miasmatic air but in viruses and bacteria that could contaminate water. It was a rapidly advancing science: in 1883 Koch identified the *Vibrio cholerae*, and in 1884 the pathologist Georg Gaffky had confirmed Karl Eberth's discovery of the typhoid bacteria, the *Salmonella enterica enterica, serovar Typhi.*

The research performed by the team at the station aimed to apply science to engineering technologies, and the primary means for doing so was sand. A variety of pollutants, ranging from blood to soap, sugar, and salt, were added to approximately fourteen tanks of sand to measure nitrification — nitrogenous organic matter being a chemical indicator of the presence of bacteria. The success of sand at filtration depended upon careful preparation and regular maintenance. It was first sifted through a series of increasingly fine sieves, then divided into portions by beaker elutriation, weighed, and its range of granule sizes measured, as much as possible, making irregular grains of material statistically regular. Once in service, it needed to be cleaned and replaced regularly to ensure the biofilm's effectiveness. Each grain of sand was subject to scrutiny. Beyond the size of the grain of sand, which was measured along three axes, the team chemist, Allen Hazen, noted that the "amount of open space depends upon the shape and uniformity ... and is independent of their absolute size." [22]

The research was the first of its kind in the United States. But quickly, the research into filtering sewage took a very specific turn. By 1890, new facilities had been built that added a biological laboratory to the existing chemical laboratories. At around the same time, the station turned from studying the chemical components, or molecules, within water as indicators of bacteria to the study of bacteria themselves, as biological species, shaped like "a rod with rounded ends ... and fine hair-like appendages." [23] In order to do this, sand, instead of being asked to filter out pollution in general, would now have to filter out specific bacteria. From today's perspective one cannot help but recognize a kind of irony: situated on one of the most foully abused waterways of the nineteenth-century United States, the work nonetheless would unintentionally begin to recast chemical waste, dyes, and industrial pollution as non-threatening in its hunt for the *Salmonella Typhi* bacteria. But first, people had to find where it originated, how it interacted with its environment, and how it was transmitted.

A fortunate, if tragic, opportunity in the quest to separate industrial pollution from malevolent bacteria presented itself in December when station biologist William Sedgwick traveled to Lowell to identify the cause of a new typhoid outbreak. Citizens in Lowell popularly attributed it to the water supply system, but local experts contested this, since Lawrence, nine miles downstream, also drew its water from the Merrimack and was not at

22 Allen Hazen et al., "Experiments on the Purification of Sewage and Water at the Lawrence Experiment Station: November 1, 1889, to December 31, 1891," *Twenty-Third Annual Report of the State Board of Health of Massachusetts* (Boston, MA: Wright & Potter, 1892), 425–601, here 432.

23 Mills, "Typhoid Fever," 525. Mills continues: "it may not be unreasonable to think of the invisible kingdom of bacteria as consisting of as many species as the visible vegetable kingdom and all of them doing as beneficent work, in the economy of nature, as the trees and plants which we see around us; but there is a small fraction, perhaps comparable with the small number of poisonous plants, which are disease producing."

24 Mills, "Typhoid Fever," 527, 528. The two towns combined had only a quarter of the population of Boston, yet in 1890 had sixty-nine more deaths from typhoid fever.

fig. 10 William Sedgwick's survey shows the cases of typhoid not attributed to the suspected canal water
Source: Plate 2 from William Sedgwick, "On Epidemics of Typhoid Fever in the Cities of Lowell and Lawrence," in *Twenty-Fourth Annual Report of the State Board of Health of Massachusetts* (Boston, MA: Wright & Potter, 1893), 667–704

25 William Sedgwick, "On Recent Epidemics of Typhoid Fever in the Cities of Lowell and Lawrence due to Infected Water Supply, with Observations on Typhoid Fever in Other Cities," in *Twenty-Fourth Annual Report of the State Board of Health of Massachusetts* (Boston, MA: Wright & Potter, 1893), 667–704, here 681. For a description of Snow's mapping process, see Steven Johnson, *The Ghost Map: The Story of London's Most Terrifying Epidemic — and How it Changed Science, Cities, and the Modern World* (New York: Riverside Books, 2006), 193–213.

26 Sedgwick, "On Recent Epidemics," 679. On January 10, 1891, Mills wrote of the findings to the Mayor of Lawrence, and stated that they should immediately inform residents to boil water before drinking. On April 10, 1891, Sedgwick presented a report to the city's water board, informing them of his findings. William Sedgwick, *A Report upon the Sanitary Condition of the Water Supply of Lowell, Mass.* (Lowell: Vox Populi, 1891).

27 Mills, "Typhoid Fever," 525.

that time experiencing an epidemic. Both towns had municipal water systems that alleviated residents' reliance upon independent wells and potentially polluted groundwater reserves, which since mid-century had been identified as a risk. **24** Given that only Lowell, and not Lawrence, was experiencing the epidemic when Sedgwick was called to investigate, local authorities favored the explanation of contaminated milk. Just as Snow had done before him, Sedgwick designed a survey and went house to house conducting interviews. Plotting personal testimony onto maps, he was able,

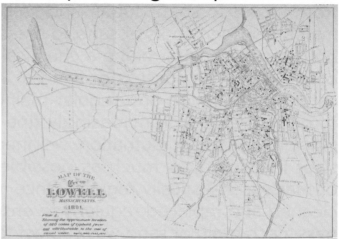

geographically and chronologically, to trace the epidemic back to a "menacingly-positioned privy" in North Chelmsford. **25** **figs. 10 and 11** Beginning with two mild cases in August — teenage girls working in a wool-scouring mill — the pandemic began when Case IV, as Sedgwick described him, contracted typhoid at the iron foundry and then spent a full day in a privy hovering over the Stoney Brook, "a small and often very foul stream emptying into the Merrimack," before dying shortly afterwards. **26** Like a detective, Sedgwick tracked down the bacteria's furtive movements, which revealed a remarkable resilience: the sturdy typhoid bacteria had traveled from Stoney Brook to the Lowell waterworks intake, through Lowell's water system, into its sewer system, nine miles down the river to Lawrence's waterworks intake, and finally made its way to the inhabitants of Lawrence. It was known that Lowell's sewers emptied, unfiltered, into the river only nine miles upstream from Lawrence's waterworks intake, but the delay was what had foiled experts: when Sedgwick arrived in Lowell, the bacteria was still on its way to Lawrence in the icy water and would contaminate that city's water supply only three weeks later.

Mills reported in 1891 that the station's main task regarding typhoid was to study "how it can get into the [environmental] system and under what conditions it can live outside of the human body." **27** Between 1890 and 1891, experiments were made by surrounding a bottle of typhoid-laden water with ice to see how long the bacteria, which bred at human body temperature, would survive in freezing temperatures. Other tests included injecting potatoes and milk with the bacteria and numerous sewage filtration experiments with sand aided by a variety of chemicals. By 1893, the station was using more than fifty filtration tanks to track the bacteria through sand. They were able to show how sand could function as a suitable filter for sewage before it entered a watercourse by removing at least 99.99 percent of harmful bacteria. [28] In 1892, Hazen, writing on behalf of Mills, summarized the refinement in purpose:

28 Hazen et al., "Experiments," 601.

"Our attention has been specially directed toward the bacteria. In sewage purification the removal of the organic matters capable of putrefaction is often of the greatest importance; but in the filtration of sewage-polluted water — water capable of causing disease — the removal of germs of disease is the all-important point." [29]

29 Hazen et al., "Experiments" 601.

This impacted the parameters that had been guiding the selectionof sand at the station.

Previously, experiments with sand at the station had been concerned with removing organic matter from sewage. The typhoid

fig. 11 The site where the 1890–1891 Lowell and Lawrence typhoid epidemic began Source: Figure B from William Sedgwick, "On Epidemics of Typhoid Fever in the Cities of Lowell and Lawrence," in *Twenty-Fourth Annual Report of the State Board of Health of Massachusetts* (Boston, MA: Wright & Potter, 1893), 667–704, plate inserted between 678 and 679

Fig. B. Privy of Foundry, overhanging Stony Brook, North Chelmsford, a Feeder of the Water Supply of Lowell. Point of Infection by T. L., (Case No. IV.)

bacteria experiments led scientists at the station now to tailor the porosity of the sand filter specifically to this new biological enemy. It certainly seems as though the changing demands placed on sand paralleled a shift in responsibility from chemists to biologists, specifically bacteriologists. More concretely, the work also began to suggest a different field for prophylaxis than Richard's emphasis on "little unclean acts." [30]

30 Richards, *Euthenics*, 100.

Despite the diagnostic success, there were few instruments available for forcing a reduction in water pollution at its source. All the towns along the Merrimack, after lobbying from the Boston Associates' related companies, had been grandfathered out of compliance with the water pollution laws of 1876, making the laws useless where they were most needed. It is hard to know if legislative roadblocks were the cause, but soon after the epidemic on the Merrimack between 1890 and 1891, the station turned its attention from technology for filtering sewage outflows to filters for drinking water: that is, for filtering inflow. In 1891, the station hired Sedgwick's student, George Fuller, to transfer sand filter technology to drinking water. He had already spent a year in Germany, working with engineers at the Berlin waterworks learning about slow sand filtration for drinking water. In 1893, instead of installing a sand filter for Lowell's sewer system, a slow sand filter was installed for the municipal water supply in Lawrence. City residents were now protected from typhoid, even if the source of their jobs had moved on to other places, and the river remained polluted.

Epilogue: From Filtration to Purification

In 1894, George Fuller was called to Louisville, on the Ohio River, to test seven different mechanical filters for the drinking water supply of the city. There, he turned his attention to the patents of private companies who provided water filtration for industrial, not municipal, purposes: a technology created for factories and mills, not for human consumption. None of the models were suitable. These filters utilized mechanical aids to clean the sand for the filters, eliminating the intensive manual labor of cleaning slow sand filters. But because of the large gaps between sand, many particles evaded capture. The sand for the American filter began to acquire very specific demands. The search for the "right" sand—the right grain size in particular—led to sand being brought from faraway Roslyn and Oyster Bay on Long Island, New York, and Hanover, New Jersey. 31 But despite the years of research that had gone into sand, ultimately what Fuller introduced to the filtration process was coagulation. Coagulation, the grouping together of smaller particles into particles large enough to be caught by the sand filter, was achieved by adding ammonia sulfate to water before it reached the filter. It was considered particularly necessary in Midwestern cities located on heavily sedimented rivers. By increasing the amount of sediment collected in filtration, coagulation increased the amount of potentially dangerous bacteria captured too, but it was largely an aesthetic requirement. Adding chemicals to drinking water meant that Fuller no longer felt he could call the end product filtered water but purified water. Somerville, New Jersey, was listed as the first implementation of a patented Hyatt mechanical filter in 1882, coupled three years later with coagulation—the indirect product of Fuller's research.

31 "It was specified that the filtering sand, which is 30ins. in thickness, should have an effective size within the limits of 0.35 to 0.42 millimeters, with a uniformity coefficient of not more than 1.50. Not more than 1 percent, by weight, of the sand was allowed to be finer than 0.25 millimeters, and not more than 0.2 percent finer than 0.20 millimeters. Considerable difficulty was experienced in getting suitable sand. The two sand dealers with whom the contract was placed by the Filtration Company failed to deliver the material, and the commencement of operations was delayed fully one month, during which time the joint efforts of all concerned were devoted to securing suitable sand from any available source. Part of the sand came from near Oyster Bay and Rosyln on Long Island, New York, and part from Hanover, New Jersey. The difficulty consisted principally in getting sand from which the fine material was properly eliminated ... Sand screening at the several places was watched by representatives of the Water Company, and Allen Hazen ... in the interests of the Water Company, also advised." George Fuller, "The Filtration Works of the East Jersey Water Company, at Little Falls, New Jersey," *Transactions of the American Society of Civil Engineers* 50 (June 1903), 394–443, here 416.

The first fully operating system to adopt Fuller's recommendations for municipal consumption was installed at Little Falls, New Jersey, in 1902. An area was set aside by the Passaic River for both concrete settling and coagulation tanks where ammonia sulfate from the Pennsylvania Salt Manufacturing Company was added. These tanks could process 1.75 million gallons of raw river water in less than an hour and a half. [32] From here the water passed down to concrete filter tanks containing the sand, which were mechanically agitated using compressed air. Water passed through the sand into a pipe gallery that fed into the city mains.

32 Fuller, "The Filtration Works," 402.

At this time, the effective benefits of rapid filtration with coagulation were still being debated. John Hill, a hydraulic engineer who built three municipal filters for US cities in this period, presented the sole dissenting voice regarding adding chemicals to water supplies in a testimony to the Washington, DC, Board of Health in 1910, stating that "I think I reflect the sentiment of the people of Cincinnati when I say that they are opposed to the use of chemicals in the water supply. That position has been taken by a number of public bodies." [33] Hill showed that any miscalculation in the amounts of chemical added to the water led to serious stomach ailments, none of which had been systematically studied. But his preference for slow filtration in the service of public health was nonetheless defeated on economic grounds, particularly because of the maintenance required to treat the sand.

33 "Statement of John W. Hill," in Charles Moore, ed., *Purification of the Washington Water Supply* (Washington, DC: Government Printing Office, 1903), 72–82, here 77.

Initially, inland waters were still the primary location for the rapid sand filter. In his own testimony at the hearings over Washington, DC's, water, Fuller divided the country into two areas: those whose reasonably clear waterways were based upon glacial drift (such as New England) that could benefit from slow sand filtration without coagulation; and regions, primarily in the South, where clay-based waters in non-glacial geological formations would always contain fine clay particulates requiring chemical treatment. [34] By the time George Johnson wrote his history of the technology in 1917, the United States had committed to it fully. For all the work performed on grains of sand, ammonia turned out to be the catch-all solution for protecting people against infected inland waters. Cincinnati had the largest version, and other major towns to install rapid filters included Columbus, Ohio; Pittsburgh and Harrisburg, Pennsylvania; Little Falls, New Jersey; Washington, DC; and New Orleans, Louisiana. [35] The technology had come to represent the primary method of bacterial defense in urban infrastructure. Instead of eliminating pollution from the environment, then, the rapid sand filter inserted itself as a prophylaxis between the domestic drinking supply and the environment, for which nothing could apparently be done.

34 "Statement of George W. Fuller," in Moore, *Purification*, 40–52, here 41.

35 Johnson, "Rapid Sand Filtration," 401–26. Rapid sand filters based on chemical coagulation were subsequently installed internationally, from Alexandria to Kyoto.

In doing this, it joined the list of inventions that form "the invisible shield, one that has been built, piece by piece, over the last few centuries" resulting in a progress "measured not in events, but nonevents: the smallpox that didn't kill you at age 2; the accidental scrape that didn't give you a lethal bacterial infection; the drinking water that didn't poison you with cholera." [36]

As with any design project, there were of course alternative paths not taken. Berlin's municipality purchased huge tracts of land for slow sand filtering of sewage. Although no longer in use, they now form a green periphery of small farms and parks. New York City has the largest filter-free water system in the United States: in 1997, the city embarked upon a major campaign of at-source pollution reduction for the enormous Catskill-Delaware watershed, with farmers and industries working together to combat pollution before it gets into the water supply system. The Hudson landscape today resembles the pastoral landscape paintings of the Hudson River School's paintings even more than it did in the nineteenth century. By contrast, the sites of the rapid sand filter—Little Falls, New Jersey, the Ohio River, the Passaic—present a kind of post-industrial sublime. The Passaic and the Meadowlands are only two of thousands of designated Superfund sites, where governments have spent millions on removing toxicity from the land after industrial profit has moved elsewhere.

Many cities in the nineteenth century were confronted with the same problem—the battle against epidemics in dense industrial settlements. While Germany, England, and France invested their public health institutions with the authority to implement sanitary measures during epidemics, including mandatory surveys, centralized health and mortality statistics, and quarantines, the peculiarity of the American response was that public health research was a state concern notably innovative in research but notoriously lax in implementation. [37] Limitations to enforcement forced adaptation in the American response: from the rapid sand filter, to the Rumford Kitchen, and the Normal Chlorine Map. Resistance to regulation was part of the "freedom" that settlers, and after them, industries, expected of this wilderness. It was politics, rather than geology, that ultimately determined the failure to treat sewerage at its source. The success of the rapid sand filter was that it enabled a detachment between the problems of environmental pollution and safe drinking water. The rapid sand filter's history was "wonderful," precisely because it facilitated massive urban growth in spite of governments impotent to stop waste being dumped into rivers.

36 Steven Johnson, „How Humanity Gave Itself an Extra Life," New York Times Magazine, April 27, 2021, www.nytimes. com/2021/04/27/magazine/global-life-span. html (accessed May 28, 2021).

37 Federalism meant that States and Commonwealths implemented community health measures independently, but implementation in itself is hardly the correct term. John Duffy, The Sanitarians: A History of American Public Health (Urbana: University of Illinois Press, 1990), 138–39, 163.

On Airs, Waters, and Places: The Construction of a Natural History of Healthcare in Twentieth-Century Greece
Lydia Xynogala

In the early twentieth century a mineral revolution took place in Greece. Healthcare, politics, science, and natural resources became entangled in Greek thermalism—a nationwide "taking the waters." Geological knowledge and attitudes towards healing were coupled with a broader environmental and healthcare movement. During this period minerals found in waters and subsoils were extensively studied and the national territory remapped.

Lydia Xynogala is a doctoral fellow at the Institute for the History and Theory of Architecture (gta), ETH Zurich.

Sites of thermalism were typically located in areas of particular geomorphology, often near sites of mineral extraction of sulfur or magnesite. The state pursued an indirect and sustainable kind of extraction—a soft form of exploitation, so to speak—acquiring minerals through hydrotherapy and positherapy, bathing, and drinking. Private investment followed public money. This momentum was manifest in medical discourse and in the numerous hydrotherapy baths that were built in locations with thermal springs. The entire country was envisioned as an open-air clinic, where waters would treat a wide range of conditions from arthritis to infertility. fig.1 The Greek Ministry of Tourism promoted thermalism abroad through iconic posters, promoting Greece as a synthesis of modernity and antiquity.

The curative properties of springs were not a new discovery, and many of the locations for bathing had been known since antiquity. [1] In this particular historical context, however, the notions of healing, therapy, and the care of *demos* became inseparable from cultural, political, and social shifts in Greece. The prior existence of *hammams* (Turkish baths), however, was neglected in this narrative, part of a broader effort to erase Ottoman cultural traces in the newly established Greek nation. Ancient practices and pagan narratives became metaphors which were deployed in the service of geopolitical aspirations; architecture was the medium through which they unfolded.

[1] Luigia Melillo, "Thermalism in Ancient World," *Medicina nei secoli arte e scienza* 7, no. 3 (1995), 461–83.

Let us begin with a single pair of islands. In the battle of the giants, during the pursuit of the giant Polyvotis, Zeus ordered Poseidon to snatch a part of the island of Kos with his trident. The giant was buried under the rock Poseidon speared, which became known as the island of Nisyros. The periodic volcanic vibrations on the island were believed to be the titan's continuous chest movements as he laid buried underground. Both Strabo's *Geography* and Pliny's *Natural History* [2] believed the island to be a fragment of Kos. Nisyros, a round island with a volcano at its center, is pungent with the sulfuric gas often released through fumaroles. Hot air comes out of vents throughout the island,

[2] *The Geography of Strabo,* trans. W. Falconer (London: Henry G. Bohn, 1854–1857), 10.5 §17, 213; *Pliny's Natural History in Thirty-Seven Books,* trans. Philemon Holland (London: George Barclay, 1847–1848), 5.36, 91.

fig.1 Poster advertising
the baths of Aidipsos
with the mythical figure
of Hercules bathing in
the waters to regain
strength
Source: Societe D'
Exploitation Vlachanis
Petropoulos

emerging from nooks in its mountainous villages and even inside homes. Earth, water, air, and fire—the elements that dominated the natural sciences for centuries as the "roots of all things"—are found side by side in the island's environment. **3**

Located in the eastern Mediterranean, Nisyros is part of the Dodecanese group of islands near the Turkish shore. **4** Kos, a larger nearby island, is not volcanic but shares geologic features with its neighbor: *solfatara* (fumarole) fields and hot springs. Both islands have a long-standing healing culture spanning ancient and recent history. In antiquity, Kos was known for its Asclepeion sanctuary; its mineral springs were used in both ancient and modern times. On the remote island of Nisyros, thermal bath complexes flourished in the first half of the twentieth century, attracting visitors from Greece, Asia Minor, and other coastal cities in the Mediterranean, such as Marseilles, who arrived by steamboats to be cured, many returning yearly. **5**

Both islands claim to be the birthplace of Hippocrates, but Kos holds the official title. **6** Nevertheless, Nisyrians still maintain that Hippocrates was born on their island. Hippocrates became a prominent representative of the Koan medical school, where he practiced according to his belief in the healing powers of nature. His treatments developed from close observation of patients and logical reasoning. Under his tenure, the school fostered a number of medical scholars who contributed to this "new science," **7** a body of knowledge that sought to understand physiology, record symptoms, and document the effect of treatments. "Hippocrates seems to be both the last witness and the most ambiguous representative" of the balance between seeing and knowing in medical experience. **8**

Hippocrates' initial reputation was as the one who saved Athens from an epidemic. When threatened by plague, Pericles invited Hippocrates to Athens to assist with the crisis. Indeed, practicing his medicine from the temple of Apollo, he managed to contain the epidemic and received great recognition for his methods.

As a practice, Hippocratic medicine integrated a holistic approach whereby the patient was treated

3 The classical theory of the elements runs through Plato to Aristotle to Empedocles, and persisted until 1661, when Robert Boyle, in the *The Sceptical Chymist* (London: J. Cadwell, 1661), put an end to the millennia-old philosophy. See, for example, James Longrigg, "The 'Roots of All Things,'" *Isis* 67, no. 3 (1976), 420–38, esp. 420.

4 From Ottoman rule, the island was transferred to Italy in 1911. In 1947, following the end of the Second World War, Nisyros was annexed to Greece.

5 Curative water and volcanic terrains were known to be connected from antiquity. The geological features of the soil gave the water which passed through it its particular qualities and temperature. According to Seneca, Empedocles had already linked hot springs and volcanism, considering the two phenomena as manifestations of the same reality. See Seneca, *Natural Questions*, trans. Harry M. Hine (Chicago: University of Chicago Press, 2010), 3.24 §1, 40.

6 Born around 460 BCE into a family of physicians, Hippocrates developed four basic principles integral to medical practice today: etiology, diagnosis, prognosis, and treatment. Hippocrates' expertise was not solely tied to Kos but was gathered from his many travels around Greece. By observing patients from various geographies, he developed theories linking the environmental qualities of a place to their effect on bodily health.

7 I refer to the ancient Greek word for science, *épistémè*, relative to Foucault's definition as the "strategic apparatus which permits of separating out from among all the statements which are possible those that will be acceptable within, I won't say a scientific theory, but a field of scientificity, and which it is possible to say are true or false. The episteme is the 'apparatus' which makes possible the separation, not of the true from the false, but of what may from what may not be characterized as scientific." Michel Foucault, *Power/Knowledge: Selected Interviews and Other Writings 1972–1977*, trans. Colin Gordon (New York: Pantheon Books, 1980), 194–228, 197.

8 Michel Foucault, *The Birth of the Clinic: An Archaeology of Medical Perception*, trans. Alan Sheridan (New York: Vintage Books, 1994), 56.

as a "psychosomatic whole ... and thus, the Hippocratic doctor treats the specific patient and not the illness." [9] Emphasis at Kos was on the broader psycho-socio-somatic state of the patient rather than on a specific illness (in contrast to the medical tradition on the nearby peninsula of Knidos). The attributes of place and environment played a role in this approach. In his treatise *On Airs, Waters, and Places*, Hippocrates analyzes the beneficial and detrimental effects of different types of winds, orientations, and water sources. [10] He indicates three key factors for investigating medicine properly: seasons of the year, the winds, and the qualities of waters. These factors must be taken into consideration in the founding of cities, for by understanding the environmental features of a place, the physician could then anticipate illnesses that would affect its population. A similar epidemiological approach to climate resurfaced in the late nineteenth century: physicians directly linked various illnesses such as cholera to particular geographic and climatic characteristics. [11]

Besides winds and broader climatic features, Hippocrates wrote extensively on the different types of water found in a region. Thermal waters were for Hippocrates almost as bad as stagnant ones:

"Next to them in badness are those which have their fountains in rocks ... they must necessarily be hard, or come from a soil which produces thermal waters, such as those having iron, copper, silver, gold, sulphur, alum, bitumen, or nitre (soda) in them; for all these are formed by the force of heat. Good waters cannot proceed from such a soil." [12]

Nonetheless, following the principles of the *pharmakon*, he recommended such waters for specific ailments.

Hippocrates rejected superstitious views, prevalent amongst his contemporaries, that illness was caused by evil spirits or vengeful gods—assertion that led to him become commonly referred to as the father of rational medicine. On Kos, however, these antithetical approaches, the traditions of ritual healing and rational Hippocratic practice, were not clearly separated. Their entanglement is manifest in the form of the Asclepeion sanctuary, simultaneously a religious center, hospital, bath complex, and medical school. **fig. 2**

Asclepeions were the healing sanctuaries dedicated to the divinity Asclepios, son of the god Apollo. [13] Their locations were selected with great care: a natural setting with views of hills, forests, and the sea was of utmost importance. Most sanctuaries were close to natural springs. The Asclepeion of Kos was considered to be one of the greatest in the Hellenistic and Roman world. [14] In the sanctuary's architecture, curative water containing iron and

9 Constantinos Trompoukis, Vasilios German, and Matthew E. Falagas, "From the Roots of Parasitology: Hippocrates' First Scientific Observations in Helminthology," *Journal of Parasitology* 93, no. 4 (2007), 970–72, here 970.

10 The Hippocratic Corpus was first printed in a Latin translation in 1525 in Rome, while the first English translation appeared in 1597. Several others followed in French and German during the nineteenth century. These publications, through their balance of healing and observation, were instrumental in the Western foundation of medical practice. For details of the Hippocratic Corpus' reception and interpretation see David Cantor, *Reinventing Hippocrates* (Aldershot: Ashgate, 2001).

11 Amanda Sciampacone, "'Epidemics in a Mist': Medical Climatology and Cholera in Victorian Visual Culture," *Journal of Victorian Culture* 25, no. 4 (August 2020), 492–511.

12 *Hippocrates on Airs, Waters, and Places,* trans. Emile Littré (London: Wyman and Sons, 1881), 3 §35, 27.

13 In mythology, Asclepius, the god of medicine, was surrounded by his healing family. The names of his daughters summarize the various facets and stages of curing an illness, from treatment to good health: Hygeia (hygiene), Panacea (remedy of all disease), Aceso (healing process), Iaso (recuperation), and Aegle (good health).

14 Built after the death of Hippocrates in the mid-fourth century BCE, it consisted of a terraced arrangement of buildings, offering visitors contemplative views amidst a scenic landscape. Other renowned Asclepeions were those of Trikke, Epidaurus, Athens, and Corinth.

sulfur minerals from the thermal springs on site was channeled into the building. 15 Later on, *thermae* (thermal bath complexes) were built by the Romans.

Temple and environment were linked through various laws, 16 an early form of environmental policy. Water played a central role in the healing practices: in order to be admitted to the sanctuary, patients had first to undergo *catharsis*, or purification. The ritual included baths and a cleansing diet. Purification of the body thus preceded any type of cure. Once completed, patients would undergo dream therapy or incubation, whereby in a hypnotic state they would be visited by Asclepius or one of his daughters for a prognosis—lying in animal skins, the divinities would tell them what they needed to do to be cured. (It was, in fact, the temple's priests whispering prescriptions for plants, exercise, fasting, and diet in their ears.) Upon waking, the patient would consult with the temple priest and recount the dream, after which treatment would follow. 17

In the words of Charles Flegel, a Lithuanian traveler to the island of Nisyros in the late nineteenth century, "the hunter [and] the fisherman can rely purely on nature, but for the goals

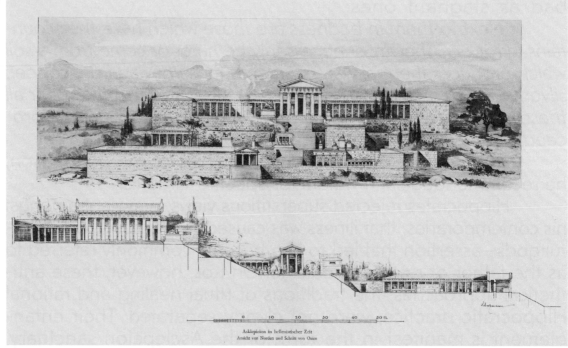

Asklepieion in hellenistischer Zeit
Ansicht von Norden und Schnitt von Osten

of hygiene, therapy and leisure, nature is in need of help by science, the arts and artistry—in other words: bathhouses, hotels, coffee shops, doctors and pharmacies." 18 Indeed, three bath complexes developed with specialized in-house doctors to care for patients. fig.3 They flourished during the first half of the twentieth century. The various names, forms and interiors of these buildings, along with their promotional material, represented a mixture of pagan and modern elements, ancient wisdom and a "European" outlook. They were a modest state-run bath building

15 A high retaining wall had fountains incorporated within it: inflow and outflow of water was used for the ritual purification of visitors and for therapeutic regimens. Marble conduits of water ran along the length of the stoa to refresh visitors. To the east of the complex, where the sacred thermal spring emerged, the water now flows from a Roman sculpture of Pan.

16 A sacred law forbade felling cypress trees within the limits of the temples of Apollo and Asclepius. A marble epigraph located at the museum located in the Ascleipeion site in Kos states "Lex Sacra prohibiting the felling of the cypresses in the sacred grove. Circa 300 BCE." Cypresses outside the demarcated area could be cut and used by the timber trade, and all profits would be used for projects related to the sanctuary.

17 H. Christopoulou-Aletra, A. Togia, and C. Varlami, „The ‚Smart' Asclepieion: A Total Healing Environment," *Archives of Hellenic Medicine* 27, no. 2 (2010), 259—63, here 259.

fig. 2 Kos Asclepeion in the Hellenistic period, perspective from the north and a sectional view from the east, from Paul Schazmann and Rudolf Herzog, *Asklipieion: Baubeschreibung und Baugeschichte*, vol. 1 (Berlin: Keller, 1932), plate 39

18 Καρόλου Φλέγελ, *Η Νήσος Νίσυρος και αι θέρμαι αυτής, Ανατύπωση* [*The Island of Nisyros and Its Thermae*] (Athens: Onnik Haleplian Galata, 2007[1899]), 8.

with in-house accommodation (Loutra), a vast private bath and hotel complex (Paloi), where the springs were discovered by Dr. Pantelidis in 1899, and a small makeshift community facility (Mandraki). These three buildings of different sizes, types of ownership, and clientele—but all solitary structures, set in the landscape—are exemplary types of twentieth-century thermalism in Greece. [19] As one local told me, "we don't live in earth. We live in lava that's been solidified. It's good to learn that the heat gets released in the water, otherwise the volcano would explode again." Geology and built tectonics are one here. The qualities of the various volcanic stones are manifest in the way they are carved to construct the island's built environment. Softer stones produce sculptural forms, while harder ones create more rigid geometries and thinner, lighter masonry. All three bath buildings utilize local stones, and their properties translate into specific architectural expressions. The baths of Dr. Pandelidis in Paloi are built from dark, hard volcanic stone—rhyolitic obsidian lava domes and pumice deposits similar to those mined on the neighboring island of Yali.

Bathing in hot water springs became a civilized form of recreation in Northern Europe during the eighteenth century. Drawing on ancient Roman practices, spa towns became popular resorts. In Greece, the beginning of thermalism coincided with the founding of the new Greek nation in 1833. Greece, in search of an identity following its independence from the Ottoman Empire, witnessed a scientific revolution of sorts. An influx of foreign scientists accompanied the Bavarian-instituted monarchy and contributed to the analysis of water and soil. Xaver Landerer, the Bavarian chemist who accompanied King Otto as his military pharmacist, became a pivotal character in the development of thermalism. As the first regular professor of chemistry and of botany at the University of Athens, he sparked interest in Greek natural resources and their potential. Landerer organized the first modestly equipped chemistry laboratory and performed chemistry experiments, not just for the students but all interested Athenians. An avid writer and traveler, he assembled a large mineral collection and wrote a number of chemical treatises. In his books on the hydrochemical properties of natural springs across Greece, he urged the state to build better infrastructure to welcome visitors. These texts became a reference point for other foreign authors who wrote guides about Greece, its landscapes, and its environmental resources. [20] Landerer started a larger movement that was not confined to scientific circles but rippled out into the wider political and social milieu: other

19 While Nisyros was not part of the Greek state until after the Second World War, a similar phenomenon of documentation and exploitation of natural resources for healing took place there. The typologies of buildings, ownership, and investment that emerged were also identical to others found in numerous locations around Greece at the time.

fig.3 Postcard showing boats from Alexandria bringing patients to the Loutra of Nisyros (n.d.) Source: Dr. Pandelidisl, Author's collection

20 See, for example, Frederick Strong, *Greece as a Kingdom* (London: Longman, Brown, Green, and Longmans, 1842).

fig. 4 C, K, Na, Mg, Ca: a periodic table of locations of terrains and waters. The ground was documented as a broad healing network. Source: Author's montage, selected crops from "Thermal Mineral Springs," produced by G. Orfanus, K. Sfetsos, and G. Ghioni-Stavropoulou for the Institute of Geology and Mineral Exploration, Athens, 1995

21 For a detailed historical record of how the state, medical, social welfare, and legal apparatus were organized in regards to hydrotherapy benefits, see Melpomeni Kostidi, "Greek Spas (Mid Nineteenth–Early Twentieth Century): Therapy, Sociability and Vacation" (PhD diss., Thessaly University, 2020).

22 Αἱ 750 Μεταλλικαί Πηγαί της Ελλάδος [Nikolaos Lekkas, The 750 Mineral Springs of Greece] (Athens: A. Dialismas, 1938).

23 Alexander More, et al. "The Impact of a Six-Year Climate Anomaly on the 'Spanish Flu' Pandemic and WWI," GeoHealth 4, no. 9 (2020), https://doi.org/10.1029/2020GH000277 (accessed May 15, 2021)

24 "Thales … says the principle is water (for which reason he declared that the earth rests on water), getting the notion perhaps from seeing that the nutriment of all things is moist, and that heat itself is generated from the moist and kept alive by it (and that from which they come to be is a principle of all things). He got his notion from this fact, and from the fact that the seeds of all things have a moist nature, and that water is the origin of the nature of moist things." Aristotle, Metaphysics, ed. W. D. Ross (Oxford: Clarendon Press, 1924), 3. See also Jaap Mansfeld, "Aristotle and Others on Thales, or the Beginnings of Natural Philosophy (With Some Remarks on Xenophanes)," Mnemosyne 38, no. 1/2 (1985), 109–29.

Greek doctors and scientists educated abroad contributed to the research. This scientific community became a vocal advocate of the benefits of the waters and the need for state infrastructure for hydrotherapy. The healing qualities of numerous locations around Greece were now confirmed through laboratory mineral analysis. **fig. 4**

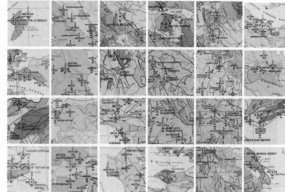

As urban centers began to grow, doctors prescribed specific waters and hydrotherapy treatments for illnesses and an escape from city life. **21** The centrality of thermalism to Greek modernization can be illustrated with a single publication, The 750 Mineral Springs of Greece, published in 1938 by the Greek Department of Healing Springs and Exhibitions. **22** This was a newly established department overseeing the function of state infrastructure at thermal springs across the country and also responsible for all fairs promoting Greece abroad. The book's author, Nikolaos Lekkas, was the department's director. Simultaneously a travel guide, geochemical cartography, and medical compendium, it addressed doctors, patients, (Greek-speaking) travelers, and politicians.

When the culture of thermalism began, its proponents, referencing popular thermal resorts, looked to the future with the aspiration of the new Greek state becoming "European." Building Loutropoli (bathing towns) was partly to achieve this desired identity. **fig. 5** A number of the bath buildings that began to crop up in thermal springs around Greece, including municipal hydrotherapy buildings in Ikaria, Kamena Vourla, and Platystomo, were named after Asclepius and Hippocrates, with Hercules appearing in advertisements for bath facilities. Medicine and the healing properties of place were once again intertwined. **fig. 6** Not least amongst the contemporary contribitors to thermalism was the Spanish Flu pandemic, which ravaged the world between 1918 and 1920. It too was analysed in terms that gave weight to the description of the health of the demos in Hippocratian terms. **23**

The water-centric philosophy of Thales, **24** Hippocratic medicine, Asclepian pagan wisdom, the legacy of Roman baths and Turkish hammams, Bavarian science: these historical, scientific, and philosophical approaches to "taking the waters" were blended in the discourse of thermalism and popular rhetoric in Greece. The discourse of prevalent historiography of the new Greek Hellenic Nation in the nineteenth century was centered on continuity from antiquity: a "national rhetoric that traced the continuous history of the Greek nation back to the first Olympiad in 776 BCE." [25]

Maria Puig de La Bellacasa writes that "care contains a notion of doing that concern lacks." [26] She points to the shared root of concern and care, coming from the Latin *cura* (cure). The

25 Introduction to Roderick Beaton and David Ricks, eds., *The Making of Modern Greece: Nationalism, Romanticism, and the Uses of the Past (1797–1896)* (London: Routledge, 2016), 1–20, here 5.

26 Maria Puig de La Bellacasa, *Matters of Care: Speculative Ethics in More than Human Worlds* (Minneapolis: University of Minnesota Press, 2017), 42.

fig. 5 A panorama of bath buildings reflecting attitudes to healing and care Source: author's collection

Greek word for care, *φροντίς*, has its roots in *φρην (frin)*; [27] a term denoting the mind, the heart, or the soul. *Φρονέω (phronéō)*, which shares the same root as care, means "to think." To care, to cure, to think, to do.

Who cared, and for whom? And healing from what? In a new nation state, born amidst ruins both ancient and modern, "healing" had an unstable meaning. From state endeavor to private interests, and from nation building to international tourism, the meaning of care implicit in Greek thermalism constantly shifted. In the 1920s, Greece was dealing with the trauma of the destruction of Izmir at the end of the Greco-Turkish war. In the aftermath of the First World War, a Greek campaign bolstered by a British alliance embarked on capturing territories of the former Ottoman Empire. "Megali Idea" or "Great Idea" was a nationalist movement aspiring to the expansion of the Greek state following its independence from the Ottoman Empire. The war, which began in 1919, ended in 1922 when the Turkish army regained control of Izmir. The catastrophic fire and destruction of the city brought waves of immigrants to Greece. In Athens alone, the documented number of refugees had reached a million, and the entire port of Piraeus had become a makeshift camp. [28] While these mass population exchanges were being brokered between the two countries, [29] hydrotherapy clinics and a culture of healing

27 Henry George Liddell, Robert Scott and Henry Stuart Jones, *A Greek–English Lexicon* (1909) (London: Simon Wallenberg Press, 2007).

28 *"Μικρασ-ιατική Καταστροφή, Πειραιάς 1922: Σπάνιο βίντεο με πρόσφυγες,"* [Asia Minor catastrophe, Piraeus 1922: rare footage with refugees], video, 5:37 mins., uploaded September 13, 2019, https://youtu.be/aeHj9xPGpaw, esp. 0:31, 1:12–2:10. (accessed January 21, 2021).

29 Sarah Shields, "The Greek-Turkish Population Exchange: Internationally Administered Ethnic Cleansing," in "Christians: Egypt, Iraq, Lebanon, Palestine", special issue, *Middle East Report 267* (Summer 2013), 2–6.

were being promoted around Greece. In the words of a medical doctor in 1926:

"All the most civilized nations ... prominently demonstrate their bath towns ... Vichy, Baden-Baden, Carlsbad, aside from the therapeutic springs that they contain, also celebrate their projects, gardens, [and] tree-lined boulevards, which contribute to well-being and satisfaction. People draw inspiration from such physical contexts. [In] the matter of such natural beauty, Greece is unsurpassable. The laced coastline of Greece is intoxicating, endless, and sun-drenched. Along it can be found our alkaline springs, which are beyond compare." [30]

Numerous descriptions in the same spirit are found in medical treatises of the time. One writer compared the excitement of the discovery of potentially therapeutic conjunctions of minerals to an El Dorado fever. [31] As Nikolaos Lekkas wrote:

"With great interest the state apparatus is moving towards the implementation of road construction, telegraph and phone communication networks, remediation and beautification works and other related projects ... Correctly, they place importance in the clearly therapeutic and mineral resources as centers, whereby the country's rate of progress and its culture can be demonstrated." [32]

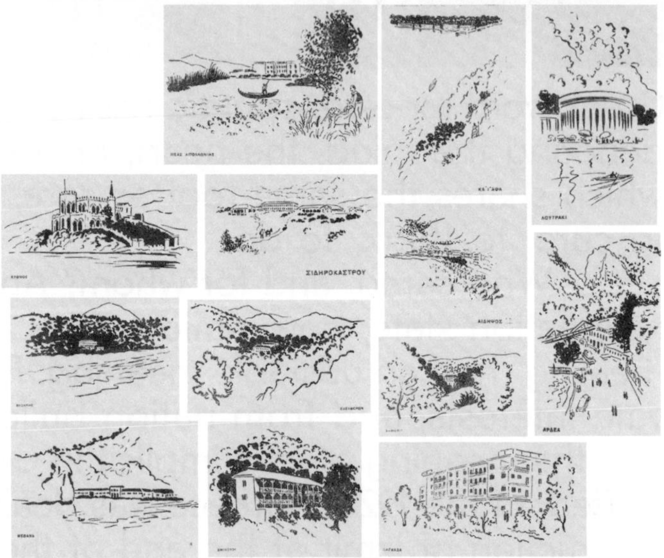

Two parallel narratives thus unfolded: the disarray of Greek domestic and foreign policy on the one hand, and the nationally inflicted celebration of a mode of healing on the other. Disorder and illness relate to balance: "illness comes from imbalance. Treatment is aimed at restoring the right balance—in political terms, the right hierarchy." [33] Since domestic and foreign disruptions to the body politic could not be reversed, the task of politics shifted to the balancing of individual and collective bodies. Greek politics became palliative.

Bathing, cleansing oneself from the past, and dreaming of a new European Greece. The figure of the bather slips from pragmatic activity to reflective metaphor, from fantasies of the glorious past to anxieties about an uncertain future, at the beginning of the twentieth century. It was not the sculpted marble of ruined temples and torsos of antiquity but a different raw matter that symbolically unified Modern and Ancient Greece: the ground.

30 Athanasios Nikitas Sioris, *Αι Ιαματικαι Πηγαί της Ελλάδας* [The Healing Springs of Greece] (Athens: *Αδελφοί Α. Τουλα*, 1926), author's translation.

31 Ioannis Palantzas, "Die Magnesitgewinnung und -verarbeitung in der griechischen Region Nord Euböa während des 19. und 20. Jahrhunderts auf der Grundlage von Archivquellen" (PhD diss., Freie Universität Berlin, 2007), 13. http://dx.doi.org/10.17169/refubium-5106 (accessed January 21, 2021).

fig.6 Building (in) nature: illustrations of bath buildings Source: Nikolaos Lekkas, *The 750 Mineral Springs of Greece* (Athens: A. Dialismas, 1938)

32 Lekkas, *750 Mineral Springs*, 37, author's translation.

33 Susan Sontag, *Illness as Metaphor* (New York: Farrar, Straus, and Giroux, 1978), 76.

Heat, water, and the minerals embedded in it reorganized society. In twentieth-century Greece, this notion of healing was both articulated and materialized in the hydrotherapy building.

On a hot summer's day, I walked through an empty square in Kos, noticing a sign pointing to the Hippocratic tree. I found a large, fenced-off tree under which, according to the story, Hippocrates wrote his treatises. Next to it is a Turkish fountain from the eighteenth century. Trees, treatises, fountains: from the Koan context of antiquity into twentieth-century Greece, it was healing that prevailed as the dominant metaphor, not illness. [34]

[34] See Sontag, *Illness as Metaphor*; Beatriz Colomina, "Illness as Metaphor in Modern Architecture," in Andrea Phillips and Markus Miessen, eds., *Caring Culture: Art, Architecture and the Politics of Public Health* (Berlin: Sternberg Press, 2011), 73–90.

Dangerous Congestions: Cholera, Mapping, and the Beginnings of Modern Urbanism
Christa Kamleithner

Christa Kamleithner is a postdoctoral researcher and lecturer in Art History at the Brandenburg University of Technology Cottbus-Senftenberg.

1 See Evelien van Es, "The Exhibition 'Housing, Working, Traffic, Recreation in the Contemporary City': A Reconstruction," in Evelien van Es et al., eds., *Atlas of the Functional City: CIAM 4 and Comparative Urban Analysis* (Bussum: THOTH Publishers/Zurich: gta Verlag, 2014), 441—44.

2 See Anna M. Cabré and Francesc M. Muñoz, "Ildefons Cerdà and the Unbearable Density of Cities," in *Cerdà: Urbs i Territori: Planning Beyond the Urban*, exh. cat., Barcelona, 1994—1995 (Madrid: Electa, 1996), 37—46.

3 Cf. Arthur H. Robinson, *Early Thematic Mapping in the History of Cartography* (Chicago: University of Chicago Press, 1982); Tom Koch, *Cartographies of Disease: Maps, Mapping, and Medicine* (Redlands: Esri, 2005); Philipp Felsch, "Wie August Petermann den Nordpol erfand: Umwege der thematischen Kartografie," in Steffen Siegel and Petra Weigel, eds., *Die Werkstatt des Kartographen: Materialien und Praktiken visueller Welterzeugung* (Munich: Fink, 2011), 109—21.

4 Enrico Chapel, *L'œil raisonné: L'invention de l'urbanisme par la carte* (Geneva: Metis, 2010). Chapel's focus is on France and the fourth Congrès International d'Architecture Moderne 4; for the latter see also Enrico Chapel, "Thematic Mapping as an Analytical Tool: CIAM 4 and Problems of Visualization in Modern Town Planning," in van Es et al., *Atlas of the Functional City*, 27—37.

Density was a constant concern of modern urbanism. When the results of the fourth Congrès International d'Architecture Moderne on the "functional city" were presented at an exhibition in Amsterdam in 1935, [1] a shocking montage warned against high population density, declared as the cause of infant mortality. The panel shows a wretched child in front of a map visualizing the density of Barcelona's districts. **fig.1** The three-dimensional cartogram rises in the medieval city center, where the population was densely packed—a fact that had already bothered Ildefonso Cerdà nearly a century before. The engineer, who planned a new, more spacious Barcelona in the 1850s and 1860s, built his urban theory on statistics, [2] making him one of the first modern urbanists. Detailed statistics on cities were first collected in the 1820s and 1830s, when population statistics and thematic cartography in general made a leap, pioneered by France and Great Britain. Subsequently, the relationship between density, disease, and poverty became the focus of interest for physicians and statisticians. One of the reasons for this was the second cholera pandemic, which—originating from India—crossed Europe in the early 1830s. [3] As is the case in the current coronavirus pandemic, the cholera pandemic caused a surge in datafication. Tables and maps of the distribution of the disease proliferated, together with statistical mapping in general, and the discourse on hygiene and urban reform gained momentum.

These new statistical maps raised awareness of social and urban differences and contributed to the discovery of the transmission routes of cholera. At the same time, these maps also created a new urban imaginary. With them, a new city emerged—a city of cloudy masses and differing zones, showing the population as a mobile and movable mass. And with these maps, modern urbanism came into existence—as a discipline monitoring demographic movements, steering the distribution of the population and ensuring its health, which meant, before everything else, the removal of congestion. Following Enrico Chapel, for whom statistical mapping and modern urbanism are inextricably linked, [4] in this essay I will draw on maps from Great Britain, France, and Germany to trace the fear of congestion that emerged in the wake of the cholera pandemics and outline the urbanist strategies that resulted. These include pioneering maps from the 1840s that pushed sanitary reform, maps from the 1870s and later that urged attention to housing, and maps from the 1910s that were used to model urban form as a whole. The point of this synopsis spanning a century is to show that these maps set a specific epistemic frame that not only changed the way the city was imagined but also how it was planned and managed. [5]

5 For more, see Christa Kamleithner, *Ströme und Zonen: Eine Genealogie der "funktionalen Stadt"* (Basel: Birkhäuser, 2020).

Cholera Maps

As Ian Hacking has put it, an "avalanche of printed numbers" was set in motion in the 1820s and 1830s. Statistical surveys, especially for military and fiscal purposes, had existed long before, but in the early nineteenth century the numbers multiplied, and above all they were no longer a state secret. Statistics were promoted

Gráfico núm. 3. Barcelona.

Densidad por hectárea.

by civic associations, driven by scientific enthusiasm as well as a number of pressing social issues, and addressed new "moral" issues such as crime and literacy. [6] Cholera was another of these topics, and an important one. The pandemic of 1831 to 1832, the first to reach Central and Western Europe, produced masses of new data as emerging experts and state commissions investigated the spread of the disease and its causes, not least using statistical maps. While many pioneering maps at this time were mainly interested in national distributions, these maps were the first to deal with differences within cities.

fig.1 Population density in Barcelona (n.d.), panel on the exhibition *Wonen, werken, verkeer, ontspanning in the hedendaagse stadt*, Stedelijk Museum, 1935, which presented the results of the fourth Congrès International d'Architecture Moderne of 1933 Source: gta Archives, ETH Zurich, CIAM 42-04-7-51-X2

6 Ian Hacking, "Biopower and the Avalanche of Printed Numbers," *Humanities in Society* 5 (1982), 279—95, here 281.

A simple way to visualize the distribution of the disease was to use different shadings that represented the average mortality of different administrative districts, as in the case of a Parisian cholera map from 1834. fig.2 The map was part of a report that made it clear that the poorest suffered the most. One of its authors, the physician and statistician Louis René Villermé, who had been studying mortality in Paris since the 1820s, was convinced that disease was a social phenomenon. Rivers and wet "miasmatic" lowlands, which older hygiene theories feared, posed no danger in his eyes. Poverty, with its many disadvantages, was for him the most likely cause of sickness—even more significant than living in a densely populated area, which often, but not always, went hand in hand with poverty. [7] Other cholera maps, such as one of Hamburg from 1836, were more detailed and analyzed the distribution of the disease street by street. fig.3 This map was later included in a report of the British General Board of Health on the cholera epidemic of 1848 to 1849, [8] which also contained a map of London with an even more nuanced shading that gave the disease its own shape. fig.4 Maps like these were used to study the relationship between disease, topography, population density, and poverty. The German cartographer August Petermann, for

7 Despite (or perhaps because of) this clarity, Villermé did not recommend any concrete infrastructural measures. Instead, the liberal hygienist put his trust in the economic progress the future would bring. See, William Coleman, *Death Is a Social Disease: Public Health and Political Economy in Early Industrial France* (Madison: University of Wisconsin Press, 1982), chp. 6, 149—80.

8 Niedersächsisches Gesundheitsamt, Deutsche Gesellschaft für Kartographie and Staatsbibliothek Berlin—Preußischer Kulturbesitz, eds., *Den Seuchen auf der Spur: 200 Jahre Infektionskrankheiten im Kartenbild*, exh. cat. (Niedersächsisches Landesgesundheitsamt: Hannover, 2012), 10.

fig. 2 Cholera map of
Paris in 1832
Source: *Rapport sur la
marche et les effets du
choléra-morbus dans
Paris et les communes
rurales du département
de la Seine: Année
1832* (Paris: Imprimerie
royale, 1834), 49

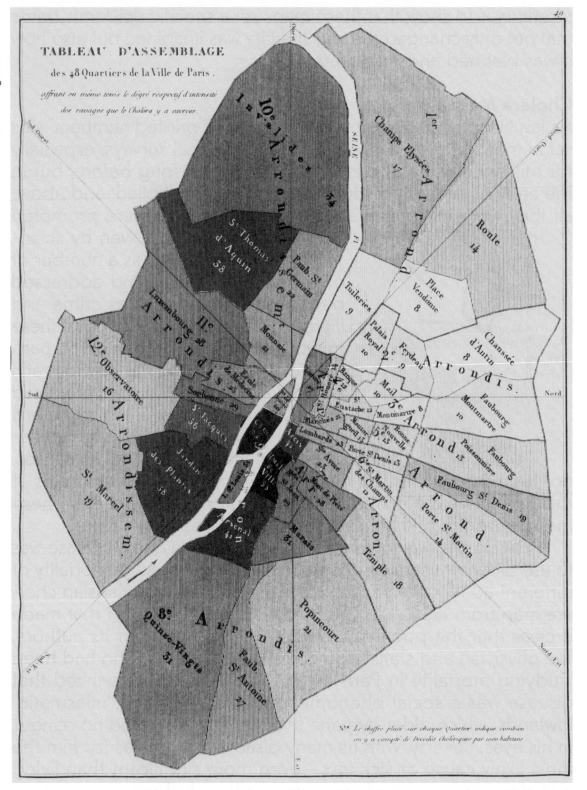

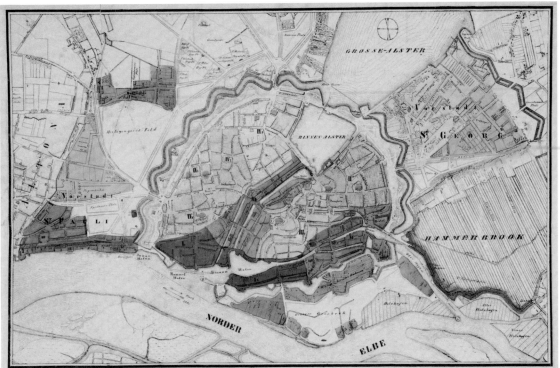

fig.3 Map of the 1832 Hamburg cholera epidemic
Source: J. N. C. Rothenburg, *Die Cholera-Epidemie des Jahres 1832 in Hamburg: Ein Vortrag gehalten in der Wissenschaft—Versammlung des Ärztlichen Vereins am 17. November 1835* (Hamburg: Perthes & Besser, 1836)

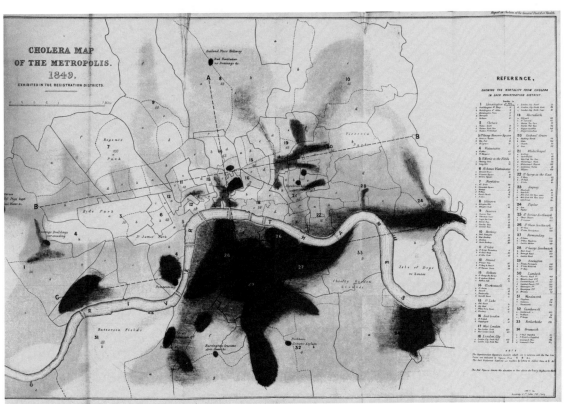

fig.4 Cholera map of London in 1849
Source: *Report of the General Board of Health on the Epidemic Cholera of 1848 & 1849. Presented to both Houses of Parliament by Command of Her Majesty* (London: Clowes and Sons, 1850), Wellcome Collection

example, who wanted to make himself known in London, made finely shaded maps of both the distribution of the disease in the British Isles in 1848 and the Isles' population—thus showing that topography was not a threat (as was still believed by some) but that population density instead was to be feared. As Philipp Felsch has pointed out, cartographers and statisticians in this period believed in the medium of the map. They actually thought they could derive meaning from the distribution of a phenomenon without further investigation. [9]

In the cholera year 1848, the long-discussed Public Health Act was passed. Inspired by Edwin Chadwick's famous *Sanitary Report* of 1842, the act obliged British communities to invest in water pipes and new sewer systems when certain death rates were reached. Chadwick's report is usually celebrated as a milestone in the history of hygiene, but it has also received harsh criticism. In

9 Felsch, "Wie August Petermann den Nordpol erfand," 115–18.

10 Christopher Hamlin, *Public Health and Social Justice in the Age of Chadwick: Britain, 1800–1854* (Cambridge: Cambridge University Press, 1998).

11 Robinson, *Early Thematic Mapping*, 172, 186.

fig. 5 Edwin Chadwick, Sanitary Map of Leeds, 1842, based on a cholera map by Robert Baker from 1833 Source: Edwin Chadwick, *Report to Her Majesty's Principal Secretary of State for the Home Department, from the Poor Law Commissioners, on an Inquiry into the Sanitary Condition of the Labouring Population of Great Britain; with Appendices* (London: Clowes and Sons, 1842), Wellcome Collection

the eyes of the historian Christopher Hamlin, its main achievement was even the reduction of existing knowledge. For the report, the secretary of the British Poor Law Commission had gathered comments on the sanitary condition of the laboring population from doctors and commissioners from all over Britain that dealt with a variety of problems—not least malnutrition, which made the poor vulnerable to all kinds of diseases. Chadwick, however, put forward a single argument: that dirt, and the miasmas that allegedly resulted from it, caused illness and misery. [10] An accompanying map of Leeds, which was based on a cholera map from 1833, [11] clarified this message: workers' quarters were not only the most densely populated and dirtiest places in the city but also the places where illness and disease were concentrated. **fig. 5** Chadwick, who advocated a new miasmatic theory that no longer believed in the danger of swamps but of man-made filth, thus radically simplified the multifaceted problem of poverty in order to propose a technical solution. And this solution, which would guide the emerging sanitary movement and housing reform, was to resolve disturbing densifications: in the future, new alluvial sewer systems in which water ran under pressure in precisely calculated pipes were to remove the dirt from the city; likewise, traffic routes were to be created where the population could be "drained" to the urban periphery. [12] Whether it was wastewater or population, in both cases dangerous congestion and stagnation had to be removed.

"Continuous Circulation"

The 1830s and 1840s were marked by a new mobility. Road networks and shipping canals were expanded, the first railway lines were built, and world trade grew. This facilitated the spread of cholera, and at the same time the disease threatened this new, interconnected world. The authorities first reacted with quarantine measures traditionally used against the plague and sealed off entire villages from the outside world. Austria reactivated the old plague front and turned its eastern borders into a *cordon sanitaire*, and Prussia did likewise. [13] To liberal minds, this seemed an act of despotism which, moreover, was not successful. New miasmatic theories therefore questioned the principle of quarantine, which was supposed to prevent direct—"contagious"—infection. According to them, the evil lay in toxic exhalations, which were to be eliminated by a general hygienic cleansing of the environment. [14]

Quarantine measures did not disappear with these theories, but within Europe these measures were both unified and loosened, and pandemic defense was shifted to the East. The countries of the Middle East were seen as buffer zones between Europe and India, the origin of cholera. This was legitimized with the assumed stasis and backwardness of the "Orient," where isolation measures seemed easier to handle than in "modern" countries with their busy trade activity and populations constantly on the move. [15] The strongest opposition to quarantine came from the British. The British Board of Health was also the first authority to embrace the new miasmatic theories and put its trust in the circulation of water when, with the Public Health Act of 1848, it required British municipalities to invest in urban infrastructure. [16] Water was to be brought in and out of every house and then purified on drain fields, and this principle of "continuous circulation" was promoted by British experts at international congresses in the 1850s, whether they were dedicated to hygiene or charity. [17] This principle, of course, has many advantages we appreciate today, and

12 Chadwick, *Report to Her Majesty*, 287–88

13 See Barbara Dettke, *Die asiatische Hydra: Die Cholera von 1830/31 in Berlin und den preußischen Provinzen Posen, Preußen und Schlesien* (Berlin: de Gruyter, 1995).

14 The classic text on this is Erwin H. Ackerknecht, "Anticontagionism between 1821 and 1867," *Bulletin of the History of Medicine* 22 (1948), 562–93.

15 Cf. Valeska Huber, "The Unification of the Globe by Disease? The International Sanitary Conferences on Cholera, 1851–1894," *Historical Journal* 49, no. 2 (June 2006), 453–76, esp. 461–62; Benoît Pouget, "Quarantine, Cholera, and International Health Spaces: Reflections on 19th-Century European Sanitary Regulations in the Time of SARS-CoV-2," in "Spotlight Issue: Histories of Epidemics in the Time of COVID-19," special issue, *Centaurus* 62, no. 2 (May 2020), 302–10.

16 Cf. Ackerknecht, "Anticontagionism"; Hamlin, *Public Health and Social Justice*, chp 8 and 9, 245–301.

17 *Congrès général d'hygiène de Bruxelles: Session de 1852* (Brussels: G. Stapleaux, 1852), 29–32; *Congrès international de bienfaisance de Bruxelles: Session de 1856*, vol. 1 (Brussels: G. Stapleaux, 1857), 67–88.

18 A discovery made with the help of maps, but maps that were embedded in in a clear chain of evidence. Steven Johnson, The Ghost Map: *The Story of London's Most Terrifying Epidemic—and How It Changed Science, Cities, and the Modern World* (New York: Penguin, 2006).

19 For more, see Kamleithner, *Ströme und Zonen*, chp. 5, 141–64.

20 For more, see Anne I. Hardy, *Ärzte, Ingenieure und städtische Gesundheit: Medizinische Theorien in der Hygienebewegung des 19. Jahrhunderts* (Frankfurt: Campus, 2005); Lorenz Jellinghaus, *Zwischen Daseinsvorsorge und Infrastruktur: Zum Funktionswandel von Verwaltungswissenschaften und Verwaltungsrecht in der zweiten Hälfte des 19. Jahrhunderts* (Frankfurt: Klostermann, 2006).

21 Cf. Karl Seutemann, "Die Städtestatistik," in Robert Wuttke, ed., *Die deutschen Städte, geschildert nach den Ergebnissen der ersten deutschen Städteausstellung zu Dresden 1903*, vol. 1 (Leipzig: Brandstetter, 1904), 864–92.

22 Statistisches Bureau der Stadt Berlin, ed., *Berliner Stadt- und Gemeinde-Kalender und Städtisches Jahrbuch für 1867*, vol. 1 (Berlin: Guttentag, 1867).

23 Hermann Schwabe, *Die Resultate der Berliner Volkszählung vom 3. December 1867* (Berlin: Kortkampf, 1869); Hermann Schwabe, *Die Königliche Haupt- und Residenzstadt Berlin in ihren Bevölkerungs-, Berufs- und Wohnungsverhältnissen: Resultate der Volkszählung und Volksbeschreibung vom 1. December 1871* (Berlin: Simion, 1874).

bacteriology, which emerged in the 1880s, promoted its implementation. As early as 1854, John Snow demonstrated the value of clean drinking water when he discovered that cholera is spread via contaminated water. [18] However, the principle of "continuous circulation" embodied an entire world view and was first of all about the removal of filth and everything connected to it. The circulation of water was not only to overcome disease but also laziness and drunkenness among the poor, and to create a clean environment that would encourage industriousness. Stagnation of any kind was to be eliminated and the "organism" of the cities perfected. Circulation formed a value in itself. [19]

Statistics and Urban Reform

In the German Empire, it was the German Association of Public Health (Deutsche Verein für öffentliche Gesundheitspflege), founded in 1873, that promoted what Chadwick had called for in his *Sanitary Report*: the introduction of alluvial sewers as well as the decongestion of the population. The association, which brought together hygienists, engineers, and city politicians, emerged from a division of the Society of German Natural Scientists and Physicians (Versammlung deutscher Ärzte und Naturforscher), which had been founded in 1867—the year after the fourth cholera pandemic had hit German-speaking countries. [20] Urban growth, the resulting logistical and density problems, and, above all, the statistics making them visible, increased the political pressure to act. The data provided by the newly established municipal statistical offices—Berlin and Vienna were the first in 1862 [21]—caused alarm. The Berlin office, in particular, drove the debate on urban reform with its publications. Its first yearbook was published in 1867—belatedly because of cholera but with a map of its distribution showing the city besieged by dark stains. [22] Maps of population density followed, included in the regular reports on the Berlin census by the director of the office, Hermann Schwabe. [23] **fig. 6**

These reports also provided detailed statistics on housing conditions which were, compared to other European cities, astonishingly detailed. Thanks to Salomon Neumann, a pioneer of public hygiene and friend of Rudolf Virchow, the census in Berlin was reformed in 1861 and thence after included information on how many rooms the dwellings had and thus how densely occupied they were. 24 The same information was available for Vienna from 1869 onwards. 25 In London and Paris, these figures were only collected three decades later. In London, the spread of cholera could already be tracked on a weekly basis in 1866, 26 but detailed housing statistics were only available after 1891, when Charles Booth—who had just published his monumental work on the distribution of poverty in London—served as a consultant to the General Register Office. 27 In Paris, too, a lot of data had long been available, but only since 1891 had the census asked questions regarding the details of dwellings to quantify overcrowding. 28 **fig.7** Jacques Bertillon, the director of the municipal service, had recently contributed to

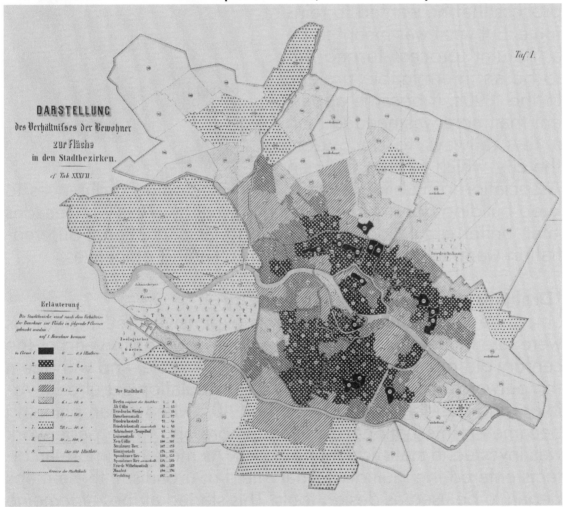

data production and its visibility when he published three map collections between 1889 and 1891, including maps of more than twenty diseases. 29

    That statistics on housing were produced so early in such detailed tables in the German-speaking countries is remarkable, as is the fact that a modern urbanist discourse, interested in steering population distribution, emerged there as early as the 1870s. This is

24 Statistisches Landesamt Berlin, ed., *100 Jahre Berliner Statistik: Festschrift zum hundertjährigen Bestehen des Berliner Statistischen Amtes* (Berlin: Statistisches Landesamt, 1962), 19–23.

25 Gustav A. Schimmer, "Gedanken über die Durchführung der nächsten Volkszählung in Oesterreich," in *Statistische Monatsschrift*, ed. Bureau der k.k. Statistischen Central-Commission (Vienna: Hölder, 1878), 169–78, here 171–72.

26 Thanks to William Farr, who oversaw the collection of medical statistics in England and Wales. See Steven Johnson, "How Data Became One of the Most Powerful Tools to Fight an Epidemic," *New York Times Magazine*, June 10, 2020.

27 Harold W. Pfautz, "Charles Booth: Sociologist of the City," in Harold W. Pfautz, ed., *Charles Booth On the City: Physical Pattern and Social Structure* (Chicago: University of Chicago Press, 1967), 1–170, here 32.

28 Diana Periton, "Urban Life," in Vittoria Di Palma, Diana Periton, and Marina Lathouri, eds., *Intimate Metropolis: Urban Subjects in the Modern City* (London: Routledge, 2009), 9–40, here 30.

fig.6 Population density of Berlin in 1867 Source: Hermann Schwabe, *Die Resultate der Berliner Volkszählung vom 3. December 1867* (Berlin: Kortkampf, 1869)

29 Antoine Picon, "Nineteenth-Century Urban Cartography and the Scientific Ideal: The Case of Paris," *Osiris* 18 (2003), 135–49, here 147.

no coincidence: Reinhard Baumeister's classic *Stadterweiterungen* of 1876 — which is, together with Cerdà's *Teoría* of 1867, one of the first books on modern urbanism — drew heavily on the writings of Berlin's statisticians. Their insights into Berlin's development were crucial for Baumeister. Not only were their numbers on over-crowding alarming, their knowledge about demographic movement also promised a solution. For them, the future of Berlin's *Innenstadt* was clear: just like the old City of London, it was about to become a business center. Shops and offices came, residents left — this was understood by them as a "natural development." [30]

When Baumeister argued for the planning and building of transport routes to support the provision of healthy housing on the periphery, he relied on this process that he wanted to reinforce. But what was meant to be a "natural" process turned out to be an interminable project. In the 1890s, it became apparent that more was needed than a few railways to decongest the city, which led the German

PARIS 1891

HABITANTS MAL LOGÉS

SUR 10.000 HABITANTS DE CHAQUE ARRONDISSEMENT, COMBIEN SONT LOGÉS TROP ÉTROITEMENT ?

(plus de 2 habitants par pièce)

Association of Public Health to promote zoning ordinances to keep building density low, at least in wealthy areas. [31] Decades later, better circulation, better housing, and functional differentiation were still the most important planning objectives.

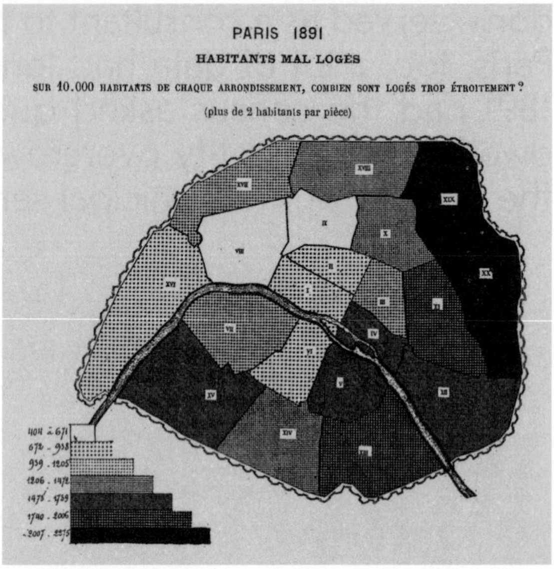

"Draining" People, Modeling the City

Since the production of maps was expensive, statistical maps were rare in the nineteenth century. Only towards the end of the century did maps became more widely available, and with them the outwards movement of the urban population acquired a visible — and designable — form. In the 1910s, when urban planning became an international discipline, more and more paperwork was invested in statistical mapping. [32] As more and more architects entered the multidisciplinary field of urbanism, these maps began to be used as design tools. This started at the *Allgemeine Städtebau-Ausstellung* in Berlin in 1910 (parts of which were shown at the Town Planning Conference in London in the same year). The planning exhibition, which was visited by many international experts and future experts like the young Charles-Édouard Jeanneret, [33] presented the results of the Greater Berlin Competition, as well as housing and extension plans from all over Europe and the United States and statistical maps and diagrams

30 Cf. Christa Kamleithner, "Concrete Abstractions: Berlin's Statistical Bureau and the Concept of Zoning, 1862–1910," in Anne Kockelkorn and Nina Zschokke, eds., *Productive Universals—Specific Situations: Critical Engagements in Art, Architecture, and Urbanism* (Berlin: Sternberg, 2019), 94–123; Kamleithner, *Ströme und Zonen*, chp. 2, 63–90, and chp. 6, 165–94.

fig.7 Inhabitants of overcrowded dwellings in Paris in 1891 Source: Jacques Bertillon, *Essai de statistique comparée du surpeuplement des habitations à Paris et dans les grandes capitales européenes* (Paris: Imprimerie Chaix, 1895), 8

31 For more, see Brian Ladd, *Urban Planning and Civic Order in Germany 1860–1914* (Cambridge, MA: Harvard University Press, 1990), chp. 6, 186–234; Kamleithner, *Ströme und Zonen*, chp. 8, 217–56.

32 To gain an overview on statistical projects in Europe at that time, see Kees Somer, *The Functional City: The CIAM and Cornelis von Eesteren, 1928–1960* (Rotterdam: NAi, 2007), 130–38.

33 Christiane Crasemann Collins, *Werner Hegemann and the Search for Universal Urbanism* (New York: W.W. Norton, 2005), 371–72.

of Berlin. 34 Probably the best-known competition entry, a joint effort by economist Rudolf Eberstadt, architect Bruno Möhring, the traffic engineer Richard Petersen, even used a map of Berlin's population density as its basis. fig.8 This map gave the impression that the population leaving the city was channeled by the railway

34 Werner Hegemann, *Der Städtebau, nach den Ergebnissen der Allgemeinen Städtebau-Ausstellung in Berlin* (Berlin: Wasmuth, 1911–13). For more on the exhibition, see Harald Bodenschatz et al., eds., *Stadtvisionen 1910/2010: Berlin, Paris, London, Chicago — 100 Jahre Allgemeine Städtebau-Ausstellung in Berlin* (Berlin: DOM, 2010). However, the volume overlooks the presence of statistics in the exhibition (and especially in the exhibition catalogue).

fig.8 Richard Petersen, population density of Greater Berlin, 1880–1905 Source: *Wettbewerb Groß-Berlin 1910: Die preisgekrönten Entwürfe mit Erläuterungsberichten* (Berlin: Wasmuth, 1911), third prize, 9

like "drainage streams," leaving the old center abandoned, 35 and the resulting zoning plan proposed to model this process by concentrating future residential areas along railways, securing green areas in between, and reducing building heights from the center to the periphery. 36

Shortly afterwards, the preparatory work for another big competition began that made statistical surveys the starting point for extension planning. The participants of the competition for the extension of Paris, which took place between 1919 and 1920, were confronted with an exhibition of a large number of statistical maps, including older ones, and a report by the architect Louis Bonnier and the historian Marcel Poëte explaining demographic trends, land use, railways, land prices, and more. The report was convinced that the working classes were leaving the center, and this movement should not be left to chance: the competition was intended to avoid future densification and wanted to distribute the population "properly." 37 The outward movement of the population had already been visualized by older maps, fig.9 but Bonnier, who had prepared the competition, was the first to use these maps in 1919 to extrapolate future growth and give the city a new form that should create a "healthy" balance between buildings and greenery. 38 Only a few years later, in 1925, as Enrico Chapel has noticed, Le Corbusier also used this data in his book *Urbanisme*. fig.10 Whereas Bonnier had concentrated on

35 This was a contemporary view, as demonstrated by a housing guide that presented the movement as "draining streams." *Die Berliner Vororte: Ein Handbuch für Haus- und Grundstückskäufer, Baulustige, Wohnungsuchende, Grundstücksbesitzer, Vorortbewohner, Terraingesellschaften, Hypothekenverleiher, Architekten u.a.m.* (Berlin: Baedeker und Moeller, 1908), XVI.

36 Peterson, *Wettbewerb Groß-Berlin 1910*; Markus Tubbesing, *Der Wettbewerb Groß-Berlin 1910: Die Entstehung einer modernen Disziplin Städtebau*, 41–144, (Berlin: Wasmuth, 2018); Kamleithner, *Ströme und Zonen*, 234–41, on the exhibition, cf. 9–19.

37 Chapel, *L'œil raisonné* 16–26, 43–65.

38 Periton, "Urban Life," 12–15, 31–35; Chapel, *L'œil raisonné*, 65–80.

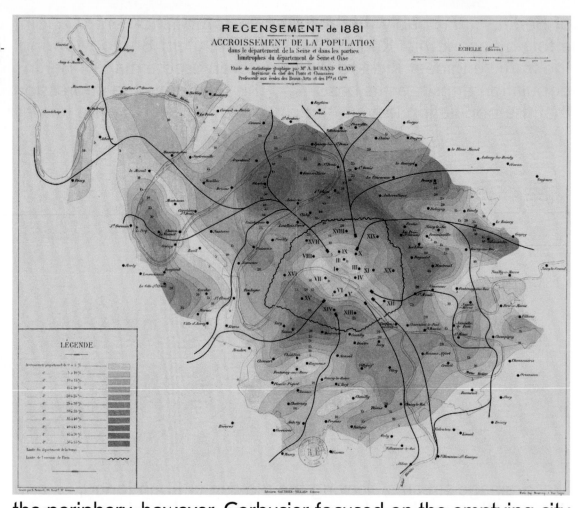

fig. 9 Alfred Durand-Claye, population growth in the surroundings of Paris, 1876–1881 Source: Recensement de 1881: Accroissement de la population dans le département de la Seine, Bibliothèque nationale de France, 1881, GE C-1838

the periphery, however, Corbusier focused on the emptying city center, using the demographic shift to justify the proposed demolition of the old Paris. [39] For Chapel, these are two quite different interpretations of the same maps — interpretations, though, that in the German planning discourse were seen as two sides of the same coin and as the future of the city in general. With London in mind (where circulation had fostered urban differentiation), for German reformers the modern city consisted of tall buildings for working in the center and spacious buildings for living on the periphery. This seemed to be a good compromise between their hygienic demands and the constraints of the booming property markets, which were pushing rents and buildings up in the center and driving residents out. [40]

The patterns of urban statistics conveyed the impression that the population could be treated as a natural phenomenon (growing, dying, moving, distributing) and, with some aptitude, be steered into healthy paths. This epistemic frame, which transformed city dwellers into a viscous mass, defined urbanism for more than a hundred years. Ebenezer Howard, the inventor of the garden city — which was to become the most important strategy for the development of large cities — gave us a hint of how strong this framing was at the beginning of the twentieth century. In 1904, after a lecture by Patrick Geddes for the Sociological

39 Chapel, *L'œil raisonné*, 37, 82–83.

40 On this readiness to compromise, cf. Juan Rodríguez-Lores, "Stadthygiene und Städtebau: Zur Dialektik von Ordnung und Unordnung in den Auseinandersetzungen des Deutschen Vereins für Öffentliche Gesundheitspflege 1868–1901," in Juan Rodríguez-Lores and Gerhard Fehl, eds., Städtebaureform 1865–1900: Von Licht, Luft und Ordnung in der Stadt der Gründerzeit, vol. 1, (Hamburg: Christians, 1985), 19–58. On the different hygienic requirements for working and living, cf. Hans Christian Nußbaum, Die Hygiene des Städtebaus (Leipzig: Göschen, 1907), 12, 20–21.

Society, Howard opened the discussion, led by Booth, with a striking image. While Geddes described the "stages by which the city grows and swells, with the descent of the population from the hillsides into the valleys," that led to a "tide" flowing "resistlessly onward to make more crowded our overcrowded tenements" and "to make the atmosphere more foul," Howard was convinced that there was a way to reverse this process by "imitating the skill ... of Nature" and "creating channels through which some of our population shall be attracted back to the fields; so that there shall be a stream of population pouring from the city into the country, till a healthy balance is restored." [41]

Even at the beginning of the twentieth century, after the triumph of bacteriology, Howard thought in miasmatic terms when he feared an "atmosphere" that was "foul" by overcrowding and should be removed by decongestion. These ideas were far from those of contemporary epidemiology. Epidemiology and urban hygiene were two different things anyway, because the latter was a practical compromise. But by the beginning of the twentieth century, hygiene had become a mere buzzword used by urban planners to indicate sound design. For them, a healthy urban development was first and foremost a healthy distribution of the population — in other words, a balanced visual pattern on a piece of paper. The visual culture of urban planning, [42] and especially of urban research, makes a difference. In this respect, modern urbanism and cholera were related: cholera pushed statistical mapping, and it was this new kind of knowledge practice — rather than specific epidemiological findings — that would change urbanism. This, quite likely, will also be true for the current pandemic. Before anything else, the pandemic will accelerate the datafication of the city, which, since in its current form is in real-time and gives us insights into individual movement patterns as well as an overview of mass phenomena, will change the way we look at cities.

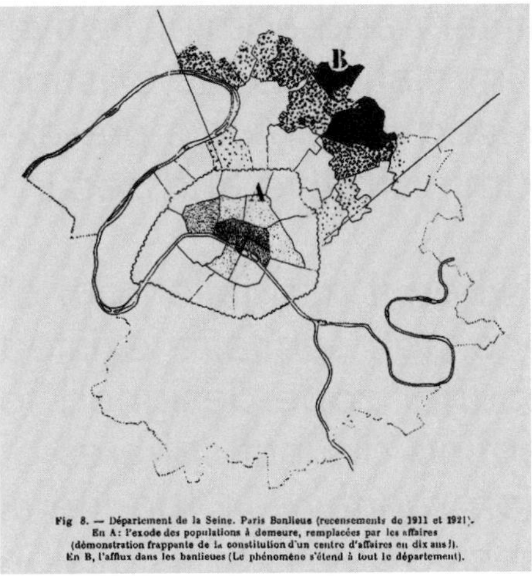

Fig 8. — Département de la Seine. Paris Banlieue (recensements de 1911 et 1921).
En A: l'exode des populations à demeure, remplacées par les affaires (démonstration frappante de la constitution d'un centre d'affaires ou city au sens). En B, l'afflux dans les banlieues (Le phénomène s'étend à tout le département).

41 Ebenezer Howard in Patrick Geddes, "Civics: As Applied Sociology," *Sociological Papers* 1904, no. 1 (1905), 103–38, here 119–20.

fig.10 Population growth in the surroundings of Paris 1911–1921 Source: Le Corbusier, *Urbanisme* (Paris: Crès, n.d. [1925]), 105

42 Andrew Shanken has only recently called for this field of research to be cultivated. See Andrew M. Shanken, "The Visual Culture of Planning," in *Journal of Planning History* 17, no. 4 (2018), 300–19.

Infection and the Politics of Space: The *Cordon Sanitaire*
Miloš Kosec and Leslie Topp

Miloš Kosec is an associate research fellow at the Department of History of Art at Birkbeck, University of London.

Leslie Topp is Professor of Architectural History at the Department of History of Art at Birkbeck, University of London.

1 This article emerged from the early stages of work in progress on a collaborative project by the authors, focusing on the *cordon sanitaire* in the context of the past and present of perimeter and boundary walls, physical and intangible. Together with historical examples, the article takes into account various ways in which movement was limited during the first and second waves of the COVID-19 pandemic up to October 2020. Since that date, the situation has evolved, but the main *cordon sanitaire* features analyzed here continue to manifest themselves, including border closures, travel bans, and the conversion of municipal and regional boundaries into restrictive barriers.

2 In a 2013 article, Eugenia Tognotti traced the decline of the use of quarantine and the *cordon sanitaire* in the late nineteenth century and its partial and inconsistent revival with the 1918 influenza pandemic. Cordons did not appear again until the SARS epidemic in 2003. Eugenia Tognotti, "Lessons from the History of Quarantine, from Plague to Influenza A," *Emerging Infectious Diseases* 19, no. 2 (February 2013), 254–59.

Since the start of the pandemic, the measures taken to control the spread of coronavirus have been consistently spatial. Some of the first responses, undertaken before the winter of 2020 ended, included the erection of *cordons sanitaires* in China and subsequently in Italy. The *cordon sanitaire* has a long history, and one of the uncanniest aspects of the pandemic has been the return of techniques of disease control—and social control—that seemed to belong to a distant past. Indeed, as we show below, cordons, by making certain forms of movement impossible, have an impact not only on space but also on time, casting people back into pre-modern forms of transport, even if augmented by the latest technological aides. We also observe how cordons—historically and now—have a complicated and shifting relationship to pre-existing boundaries and barriers, both military and administrative. Cordons are for the most part arbitrary in relation to the existing built environment, but at the same time tend to reinforce pre-existing and predominantly intangible administrative and security infrastructure. **1**

In the decades of the Cold War, when it had fallen out of use as a public health technique, the *cordon sanitaire* existed primarily metaphorically as a political buffer zone designed to avoid triggering conflict by tacitly accepting distinct spheres of influence. The resurrection of the *cordon sanitaire* in the literal sense has turned our attention to the specific details of its design and operation. **2** A *cordon sanitaire* is, strictly speaking, a physical barrier restricting individuals' and goods' entry into, and exit from, an area, for the primary—or ostensible—purpose of controlling the spread of infectious disease. Often it operates in conjunction with a quarantine system—that is, with the isolation of people or goods in transit until they are deemed to be free of infection and can continue on their way. A cordon can be intended either to keep a defined region free from disease coming from the outside, or it can be to contain the disease within a given area to prevent it from spreading into regions further afield. A close relative of the *cordon sanitaire* is the boundary enclosing an area (usually with what is deemed to be an exceptionally high rate of infection) within which a set of restrictions on individuals and businesses operate. The boundary differentiates it from the areas beyond—but these restrictions do not necessarily include a ban on movement into or out of the area.

Cordons vary widely, both in the shape they take and in the extent and nature of their material existence. Some are rings around urban centers or islands. Others are lines, often across great distances or extending from one coast to another. They can be continuous (a fence, wall, or unbroken and controlled protective barrier) or discontinuous (blocks or checkpoints set up across selected transport routes but without barriers between them). Elements of the cordon might also exist within the perimeter of an enclosed area—for instance, at the entrance to railway stations in the center of a city. And of course, the "barrier" can consist of legislation or fiat to suspend the operation of mass transport into or out of an area, or laws (or advice) against individual travel beyond a particular boundary, either in conjunction with, or in place of, physical boundaries such as roadblocks. Both tangible and intangible cordons depend on surveillance for enforcement, whether in the form of military or police patrols, civilian informants, or remote video monitoring.

The elements that make up a cordon respond to the mode of transport that is most often used to enter or leave an area. Before mass air travel, regions and cities on maritime trade routes used cordons during times of plague, yellow fever, and cholera to maintain strict control over access from the sea. [3] The officials governing the Spanish island of Majorca, for instance, set up cordons around the island twenty-eight times between 1787 and 1899; these consisted of "defensive rings set up in order to guard the whole of the island perimeter intensively from the land, with the support of coast guard boats." [4] New Zealand was highlighted during the 2020 pandemic as one of the nations that has most successfully kept the virus at bay, ensuring freedom of movement within the nation in large part by closing its borders and keeping any infected parties out. The fact that it is an island nation has naturally played a role in this, but the crucial element of its cordon is the restriction of air travel, not a defensive ring of coastal lookouts and patrolling boats. [5]

Similarly, the type of land-based transport used to access an area and connect it to other significant population centers determines the form a cordon takes. In Wuhan, as the urban studies academic Fei Chen explains, urban design decisions concentrating the land access to the city into a few channels (rail lines and multi-lane motorways) meant that the strict cordon established there in January 2020 consisted of a limited number of road blocks (some of which were reinforced toll barriers) and government orders cancelling rail services. "People who live on the periphery of the city may still be able to get out through small local road networks that mainly lead to villages or the countryside," she wrote. "As long as the major roads are closed off, they are not able to reach other major cities with a large, concentrated population and the quarantine remains effective." [6]

3 Pere Salas-Vives and Joana-Maria Pujadas-Mora, "*Cordons Sanitaires* and the Rationalization Process in Southern Europe (Nineteenth-Century Majorca)," *Medical History* 62, no. 3 (July 2018), 314–32, here 315–16.

4 Salas-Vives and Pujadas-Mora, "*Cordons Sanitaires*," 319.

5 Michael Plank et al., "How New Zealand Could Keep Eliminating Coronavirus at Its Border for Months to Come, Even as the Global Pandemic Worsens," *The Conversation*, July 16, 2020, https://theconversation.com/how-new-zealand-could-keep-eliminating-coronavirus-at-its-border-for-months-to-come-even-as-the-global-pandemic-worsens-142368 (accessed October 8, 2020).

6 Fei Chen, "Coronavirus: Why China's Strategy to Contain the Virus Might Work," *The Conversation*, January 30, 2020, https://theconversation.com/coronavirus-why-chinas-strategy-to-contain-the-virus-might-work-130729 (accessed October 8, 2020).

A press image of a roadblock on a motorway leading out of Wuhan conveys the vast scale of transport infrastructure but also the way the rationalization and concentration of travel into a few enormous corridors means that the infrastructure contains within itself the means of stopping as well as facilitating travel. fig.1 The block is positioned at a place where traffic pauses anyway at a toll barrier. While evoking the pleasure of rapid mechanical movement with its swooping, roller coaster-esque superstructure, the barrier has, with only a few lightweight, ephemeral, and multicolored barriers, been converted into a link in the cordon "chain"

fig.1 Roadblock on motorway leading into Wuhan, China, January 25, 2020
Source: Hector Retamal — Getty Images

around Wuhan. The image conveys the unique morphology of this barrier. It is a field rather than a line, the toll barrier itself just one element in a thick, layered composition consisting of supplemental barriers, empty space, and human patrols. The woman waiting with her suitcase in the foreground (a nurse waiting for a lift back into Wuhan, according to the caption) seems transplanted from a slower world of pedestrians and taxi lines; the space behind her suddenly emptied of the streams of speeding vehicles that would normally eradicate the possibility of the stationary, unprotected human body. A channel of movement has become an empty square. This local spatial transformation signals a citywide one, which is also a temporal transformation. The people of Wuhan during the period of the cordon, with the channels of mass transport switched off, were projected back into a past era of transport, relying, if they wanted to leave the city, on the small-scale, unplanned web of city — countryside connections which continued to exist, neglected, on the periphery.

A much more intimate, continuous, and obviously confining type of *cordon sanitaire* comes about when the area being contained or cut off is relatively small and the routes into it are many (especially when people normally enter and leave by car, by horse, or on foot). This kind of cordon can be seen in a 1911 image from the *Illustrated London News*, in which the artist depicts a fenced-off rural village. 7 **fig. 2** The accompanying text tells us that this is a village in Romania that has been isolated during the cholera pandemic that affected large swathes of Asia, the Middle East, Russia, the Balkans, and parts of Europe. 8 In the image's middle ground is a continuous fence, about six feet high, made of woven willow. Behind the fence, presumably having climbed up on supports, are three young women in local costume, and directly behind them is a picturesque jumble of thatched cottages. The women are speaking with two men in military uniform in the foreground; these men stand on a track which runs along the fence; two more soldiers patrol in the middle distance along another stretch of the fence, which, with its accompanying track, disappears into the distance. The text tells us that the image represents an "infected hamlet," which has become "the center of a circle of soldiers" — we are meant to imagine the willow fence, track, and the soldiers tightly enclosing the village, cutting across and rendering impassable a web of roads and tracks leading from the settlement into what we imagine to be the agricultural land surrounding it. 9

The cordon here, then, is a single continuous physical barrier, like an ephemeral city wall — though without, at least in this image, any gates. But whereas in the image of the Wuhan road block the bodies being contained within the cordon are only implied as anonymous inhabitants of the shadowy tower blocks in the distance, this image and the cordon it represents operate at such a small scale that we see the contained bodies and their dwellings straining against the barrier and its miniature militarized zone beyond.

In this early twentieth-century image of disease control measures in the rural Balkans for the London reading public, we see the alluringly disordered and dangerous past under control by a scientifically minded present, but only just. The barrier containing the villagers is flimsy, and the soldiers, representatives of the state, are susceptible to the charms of the three women, whose embroidered linens and head scarves allude to prevalent stereotypes of Balkan women as standing for a continuous, pre-industrial past existing within the present. 10 The tree branches and stakes bearing broken pots and an ox skull hovering significantly over the head of one of the soldiers may allude to

7 "The Universal Enemy: A Dread Foe the World Is Fighting," *Illustrated London News*, November 18, 1911, 13.

8 "The Universal Enemy," 13. The text also relates that the village represented had been a particular target for isolation since the rumor had taken hold there that doctors were killing infected people, and therefore inhabitants refused to be treated. There is no commentary on the skull and other ornaments on the fence—we presume they are meant to represent talismans, warding off the evil which the villagers see as coming from outside.

9 "The Universal Enemy," 13.

10 Thank you to Katarzyna Murawska-Muthesius for sharing forthcoming material on the topic of the trope of Eastern European women in ethnic dress. Katarzyna Murawska-Muthesius, *Imaging and Mapping Eastern Europe: Sarmatia Europea to Post-Communist Bloc* (New York: Routledge, 2021).

the more archaic past of pagan tree-cults. [11] The project of cordoning off disorder and disease seems a precarious one, undermined by unruly elements of a past that lives on into the present.

The *Illustrated London News* image, with its play on tropes of the "wild East," echoes in miniature the historically most-notorious *cordon sanitaire*, which until 1871 formed an entire border region on the eastern edge of Europe. The so-called *Militärgrenze* (military frontier), a deep strip of land along the edge of the Habsburg Empire where it met the border with the Ottoman Empire, was established in 1522 and consisted materially of a series of fortified outposts and military garrisons. The *Militärgrenze* was meant to defend the empire from Ottoman military attack. Beginning in the early eighteenth century, the border, which extended from the Adriatic to Transylvania, gained the additional function of a permanent *cordon sanitaire*, intended to prevent the spread of bubonic plague from outbreaks in the Ottoman Empire. [12] A map from 1830 shows that this was not just a border but a wide, ribbon-like region. fig.3 According to William O'Reilly, over time, "the 33,422 square kilometers of land that comprised the military frontier metamorphosed into a complex region with different law codes, privileges, and customary duties when compared with other areas in the empire." [13] Boro Bronza refers to it as a "living wall." [14]

The fortresses and military garrisons along the border were designated the task of defending the Austrian Empire as well as enforcing border, customs, and refugee regimes. This existing military infrastructure provided a good base for the complex *cordon sanitaire* system, and since the 1970s, historians have revised the traditional military historians' views of the *Militärgrenze* to stress its significance not only as a military but also as a *Pestfront* or sanitary frontier, especially after the threat of Ottoman invasion grew smaller in the late eighteenth and early nineteenth centuries. [15] Gary Magee describes how the cordon:

"consisted of a chain of manned lookouts, each within musket range of each other, regular patrols and Bauernsoldaten stationed ... along the frontier. Guards

11 Tree worship, its roots in ancient religions and its continuation among the European peasantry, were discussed at length in James George Frazer's widely read *The Golden Bough* (London: Macmillan, 1890). Thank you to the editors for alerting us to this reference.

12 "Militärgrenze (English), AEIOU," in Austria-Forum, *das Wissensnetz*, https://austria-forum.org/af/AEIOU/Militärgrenze (accessed February 10, 2021); Gary B. Magee, "Disease Management in Pre-Industrial Europe: A Reconsideration of the Efficacy of the Local Response to Epidemics," *Journal of European Economic History* 26, no. 3 (January 1997), 605–23, here 610–11. The measures establishing quarantine were taken gradually beginning in 1710, but Bronza dates the beginning of the *cordon sanitaire* proper to 1728, when a patent was issued for the construction of a system of quarantine along the border. Boro Bronza, "Austrian Measures for Prevention and Control of the Plague Epidemic Along the Border with the Ottoman Empire During the 18th Century," *Scripta Medica* 50, no. 4 (December 2019), 177–84, here 179.

13 William O'Reilly, "Fredrick Jackson Turner's Frontier Thesis, Orientalism, and the Austrian *Militärgrenze*," *Journal of Austrian-American History* 2, no. 1 (2018), 1–30, here 9.

14 Bronza, "Austrian Measures," 179.

15 O'Reilly, "Fredrick Jackson Turner's Frontier," 10, 12; Bronza, "Austrian Measures," 177–79.

fig.2 "The Universal Enemy: A Dread Foe the World Is Fighting," *Illustrated London News*, November 18, 1911, 13 *were under orders to fire on all illegal traffic attempting to enter the Empire without passing through a quarantine station."* **16**

16 Magee, "Disease Management," 610.

17 We are grateful to Richard Kurdiovsky for his assistance in determining the approximate date of this drawing through reference to comparable design drawings by architects working for the imperial bureaucracy.

Three watchtower designs—dating from the late eighteenth or early nineteenth century—emphasize viewing angles for spotting smugglers and potential plague carriers. **17** **fig.4** This is the type of *cordon sanitaire* infrastructure of the Austrian *Militärgrenze* that would have been experienced by the British writer Alexander William Kinglake while traveling over the border into the Ottoman Empire. In his 1844 travel narrative *Eothen*, which recounted a journey from ten years earlier, he describes the strict separation of two frontier towns which "are less than a cannon-shot distant, and yet their people hold no communion. ... It is the Plague, and the dread of the Plague that divides the one people from the other." The strict enforcement of frontier quarantine was administered by the Austrian officials who were themselves living in

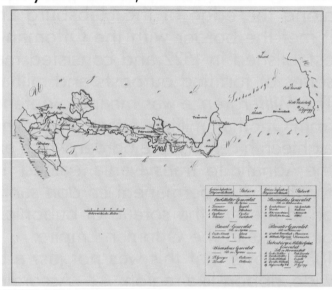

fig.3 Map of the Austrian *Militärgrenze* from 1830. J.N. von Metzberg, "Übersichtskarte von der Militärgrenze," *Tafel zur Statistik der Österreichischen Monarchie*, 3 (1830), n.p.
Source: Austrian National Library, Bildarchiv

a state of "perpetual excommunication" as "compromised" individuals; that is, those who were "in contact with people or things supposed to be capable of conveying infection." The punishment for transgressing the cordon was severe: "if you dare to break the laws of quarantine, you will be tried with military haste; the court will scream out your sentence to you from a tribunal some fifty yards off; the priest, instead of gently whispering to you the sweet hopes of religion, will console you at a dueling distance, and after that you will find yourself carefully shot, and carelessly buried in the ground of the Lazaretto." **18**

18 Alexander William Kinglake, *Eothen, or Traces of Travel Brought Home From the East* (Evanston, IL: Northwestern University Press, 1997 [1844]), viii, 1–2.

O'Reilly has shown that, despite the sanitary effectiveness and rational military organization of the frontier area, the image of the *Militärgrenze* was that of a wild territory of crime and adventure in the minds of Westerners and Austrians alike. In the widespread image of Balkanism, the military frontier was seen as "a place simultaneously forbiddingly unknown and desirably exotic, hostile and romantic." **19** We can see these kinds of Orientalist tropes still at play in the 1911 image of the isolated Balkan village discussed above. The soldiers in the foreground could be from any of the European armies; their uniforms and military technology are familiar to the readers of the *Illustrated London News* and could be taken to represent modernity, framing as

19 O'Reilly, "Fredrick Jackson Turner's Frontier," 15.

well as containing the uncontrollable (cultural, infrastructural, or epidemic) wilderness beyond the *cordon sanitaire*.

In an April 2020 opinion piece for the *Wall Street Journal*, the historians of Habsburg Austria, Charles Ingrao and A. Wess Mitchell (who served as Assistant Secretary of State for Europe-

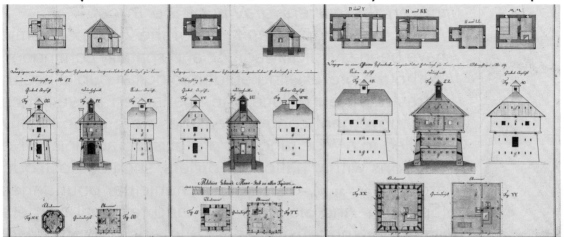

fig. 4 Designs for watchtowers forming part of the cordon on the Austrian *Militär-grenze*
Source: Historical Archives of Belgrade, collection of plans and maps, inventory number IAB-1184-IG-1/9

an and Eurasian Affairs in the Trump administration between 2017 and 2019), drew parallels between the *cordon sanitaire* along the Habsburg *Militärgrenze* and the US restrictions on travel from China (source of "the world's worst contagions—SARS (2002–2003), avian flu (2005) and now Covid-19") in March 2020. [20] As we write this article in October 2020, the parallel with the United States' extensive land border with Canada seems more apposite. An existing enforced border stretching thousands of miles has become a *cordon sanitaire*; at this stage in the pandemic, Canada, with its science-focused government and relatively low rate of infection, is in the role of the Hapsburg Empire, defending itself against infection from the "wild," irrationally governed, and COVID-19-ridden United States. [21] Of course in 2020, the measures taken to control infection by no means end at the border, with Canada (along with almost all other countries across the world) employing increased surveillance and limiting movement via mobile applications, voluntary and imposed quarantine measures based in people's homes, and different regimes of movement and selective population control for different groups of people within the same geographical area. A delineation of territory along a single line controlled by border posts, fences, and walls exists alongside a much deeper zone of surveillance and movement restriction. On closer inspection, such one-layered delineation perhaps never existed on its own. A zone made up not only of the border line itself but crucially supplemented by the auxiliary infrastructure both in front and behind the line of control is a characteristic of many of the older, even pre-modern *cordons sanitaires*. This depth existed in the operations of the *Militärgrenze*. As Magee describes:

20 A. Wess Mitchell and Charles Ingrao, "Emperor Joseph's Solution to Coronavirus," *Wall Street Journal*, April 6, 2020, https://www.wsj.com/articles/emperor-josephs-solution-to-coronavirus-11586214561 (accessed February 10, 2021). One of the "insights for our times" that the history of the Habsburg *cordon sanitaire* provides, according to the authors, "is that physical space matters in fighting epidemics. Hard as it is to swallow for Western publics habituated to globalization, well-regulated, rational borders contribute substantially to the public good. Early critics of the Trump administration's travel restrictions failed to appreciate the urgent medical rationale. As Anthony Fauci testified to Congress, no public-health strategy can contain a contagion already inside the country without stopping the influx of new carriers."

21 Paula Newton, "Covid-19 Built a 'Northern Wall' between the US and Canada and It Could Stay Up Longer than Anyone Expected," *CNN Travel*, September 1, 2020, https://edition.cnn.com/travel/article/covid-wall-canada-us-trnd/index.html (accessed November 17, 2020).

22 Magee, "Disease Management," 610–11.

23 "Covid-19 Local Lockdown—Postcode Checker," *Tableau Software*, 2020, https://public.tableau.com/views/Covid-19Local-Lockdown-Postcode-Checker/Postcodes (accessed October 1, 2020).

24 Sam Jones, "Protests in Madrid over Coronavirus Lockdown Measures," *Guardian*, September 20, 2020, https://www.theguardian.com/world/2020/sep/20/protests-madrid-coronavirus-lockdown-measures-spain (accessed October 7, 2020).

25 "STA: Janša Says Restrictions Here To Stay, No Inter-Municipal Movement During Holidays," *English.Sta.Si*, April 25, 2020, https://english.sta.si/2756863/jansa-says-restrictions-here-to-stay-no-inter-municipal-movement-during-holidays (accessed October 7, 2020).

26 Rhea Mahbubani and Alison Millington, "Italy Has Put 16 Million People on Lockdown to Control the Escalating Coronavirus Outbreak," *Business Insider*, March 8, 2020, https://www.businessinsider.com/italy-lockdown-lombardy-11-provinces-coronavirus-crisis-2020-3 (accessed October 7, 2020).

27 "Coronavirus: Australia to Close Victoria-New South Wales Border," *BBC News*, July 6, 2020, https://www.bbc.com/news/world-australia-53303317 (accessed October 7, 2020).

28 "Coronavirus: Leo Varadkar 'Now Is the Time for Further Action,'" *BBC News*, March 27, 2020, https://www.bbc.com/news/world-europe-52071733 (accessed October 7, 2020).

29 The main extra restriction imposed in Leicester was a ban on households mixing with each other, either at home or elsewhere. Department of Health and Social Care, "Leicester: Local Restrictions," July 17, 2020, https://www.gov.uk/guidance/leicester-lockdown-what-you-can-and-cannot-do (accessed October 6, 2020).

"Supplementing the cordon was a network of government agents, operating within the Ottoman Empire, who sought out information on the current status of the plague in Turkey … Based on this information, the cordon could be strengthened or relaxed, depending on the current gravity of the threat." [22]

The *cordons sanitaires* of the 2020 pandemic have been stylistically ad hoc and spatially contingent. Without a pre-existing epidemiological public health infrastructure in place, the spatialized surveillance and movement control measures were often hastily applied to a wide range of pre-existing administrative divisions within national borders, such as postcode areas (UK [23]), district and municipal boundaries (Spain [24] and Slovenia [25]), and regional borders (Italy [26] and Australia [27]). In addition to these, other more spatially abstract limitations on freedom of movement were devised, such as a two-kilometer radius around one's home (Ireland [28]).

What all these ways of defining the *cordon sanitaire* share is the almost complete intangibility and invisibility of the border. In contrast to the sentry towers of the *Militärgrenze*, and the fencing surrounding Balkan villages during cholera outbreaks, these boundaries are visible only on maps. The continuous updating of digital map data obscures the history of the movement of the cordon. Unsurprisingly, they have also given rise to much confusion. When, after a local increase in COVID-19 cases, the city of Leicester in England had extra restrictions imposed on it in July 2020, a question about the precise boundaries of the city and the quarantine area was raised immediately. [29] It was only at this point that the archaic nature of such a question became evident. The precise boundary of the city in pre-modern Europe was a question of pragmatic importance, because of different legal, taxation, and security regimes that the position on one or the other side of the line brought with it. The most extreme form of this boundary, the city wall, presented the limit as a physical fact. It has been over a century since the last cities were stripped of functioning walls, and the border shifted to the exterior perimeter of the nation state (or, more recently, of a group of states like the Schengen states in the European Union). 30 Therefore, the dismay over the spatial re-imposition of boundaries around elements of the state, like cities, is understandable.

In the case of Leicester, the city council's original solution was to publish a city map (based on an Ordnance Survey map) with a red line delineating the area of the lockdown. fig.5 Furious reaction over the unclear boundary due to the width of the line and the small scale of the map (that put parts of the city into an ambivalent zone that was neither within nor outside of the lockdown zone) followed, and, after the unclear status of those living in the area "on the line" was realized, the city officials acknowledged the deficiency of the mode of representation of the ad hoc boundary with a statement: "nothing is perfect and that includes this map." 31 Instead of the map, the city council set up a website with the list of postcodes included in the lockdown. 32 This measure was more precise but even more abstract than the map and hard to navigate due to the large number of postcode areas arranged in an administrative and alphabetical order, rather than spatially (that is, corresponding with how the postcode areas are actually perceived, used, and connected to one another). The city council soon published a code checker where it was possible to check whether one's postcode was within or outside of the lockdown zone. 33 Finally, on July 16, 2020, the Secretary of State for Health, Matt Hancock, changed the lockdown boundary definition. Local media informed the public that, from July 18, 2020, "only residents who live in the City of Leicester and the borough of Oadby and Wigston are in the lockdown zone. This means that if you pay your council tax to Leicester City or Oadby and Wigston Borough Council, you remain in the restricted area." 34 There was an uneasy coupling of reliance on the individual resident to determine whether or not they lived in the restricted zone (via the postcode checker or their own tax records) with coercive top-down enforcement through policing and penalties. 35 Thus, we can see that the definition of the swiftly imposed *cordon sanitaire* changed three times over the course of fourteen days. Each of the three definitions was based on a different set of spatial parameters: the first was based on a general survey map, the second on a postal service administrative division, and the third on the taxation register. This raises the question of the difficulty and arbitrariness of imposing and enforcing ad hoc delineations within the largely seamless urbanized space, within which liberalized rules of movement operate in contemporary societies.

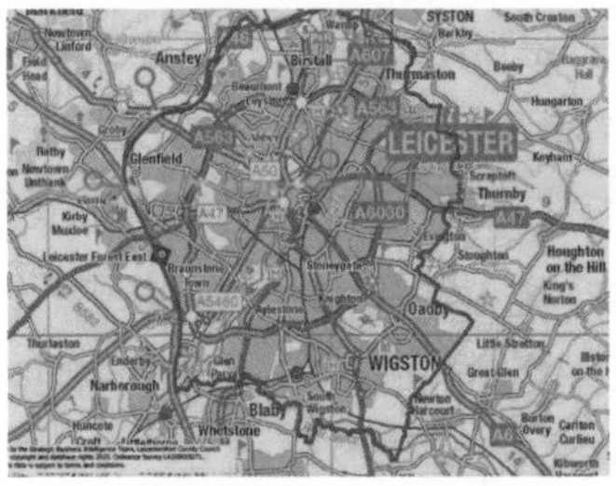

30 John Torpey, *The Invention of the Passport: Surveillance, Citizenship and the State*, 2nd ed. (Cambridge: Cambridge University Press, 2018), 1—3.

fig.5 Initial Leicester July 2020 lockdown boundary Source: Dan Martin/ Leicestershirelive, July 2, 2020, https://www. leicestermercury.co.uk/ news/leicester-news/ council-explains-leicester-lockdown-zone (accessed October 3, 2020)

31 Dan Martin, "Council Explains Lockdown Zone Boundary After Furious Reaction," Leicestershirelive, July 2, 2020, https://www. leicestermercury.co.uk/ news/leicester-news/ council-explains-leicester-lockdown-zones-4287492 (accessed July 9, 2020).

32 "Covid-19 Local Lockdown—Postcode Checker."

33 Dan Martin and Amy Orton, "This Is the Postcode Checker for the Leicester Lockdown Zone," *Leicestershirelive*, 2020, https://www. leicestermercury.co.uk/ news/leicester-news/ postcode-checker-tell-you-you-4280178 (accessed July 9, 2020).

34 "Covid-19 Local Lockdown—Postcode Checker."

35 The main UK government guidelines for Leicester residents stated that "the police will be able to take action against those who break these rules," and stipulated a scale of fines for individuals and business, increasing for multiple offenses. Department of Health and Social Care, "Leicester: Local Restrictions."

If the contemporary *cordons sanitaires* have been improvised on the existing foundations of administrative and largely intangible divisions quite unlike the physical *cordons sanitaires* of the past, the desired effect of the cordon has hardly changed at all. The limitation of movement to the radius of a city, municipality, or even a walkable two-kilometer radius (as in the case of Ireland) seems to invoke the transport and physical movement patterns of a pre-modern society, even if the measures for implementing these limitations have become high-tech, digital, and virtual. Wuhan, with its mobile applications and drone surveillance but also with its improvised roadblocks and controlled checkpoints that are merely an update of the *cordon sanitaire* from the *Illustrated London News*, has became both more of a pre-modern and technologically advanced city than before the outbreak. Something similar can be observed in the case of Leicester, although the cordon was enacted with surveillance and enforcement techniques more in tune with the standards of liberal democracy. For both Wuhan and Leicester, the present-day physical city fabric, largely dating from the nineteenth and twentieth centuries, represents neither a hindrance nor a welcome infrastructure. The cordon exists quite independently of the physical fabric of the city, which can accommodate both the archaic movement patterns and the high-tech surveillance techniques equally well. The *cordon sanitaire* city of 2020–2021 is more determined by invisible administrative borders, controlled checkpoints, and virtual geolocation applications than by its walls and surfaces.

This short and by no means comprehensive overview of the history of the *cordon sanitaire* suggests that certain elements of the sudden and spatially arbitrary rewriting of the use of space reoccur. Cordons past and present may differ strikingly in appearance, location, and function, but they often share a similar negating relationship to the contexts in which they are imposed. They upend the ways we delineate and move through space because they act as barriers against a dynamic occurrence (such as a pandemic) that spreads through the existing infrastructure of communication, culture, and trade networks. In that sense, the *cordon sanitaire* can be seen as a contextual negation of the preceding and surrounding space. In many of the cases of the *cordon sanitaire*, both historical and contemporary, its area and operations are targeted precisely against the very spatial qualities that are meant to make infection possible: unbounded movement, liberalized trading, unlimited connection, and easy transgression of borders that have shed their physical properties, keeping merely their administrative and abstract lines on maps.

The Habsburg *Militärgrenze* represents a spatial model of reinforcement rather than negation. Here the *cordon sanitaire* evolves on top of a pre-existing militarized infrastructure and shares the longevity of that infrastructure. The 2010s were a period in which armed boundaries and borders were erected anew across the globe; it will be interesting to see whether this relatively fresh, armed infrastructure leads to a more durable system of *cordons sanitaires*. Together with the newly imposed *cordons sanitaires* that include district, municipal, and regional borders, they might with time evolve, transmute, and solidify into permanent and overt social control, exclusion, or containment infrastructure.

Gregorio Astengo is a scientific assistant at the Institute for the History and Theory of Architecture (gta), ETH Zurich.

1 Daniel Defoe, A Journal of the Plague Year (London: E. Nutt, 1722), 19.

2 Paul Slack, The Impact of Plague in Tudor and Stuart England (London: Routledge and Kegan Paul, 1985), 187.

3 Gary W. Shannon and Robert G. Cromley, "The Great Plague of London, 1665," Urban Geography 1, no. 3 (1980), 254–70; Slack, Impact of Plague; Justin Champion, London's Dreaded Visitation: The Social Geography of the Great Plague 1665 (London: Historical Geography Research Group, 1995); Edward Copeland, "Defoe and the London Wall: Mapped Perspectives," Eighteenth-Century Fiction 10, no. 4 (July 1998), 407–28.

The London Wall and the Great Plague of 1665
Gregorio Astengo

"The Face of London was now indeed strangely alter'd, I mean the whole Mass of Buildings, City, Liberties, Suburbs, Westminster, Southwark *and altogether; for as to the particular Part called the City, or within the Walls, that was not yet much infected."* [1]

During a period of about ten months over the summer of 1665, almost 20 percent of the population of London died from an epidemic of bubonic plague. Known as the Great Plague, this was the last of a long series of outbreaks—occurring in England previously in 1603, 1625, and 1636—which killed about one fifth of London's overall population as part of the centuries-long "second plague pandemic." [2] Among other major epidemics, the Great Plague of London stands out not only for its high body count and the rate at which it killed victims but also for the vast documentation produced at the time. This includes burial counts, especially the weekly "Bills of Mortality" (the weekly reports collected by parish officials and built up to create burial chronicles for all London parishes) as well as personal accounts and narratives, like those of Daniel Defoe and Samuel Pepys, which provide insights into the epidemiology and cultural dimension of the plague. In fact, the vast scholarship on the Great Plague has systematically focused on these sources to produce comprehensive spatial patterns of the plague upon the social geography of London. [3]

In line with existing studies on the urban dimension of the plague, this paper investigates the role of an overlooked yet fundamental element of the city, the London Wall. Since the Middle Ages, the ancient Roman fortification surrounding the central portion of London changed from a military installation into an important piece of administrative infrastructure, separating the wealthier 30 percent of the population living inside its perimeter from the rest of metropolitan London. During the summer of 1665, the Wall turned into an active participant in the movement, management, and cultural conception of the pandemic. It not only drove the spread of the plague but, more importantly, offered to the authorities a system to control the displacement of civilians, at the same time producing the powerful image of a barrier against the "invading" disease. In establishing the Wall as a physical presence, containment system, and cultural imaginary, I argue that the nature of the London Wall as a mechanism for social segregation already existed "within" the Roman structure and was reactivated during the months of the plague. Thanks to its accepted institutional dimension within the political geography of London, the Wall temporarily reacquired previously latent characteristics, directing the plague, generating policy, and filtering perceptions of the disease. fig.1

London and Its Wall

As in many urban settlements with a fortified past, since its Roman inception in the first century CE, London had always been surrounded by a defensive wall. While the presence of a wall may not be particularly noteworthy, the London Wall had, since the Norman Conquest in the eleventh century, come to shape the political geography of the city along two autonomous and interdependent centers of governance. The Royal Government held general power over metropolitan London and its region, with headquarters located in the palace of Whitehall in Westminster along the River Thames to the southeast. Meanwhile, the central area of London was governed by a distinguished local authority known as the Corporation. The Corporation held jurisdiction over an area encompassing the central and more ancient portion of the city, the so-called Square Mile. It appointed its own mayor, police force, and guilds, and held substantial independence from the Crown. This area was often simply known as "the City," distinguishing it from the rest of London, whose political territory continued in all directions into the countryside. [4]

The jurisdiction of the City was made up of 113 parishes, of which ninety-seven constituted its primary political body. [5] These ninety-seven parishes were physically separated from the sixteen outer "liberties" and from the rest of London by the imposing presence of the Roman Wall, a brick-and-stone defensive fortification surrounding the City towards the west, north, and east. Originally erected around the third century to defend the Roman settlement of Londinium, the Wall was a substantial feat of engineering and one of the largest Roman fortifications in the British Isles. Despite being abandoned after the fall of the Empire, it was subsequently renovated during the Middle Ages. As a result, in the seventeenth century the Wall remained a continuous and imposing presence in London: up to nine meters tall, it ran for more than three kilometers around three sides of the City. [6] Its oldest portions, up to two meters thick, were made of ragstone mixed with mortar, upon which newer segments of brickwork were added, often with battlements on top. fig.2

Despite its impressive appearance, since the Late Middle Ages the Wall had retained no military function, progressively turning into an organic component of the urban fabric. [7] Since the early sixteenth century, dozens of houses, churches, shops, and scrapyards encroached along both sides of the Roman structure, and London continued for miles beyond it. Its seven primary

4 Steen E. Rasmussen, London: The Unique City (London: Jonathan Cape, 1937), 33–36.

5 The jurisdictional division of early modern London was subject to some debate. For the purpose of this essay, the system adopted is the one proposed by Vanessa Harding, "The Population of London, 1550–1700: A Review of the Published Evidence," London Journal 15, no. 2 (1990), 111–28, here 111–14.

6 Walter G. Bell, F. Cottrill, and Charles Spon, London Wall through Eighteen Centuries: A History of the Ancient Town Wall of the City of London (London: Simpkin Marshall, 1937); Brian Hobley, "The Archaeology of London Wall," London Journal 7, no. 1 (1981), 3–14.

7 Even during the English Civil War, just some twenty years earlier, it was decided to defend the perimeter of London by erecting a new system of lines of communication, an eighteen-kilometer-long rampart encompassing both the city and its suburbs. Hobley, "Archaeology," 13; Simon Marsh, "The Construction and Arming of London's Defences 1642–1645," Journal of the Society for Army Historical Research 91, no. 368 (Winter 2013), 275–98.

fig. 1 Wenceslaus
Hollar, map of London
from the *Atlas Van
der Hagen*, late
seventeenth century
Source: Koninklijke
Bibliotheek, Nether-
lands

8 From east to west, they are: Ludgate, Newgate, Aldersgate, Cripplegate, Moorgate, Bishopsgate, and Aldgate. Thomas De Laune, *Angliæ Metropolis: Or, the Present State of London* (London: George Larkin, 1690), 11.

fig. 2 Remaining portion of the eastern end of the London Wall in Tower Hill
Source: Brian Hobley, "The Archaeology of London Wall," *London Journal* 7, no. 1 (1981), 3–14, here 12

9 Ian Doolittle, "'The Great Refusal': Why Does the City of London Corporation Only Govern the Square Mile?" in "A Review of Metropolitan Society Past and Present," special issue, *London Journal* 39, no. 1 (2014), 21–36, here 24–25.

gates had been progressively enlarged to make way for increasing traffic. **8** In addition, over the centuries, the Wall had also been pierced with smaller additional openings known as posterns, becoming increasingly more permeable.

At the same time, the Wall still acted as a partition, and its presence was a determining factor of urban life. For example, its gates guided the development of the major thoroughfares departing from London, such as Aldersgate Street to the north and Whitechapel Street to the east. More importantly, the Wall identified the ninety-seven parishes inside from the rest of London and established the main territory of the City's governance. With the so-called "Great Refusal," a political move dating back to the 1630s and further confirmed in the 1660s, the Corporation had officially withdrawn the suburban land beyond the Wall from its primary authority. **9** This division, generally distinguished as "within" and "without" or "infra" and "extra," was in turn reflected in the name of its parishes, such as St. Giles-without-Cripplegate or St. Audoen-within-Newgate.

As a result, the London Wall operated both as an immaterial urban presence and a substantial piece of political infrastructure. Rather than a tectonic object with any sort of military or even archaeological interest, the Wall existed essentially as a foundational threshold between two layers of London, a condition visible primarily through the simplified, diagrammatic language of maps. In his survey of 1642, graphic artist Wenceslaus Hollar exemplified the nature of the Wall by representing the territory of the City as a dense and coherent entity existing autonomously from the rest of London. **fig. 3** Absent from the engraving, the presence of the Wall is established by the shape and limits of the area, becoming an invisible yet powerfully present demarcation between a sort of citadel and its outer territory. Hollar's bird's-eye view turned a political boundary into a geographical threshold, transforming the City itself into an island, almost metonymic for England's own geography. The Wall negotiated with its presence the system of London's jurisdiction and at the same time limited and contained any sort of territorial expansion, petrifying the image of an immobile, stable City. [10] It is exactly this role, at once invisible and fully present, that determined the social, political, and urban roles of the Wall during the months of the plague.

10 Rasmussen, London, 33.

Pestering Places

With its infrastructural presence, the London Wall both separated and bound two distinct and highly uneven portions of London. Alongside a significant territorial disproportion (the extent of the parishes "without" was about three times that of those "within"), the demographic balance between the London "within" and "without" was also highly uneven. Vanessa Harding has estimated that around 1664, between 88,000 and 100,000 people lived in the ninety-seven parishes inside the Wall, against 172,000 to 200,000 living in the sixteen parishes outside, and even more in the suburban territories beyond. [11] As in other notable cases like Florence or Madrid, this demographic imbalance, in which the presence of the Wall was a determining factor, also carried important socioeconomic consequences. It has been estimated that around the mid-seventeenth century between 25 and 50 percent

11 Harding, "Population of London," 123. Suburban London was itself also highly uneven, with western portions, especially long the Thames and towards Westminster, significantly wealthier than in the east. See for example Michael Power, "The East and West in Early-Modern London", in Wealth and Power in Tudor England. Essays Presented to S. T. Bindoff, ed. Eric William Ives, Robert Jean Knecht, and J. J. Scarisbrick (Bristol: The Athlone Press, 1978), 167–185.

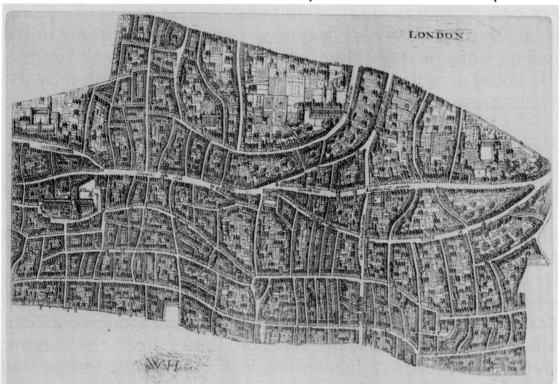

LONDON

fig. 3 Wenceslaus Hollar, survey of the City of London, 1642 Source: University of Toronto

12 This is according to the "hearth tax," a system of contributions introduced by Charles II and based on the number of fireplaces per household. Cf. Vanessa Harding, "Housing and Health in Early Modern London," in Virginia Berridge and Martin Gorsky, eds., Environment, Health and History (Basingstoke: Palgrave Macmillan, 2012), 23–44, here 32; M. J. Power, "The Social Topography of Restoration London," in A. L. Beier and Roger Finlay, eds., London 1500–1700: The Making of the Metropolis (London: Longman, 1986), 208; Slack, Impact of Plague, 159.

of households along and outside the Wall were poor, against less than 2 percent inside, an economic divide which had been growing dramatically since the previous century. [12]

The presence of the Wall then also carried important effects for the social economies of London. Indeed, at the time of the plague, London beyond the Wall was experiencing an unprecedented building boom, driven by immigration and commerce.

13 William C. Baer, "The Institution of Residential Investment in Seventeenth-Century London," *Business History Review* 76, no. 3 (Autumn 2002), 515–51, here 516.

Over the course of a century, more than fifty-five thousand new houses were built in the suburbs, especially towards Westminster, and the population more than tripled. [13] Inside the Wall, this growth was mirrored by a vast densification of the existing built environment, the only possible development of the City's limited urban form, immobilized as it was by the presence of the barrier. This was a notable "annoyance and nuisance" and a cause for concern. John Evelyn's pamphlet *Fumifugium* (1661), devoted to "dissipating" the "epidemicall" miasmas of London's pollution, proposed to move all coal factories towards the periphery and to establish a green belt of trees, orchards, and aromatic shrubs in the "low-grounds circumjacent to the City." [14]

14 John Evelyn, *Fumifugium* (London: W. Godbid, 1661), 24.

Evelyn was perpetuating a paradigm of social and economic layering which, as was the case in many early modern walled metropolises, occupied much of the public perception of London. Also known as "pestered places," the parishes and suburbs beyond the Wall were almost universally associated with dirt, danger, and disease. Epidemics were called "the poores plagues," insisting on an epidemiological distinction between the two social faces of London. In the public eye, the Wall was not only a political entity but a demographic and sanitary one, establishing an immovable border between two distinct urban realms. Unsurprisingly, then, when the Great Plague hit London, the social paradigms of confinement already suggested by the Wall's presence were cemented and heightened.

Moving the Plague

It was in St. Giles-in-the-Fields, one of the largest and most populated parishes of suburban London, almost two kilometers west of the Wall, that the Great Plague was said to have originated, sometime in the early months of 1665. The bubonic plague is a highly contagious disease with a quick and equally high mortality rate. Its agent, *Yersinia pestis*, is a bacterium which primarily infects small animals and is transmitted to humans through infected fleas. [15] However, human blood rarely contains enough bacilli for a flea to catch and carry the infection. That is to say, the bubonic plague rarely follows a human-flea-human sequence. Instead, the disease is generally carried around by animals and spread via fleabites. People normally act as secondary carriers, transporting fleas on their clothes.

15 Slack, *Impact of Plague*, 27

In the case of London, the primary carrier of the bubonic plague was its vast population of black rats. The rat population of seventeenth-century London, a growing capital of commerce and trade, proliferated around granaries, docks, slaughterhouses, factories, landfills, and overcrowded and decaying households, all consistently found in the vast and fast-growing suburban parishes of outer London.

During the month of May 1665, the presence of the plague became substantial and started moving across London through the slow but extensive, and mostly unnoticeable, movement of black rats. The primary public records available to trace the movement of the disease are the "Bills of Mortality". Despite certainly offering an incomplete picture, the "Bills of Mortality" still constitute an important yardstick to investigate the spatial patterns and intensity of the disease, especially in relation to the social and urban geography of London. [16] For instance, the very structure of the Bills followed the infrastructural layering already established by the London Wall. Burial counts were strictly divided between the ninety-seven parishes "within the wall," the sixteen "without the wall," and the rest of London and Westminster, reflecting both the jurisdictional and civic distinction imposed by the Roman barrier.

According to the Bills, from late May onwards the epidemic quickly moved across London, reaching the southern side of the Thames by mid-June. Mortality grew throughout the summer, peaking in September with more than three thousand deaths in a fortnight across five outer parishes. Inside the Wall, the situation was considerably different. Here, plague-related deaths were not reported until the beginning of June, nearly two months after the disease had gained significant momentum. According to H. F., the protagonist of Defoe's *A Journal of the Plague Year*, "we perceiv'd the Infection kept chiefly in the out-Parishes, which being very populous, and fuller also of Poor, the Distemper found more to prey upon than in the City." By mid-July, Defoe remarked, "the City, that is to say within the Walls, was indifferent healthy still." [17] When the plague peaked in early September, deaths inside the Wall remained five times lower than outside, and when the pandemic finally subsided, parishes "within" were the first ones free of deaths. [18] By the end of the epidemic, during the final months of 1665, reported plague deaths reached eighty thousand. [19] Of these, nearly 90 percent were registered outside the London Wall. [20]

As this data suggests, the densely populated City "within" the Wall suffered significantly less than the rest of London. [21] Alongside obvious social and demographic factors — wealthier and healthier parishes ran a lower risk of rat-carried contagions — the significant physical presence of the Wall played an active part in directing the propagation of the plague. [22] The epidemic circled around the Wall and moved across the river before entering its perimeter. The Roman barrier thus turned into

[16] Shannon and Cromley, "Great Plague," 257.

[17] Defoe, *Journal*, 17. With his *Journal*, Defoe was probably compiling something of a "manual," in the form of a narrative, to inform the public about the effects of the plague. Defoe was writing in response to the Great Plague of Marseille, which had been killing hundreds of thousands since 1720 and which at the time threatened to move towards England. Curiously, to contain the spread of the disease, the French authorities erected the so-called *mur de la peste*: a two-meter-high, seventy-centimeter-thick, and twenty-seven-kilometer-long drystone wall stretching across the countryside of Provence to protect the region from Marseille. The *mur*, however, did little to contain the disease. See Ernest B. Gilman, *Plague Writing in Early Modern England* (Chicago: University of Chicago Press, 2009), 230.

[18] Shannon and Cromley, "Great Plague," 263–266.

[19] This number is likely to have been under-reported, and deaths have been estimated as reaching one hundred thousand. See Slack, *Impact of Plague*, 151.

[20] Shannon and Cromley, "Great Plague," 258.

[21] This can still be held true, even though many reported deaths probably occurred inside the Wall, and the bodies were subsequently moved outside for burial and recording.

[22] Shannon and Cromley, "Great Plague," 268.

a true line of defense, making the once-metaphoric image of the City as an "island" into a tangible geographical property. As Defoe put it, "the City was preserv'd more healthy in Proportion, than any other Places all the Time of the Infection." [23] As shown hereinafter, this territorial distinction was only in part determined by the inert presence of the Wall. Instead, the detachment of the City was primarily the result of the enforcement of public policies and protocols put in place to control the spread of the Great Plague, of which the Roman defense became an active component.

23 Defoe, *Journal*, 45.

Defense Mechanisms

In late seventeenth-century London, most of what we now know about the bubonic plague was unfamiliar. The medical explanation of the plague was based on a combination of individual predisposition (the "humors" of the body) and theories of contagion (physical contact and "miasmas"). A further, fundamental component in the early modern epidemiology of the plague was geography. [24] It was in the "pestered places" of suburban London that plague was known to proliferate, and it was there that it had to be confined. However, urban containment measures were, in reality, difficult to enforce. A system of *cordons sanitaires* established between the outer parishes of London in early 1665 was soon abandoned, as it became clear that the plague could easily travel through it. Similarly, the establishment of large pest-houses in the outskirts of the city, despite being a useful and official procedure, was never carried out. [25]

24 Paul Slack, *Plague: A Very Short Introduction* (Oxford: Oxford University Press, 2012), 32.

25 Alanson L. Moote and Dorothy C. Moote, *The Great Plague: The Story of London's Most Deadly Year* (Baltimore: Johns Hopkins University Press, 2004), 14.

In the end, the primary systems employed to counter the spread of the Great Plague were quarantine and eviction. Both were often carried out as a preventive measure and followed unwritten customs. The vast suburban working class inhabiting London's "pestered places" was the first to be isolated, frequently without a diagnosis and solely as a precautionary measure. Humble clothing and other illnesses became signifiers of the plague-ridden, who were forcibly confined to their homes by inexperienced, publicly employed "searchers." In addition, potentially "dangerous" individuals were also pushed out of the perimeter of the Wall and into the outer parishes. On July 4, 1665, the Lord Mayor of the City issued the following order to the Aldermen of the wards:

"That a carefull Watch and Ward be constantly kept at the Gates and Landing Places, to restrain and prevent the ingress of all Vagrants, Beggers, Loose and Dangerous people, from the out parts into this City and Liberties; and to bring to punishment such as shall be apprehended doing the same, according to Law." [26]

26 Quoted in Charles J. Ribton-Turner, *A History of Vagrants and Vagrancy* (London: Chapman and Hall, 1887), 171.

Already a political artifact, establishing the systems of governance between the wealthier City and London's poorer neighborhoods, in the summer of 1665 the London Wall was made into a contamination shield. The protective nature of the Wall became reactivated in official containment protocols, with inevitable repercussions for London's social body. The high mortality of the disease, combined with its unpredictability and association with poverty, turned the City into a sort of fortified citadel, where control and health were maintained through segregation and removal. Entrances to the City were patrolled by armed "watchers," usually employed only during times of conflict, with access generally granted only to the wealthy few. In the orders of 1646, which were adopted again in 1665, it was similarly established that "no wandering beggars be suffered in the streets of this city, in any fashion or manner whatsoever." [27] Unemployment and homelessness were crucially linked to the spread of diseases. [28] Plague victims had to be secluded not only for a matter of health and safety but also to maintain public order. While in Stuart London rudimentary systems of social welfare and charity were present, their effects were often limited. [29] The poor and unemployed were often seen as menacing carriers of both physical disease and moral decay, and as such their movement had to be limited and circumscribed. The presence of disease, it has been suggested, could be systematized into public procedures of close observation and detailed seclusion, meant not only to "purify" the early modern city but to exercise centralized supervision and close monitoring. [30] In this way, the plague turned a pre-existing popular perception into a policy, of which the Wall became the ideal facilitator as a sort of mass-scale "social-distancer." As Paul Slack puts it, "what plague did was to exaggerate features of the demographic scene which would not without it have been so obvious." [31]

If the black rat was the primary carrier of the disease, the articulation of its impact upon the city was man-made. By moving towards defensive strategies to control the pandemic, what was previously an unnoticeable dimension of the London Wall expedited military forms of isolation and forced displacement which in turn shaped the progress of the epidemic.

Under Siege

Like other notable cases, such as Rome and Naples, the plague was seen, essentially, as an enemy. [32] Earlier in the century, the Elizabethan writer Thomas Dekker talked of "the cannon of the Pestilence," insisting on the military dimension of contagion. [33] Plague was an invader, and it had to be defeated by activating systems of urban defense, such as the "watchers". This "process" aligned itself with the common early modern project of isolating sickness,

27 *Orders Conceived and Published by the Lord Major and Aldermen of the City of London, Concerning the Infection of the Plague* (London: James Flesher, 1665), 12.

28 Harding, "Population of London," 32.

29 Wilbur K. Jordan, *Philanthropy in England, 1480–1660: A Study of the Changing Pattern of English Social Aspirations* (New York: Russell Sage Foundation, 1959), 47.

30 Alan McKinlay, "Foucault, Plague, Defoe," *Culture and Organization* 15, no. 2 (2009), 167–84, here 174.

31 Slack, *Impact of Plague*, 187.

32 Slack, *Impact of Plague*, 14.

33 Slack, *Impact of Plague*, 153.

34 Slack, *Impact of Plague*, 308; Robin Evans, "The Rights of Retreat and the Rites of Exclusion: Notes Towards the Definition of Wall," in *Translations from Drawing to Building and Other Writings* (London: Architectural Association, 2003), 35–54.

35 Henry Wheatley, ed. *The Diary of Samuel Pepys*, vol. 8 (Boston: Francis A. Niccolls, 1896), 407.

36 Defoe, *Journal*, 6.

37 Defoe, *Journal*, 19.

38 Copeland, "Defoe and the London Wall," 413.

39 Mark S. R. Jenner, "Plague on a Page: *Lord Have Mercy Upon Us* in Early Modern London," *The Seventeenth Century* 27, no. 3 (2012), 255–86, here 269.

fig.6 Woodcut from *Londons Loud Cryes to the Lord by Prayer*, 1665 Source: British Library

idleness, and insanity. **34** The defensive nature of the Wall then also became an active instrument in the popular perception of a "war on plague." On June 10, 1665 diarist Samuel Pepys heard "that the plague is come into the City (though it hath these three or four weeks since its beginning been wholly out of the City)." **35** The event was noteworthy, as the City was evidently considered the safest place to be. Defoe similarly noted how discouraging it was when, at the beginning of May, "to the great Affliction of the City, one died within the Walls." **36** In his novel, we read of the exact moment when the plague breached through and "the City itself began now to be visited too, I mean within the Walls." **37**

The "political and mystic powers" projected by Pepys and Defoe onto the Wall was a common topos during times of plague. **38** For instance, the 1665 *Londons Loud Cryes*, a widespread medical, religious, and statistical broadsheet also known as *Lord have Mercy Upon Us*, was accompanied by an eloquent woodcut, previously used during the plague of 1636. **39** **fig.6** London is represented as a unified assemblage of houses standing behind the Wall. Outside, after a single row of houses, an empty land

opens in the foreground, suggesting the vastness of a battlefield, with citizens fleeing, priests praying, and the powerful image of Death itself besieging the citadel. Instead of the unregulated and fast-growing built panorama of suburban London, the illustration offers the idealized portrait of a closed-off, clearly defined enclosure protected by the Wall. Access through one of the gates, shown on the left side of the picture, is guarded by "watchers," who can also be seen patrolling the territory around the City.

This image of London as a citadel reflected a common perception of the City as a heavily guarded place of safety, existing within London but otherwise fully separate from it. As already suggested in Hollar's survey, the City could be construed as an "island," immobile and secure behind the perimeter of the Wall. In fact, this perception was powerful enough to shape popular behavior. Exodus, for example, which from the earliest signs of the plague was a desirable option for those who could afford it, became a compromise between the risk of contagion and the protection provided by the Wall. During the summer of 1665, an estimated two hundred thousand people fled London, the largest mass migration in the capital's history. [40] Even then, the Wall, it was thought, would protect the gentry who lived in the City. Defoe noted how:

"The City, and those other Parts, notwithstanding the great Numbers of People that were gone into the Country, was vastly full of People, and perhaps the fuller, because People had for a long time a strong Belief, that the Plague would not come into the City." [41]

According to Defoe, during the months of the plague, the infrastructural presence of the London Wall became intertwined with the primordial imaginary of an autonomous entity, an imposing institutional presence that promised continuity by the mere fact of its antiquity.

As Defoe noted, the plague had a profound impact on London's built environment. It altered "the face" of the entire city, displacing its people, emptying its streets, shutting off its houses, and closing its gates. As a landmark of sovereignty, the Wall was a substantial filter through which the people of London perceived and experienced this new city. The part that the Wall came to play was also a magnification of pre-existing paradigms. As Slack puts it, "plague simply exaggerated an established feature of metropolitan life." [42]

The territorial autonomy of the City of London, emerging from Hollar's survey as a subtext to his clearly bordered map, was a tacit political fact. During the summer of 1665, it became a visible urban mechanism against contagion, visually delineated in the explicit military analogies of *Londons Loud Cryes.* The "changing face" of London noted by Defoe identified a movement in the meaning of the Wall that restored its ancient veiled attributes once more. The progressive growth of suburban London had softened the Wall from a military installation into an infrastructure,

40 Moote, *The Great Plague,* 89.

41 Defoe, *Journal,* 219.

42 Slack, *Impact of Plague,* 160.

deeply associated with administration, governance, and urbanity. Through the immutable presence of the Wall, the City within was crystallized and preserved as a steadfast entity, existing almost in opposition to the everchanging suburbs of London. Already an administrative "island" with its own governmental authority, social and demographic identity, and urban character, during the months of the Great Plague, the City again turned into a fortified citadel. In being adopted to enforce the politics of seclusion and isolation, the Wall provided the suggestive image of a protected enclave, almost a Noah's Ark. The Roman structure reacquired its ancestral *raison d'être* from the catastrophe; it had been reactivated to become a key component of epidemic containment strategies and in the City's evolving capacity for social control. [43]

43 In the aftermath of the plague, and especially after the Great Fire of 1666, the Wall was slowly but consistently taken down as a consequence of the City's growing jurisdiction and of London's massive urban expansion. Hobley, "Archaeology," 13.

The Villa
Britta Hentschel

"Yesterday I came to the villa of Careggi, not to culti-vate my fields but my soul," is how Cosimo de' Medici described his motivation for visiting one of his villas outside Florence in a letter around 1460. His comment set the tone for generations to come, and contin-ues to resonate with our collective perception of the Renaissance villa.

Around fifteenth-century Florence, the ancient Roman villa culture underwent a full revival, and bank-ers, rich merchants, and statesmen invested in elegant abodes outside the city walls. The builders and their architects were inspired by the opulent and detailed descriptions of villas by Pliny the Younger from the first century CE. In the spirit of the Ciceronian topos *otium cum dignitate*, or "dignified leisure," the mer-chants and politicians of the Renaissance devoted time to antique literature, art, and philosophy in man-icured gardens and delicately frescoed loggias far from the madding crowd. Here, in the company of the intellectuals of their time, they reflected on the meaning of the good life and the conduct of state-craft, and were entertained with stories and per-formances, as Boccaccio had previously described in his mid-fourteenth-century *Decameron*.

Cosimo de' Medici even gave the lead-ing Florentine humanist, philosopher, and physi-cian Marsilio Ficino a country house in Careggi in 1463, so that he would always be close to him. The famous Platonic Academy, which Ficino is said to have maintained at Careggi on de' Medici's behalf, however probably corresponds more to a wishful projection of the seventeenth century. Nevertheless, the villa became, over the centuries, an ideal place for the exchange of ideas and the contemplation of art in Arcadian surroundings. Even in contemporary wealthy suburbia, this aspiration still resonates quietly as an urtext.

But this is only one side of the story. The passion for culture and art as a compensation for the harsh realities of economic and political life alone does not explain the enthusiasm for villas in fifteenth- and sixteenth-century Italy. More than six hundred villas and villa-like buildings were located in the vicinity of Florence during the Renaissance. The villa as a counterpart to the palazzo in the city was thus a mass phe-

La Real Villa di Careggi

nomenon in which even apothecaries, rich craftsmen, and successful artists partook. A desire for prestige and improved social standing were unquestionably other factors. The villa also indirectly provided the economic basis of the modern capitalist banking system: mortgaged land created the security against which the tradable share certificates of the Florentine banks were issued.

Villa and garden are also often understood as a sign of bourgeois republican liberties, or as an expression of a culture of bourgeois emancipation. This, too, is an eminently possible explanation. In addition, until the nineteenth century the villas were large farms, which guaranteed the patrician family a year-round supply of food, provided by tenant farmers on half-leases. This could prove decisive in the event of an epidemic.

Between 1347 and 1351, the plague swept through Europe. Within just four years, seventy-five to eighty million people succumbed to it, about a third of Europe's population at the time. According to medical historian Klaus Bergdolt, the plague "represents one of the great European memories." Suffering, despair, a lonely and agonizing death, the dissolution of social ties, the loss of religious and ideological securities, utilitarian restrictions on freedom, and the internalization of a state of emergency shook first Italy and then other European countries.

The two modes by which the bacterial infection spread, firstly via fleas which used the rat as an intermediate host, but then also by droplet infection from person to person—analogous to the novel coronavirus—made the pandemic both incomprehensible and effectively uncontrollable. In the face of the collapse of administrative and charitable institutions, many saw flight from the cities as the only remaining option for protection against the disease.

Galen, the famous physician of antiquity, blamed winds and damp for the spread of the plague, in

CA

accordance with his theory of the humors. Yet even this doctor, whose doctrines misled European medicine for centuries, left Rome in 166 CE because of the Antonine Plague.

"Ruptures of civilization" (*Zivilisationsbrüche*), in Norbert Elias's sense, regularly accompany unpredictable, deadly epidemics. In the 1350s, the Black Death dealt a blow to the late medieval aristocracy of Tuscan cities and led to the rise of new state-supporting groups such as the guilds, the craftsmen, and the bankers—above all, the Medici family. And they relied on prevention: in defense against the plague that had made their rise possible in the first place, the Medici bought a villa in Cafaggiolo, north of Florence near Lago di Bilancino.

Visually unlike the light and airy Renaissance villas, Cafaggiolo was a self-sufficient medieval fort that could serve as a refuge in times of epidemics as well as political turmoil. Such a place was perfect for whiling away the time, as Boccaccio noted in the *Decameron*, the ultimate plague book, written between 1349 and 1352. In the *Decameron*, seven young women and three young men flee to a country house near Fiesole, above Florence, and tell each other frivolous tales while the plague rages in the city.

It was only shortly beforehand that the progressive securing of the territory had even made it possible to settle safely in the countryside. Throughout the Middle Ages, spending the night outside city walls was considered mortally dangerous, and only those who could not avoid doing so would undertake the risk of travel.

A decade before the Great Plague, Ambrogio Lorenzetti impressively depicted the effects of good and bad government on city and country in his cycle of frescoes for the Palazzo Pubblico in Siena (1338 to 1339): tyranny plunges city and country into war, destruction, and disease, but good government secures the territory. Agriculture, hunting, trade, and architecture can then flourish.

The good government of the Florentine Republic made the acquisition and leisured enjoyment of country estates possible from the fourteenth century onward. The Medici, however, took a strategic approach. The family's villas grew out of old defenses in places where it seemed politically advisable to have a presence: near borders and mineral resources, or close to administrative centers for agriculture and fish farming, as in the case of the aforementioned and particularly prized villa in Careggi.

The great reconstructions and designs of Renaissance architecture that followed the formal vocabulary of antiquity, and the semantic connotations that established the villa as a place of longing, were realized above all under Cosimo de' Medici and his house and court architect Michelozzo, who also extended the Medici parish church, San Lorenzo, in Florence — albeit according to the plans of the already deceased Brunelleschi — and created the family palazzo on the Via Larga.

The hybrid of the Renaissance villa as a place of protection from epidemics — the plague returned to Florence every twenty years and could therefore mark a generation's life experience several times over — as well as a place of leisure, agricultural production, and social representation, finally found its definitive Renaissance manifestation with the Medici villa in Poggio a Caiano of 1490, designed by Giuliano da Sangallo.

Palladio's famous villas in Veneto also date back to a large-scale campaign by Alvise Cornaro in the mid-sixteenth century to drain Venice's hinterland by digging canals. The heat and humidity of the lagoon was a dreaded source of infection for humans and animals, and drainage works brought it under control. It was these canal constructions that made it possible to access the villas by boat from Venice in the first place. As the most important trading city and goods hub of the Mediterranean, Venice was affected by epidemics and infections like no other city. Between 1348 and 1576 alone, it was struck by the plague twenty times — hence the considerable need for villas as places of refuge in times of the Black Death.

At present, many wealthy individuals have retreated to their villas and chalets in fear of the COVID-19 pandemic. The coronavirus crisis thus also raises the question of what the potentially enduring social distance rules will do to space. How should a city be formed if it is to offer both quality of life and prevent epidemics? One answer to the Spanish Flu was international modernism, with its emphasis on light, air, and washable surfaces.

But what will COVID-19 mean for office buildings, public transport, settlement density, and the landscape? The plague—and, in its swan song, the Renaissance—led to a new, altered perspective on both landscape and architecture. We have retained much of this perspective to this day, but it does not adequately meet all the current challenges of social distancing and the coronavirus pandemic.

The postwar generation, shaped by enforced communal experiences such as the military, camps, or bunkers, had had enough of collective space after 1945. The desire for a prelapsarian world, the retreat into the private, into the apolitical, and, in the best case, into one's own suburban home—the miniature villa *par excellence*—led to deserted, anti-urban spaces, to commuter traffic and to the desolation of the cities. A repetition of this movement, however, seems ill-advised in the twenty-first century, given the higher population, scarcity of space, and the climate change that is taking place. Nonetheless, we must now rethink densification in line with the pandemic.

Britta Hentschel teaches History of Architecture, Art, and Urban Planning at the University of Liechtenstein.

fig 1. Giusto Utens, *Lunette of the Medici Villa in Cafaggiolo*, (1599–1602)
Source: Museo Villa medicea della Petraia, Florence

fig 2. Giuseppe Zocchi, *Villa di Careggi* (1744)
Source: Wikimedia commons

An earlier version of this article appeared in the *Neue Zürcher Zeitung*, May 5, 2020, under the title
"Die Seuche produzierte nicht nur Tod und Verderben, sondern brachte auch die Villa hervor."

From the gta Archives
Selected by Daniel Weiss

1 Libéral Bruant and
Jules Hardouin-Mansart,
Hôtel des Invalides in
Paris, 1670–1671; plate
27 from Jean-Nico-
las-Louis Durand,
*Recueil et parallèle des
édifices de tout genre
anciens et modernes,
remarquables par
leur beauté, par leur
grandeur, ou par
leur singularité*, Paris
1800; Bequest of Dolf
Schnebli, gta Archives,
ETH Zurich.

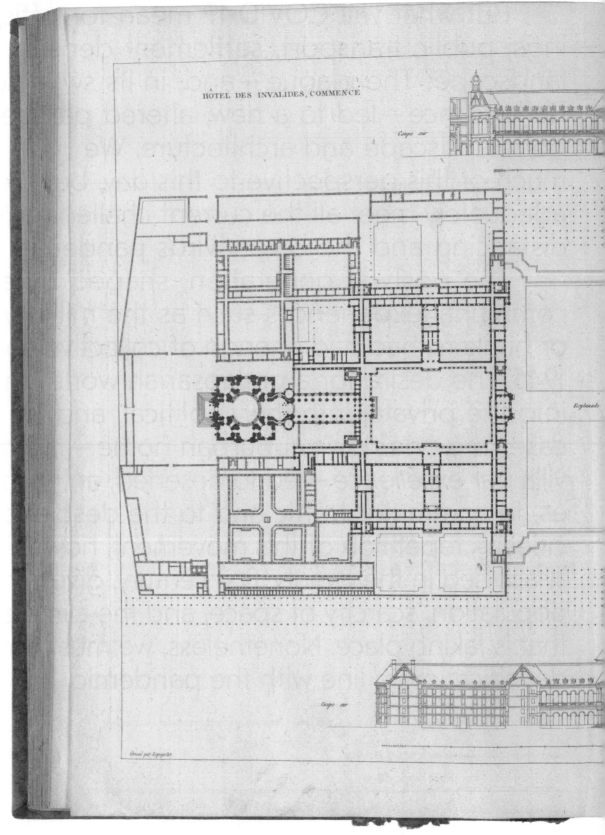

HÔTEL DES INVALIDES, COMMENCE

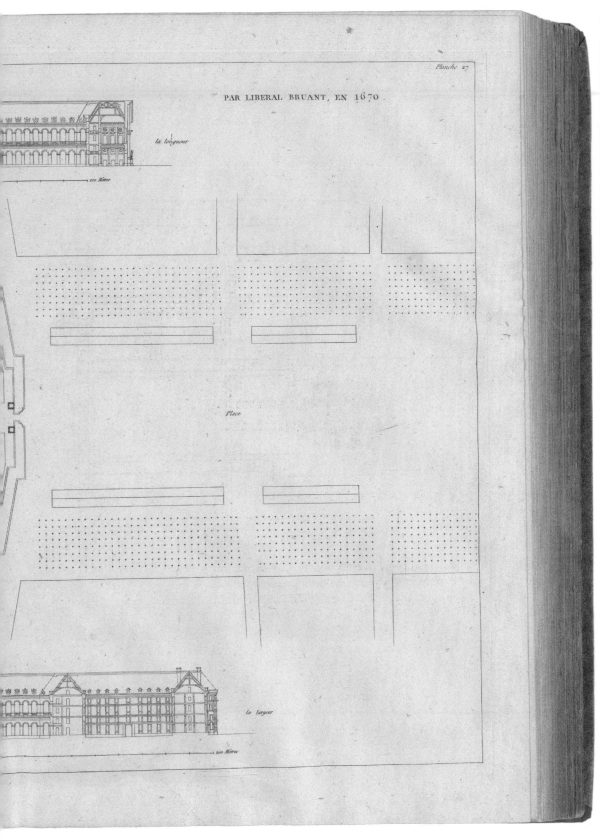

PAR LIBERAL BRUANT, EN 1670.

la longueur

la largeur

Place

Durand's encyclopedic standard work included, among studies of numerous other building types, an entire section on hospital buildings and homes from various eras. The Hôtel des Invalides in Paris, commissioned by Louis XIV, is described in detail on a double page spread. The monumental complex, typologically a mixture of palace and monastery, was intended as a home for war-disabled, old, impoverished, or homeless soldiers. In this building project, the absolutist ruler was not only concerned with solving a social problem but also with demonstrating munificence and magnificence. In return for shelter, the inmates were to follow a regular daily routine of religious services and manual labor behind the walls of their magnificent asylum.

2 Folder on the topic of sanatoriums, nursing homes, and prisons with a perspective drawing of the County Devon Lunatic Asylum (opened 1845); Bequest Bauschule, gta Archives, ETH Zurich.

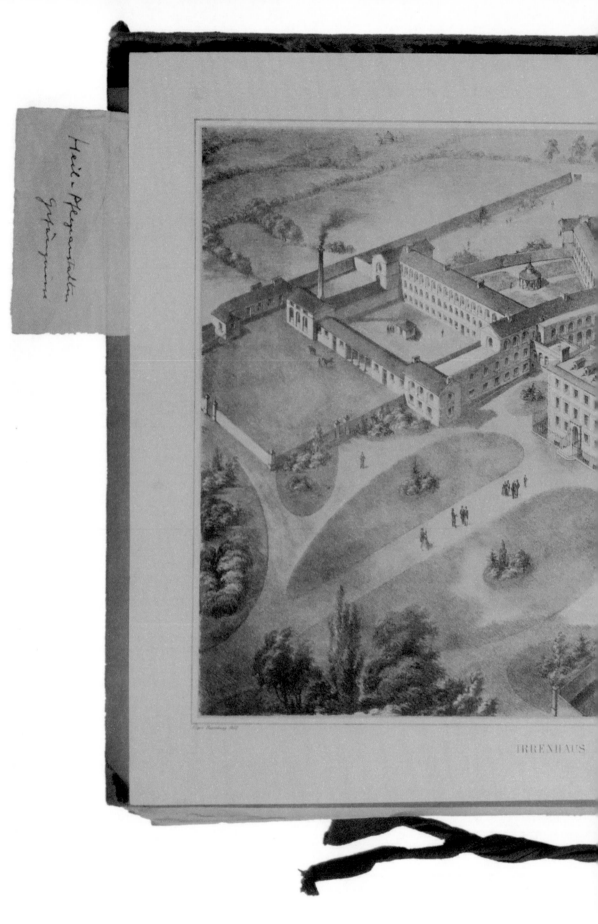

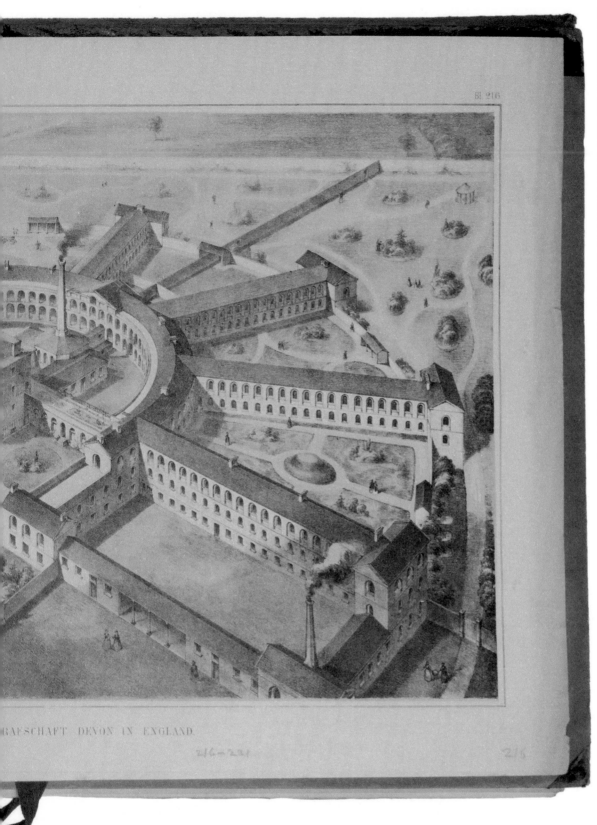

GRAFSCHAFT DEVON IN ENGLAND.

In his now-classic *Discipline and Punish* (New York: Pantheon Books, 1977), Michael Foucault examined how purely repressive techniques of power were gradually replaced during the modern era by a comprehensive disciplining of society in which the education and the social and health care of the population played an essential role. In his view, this process found its structural expression in the panoptic prison but also in the form of citizens' asylums, hospitals, insane asylums, or schools. In this context, one of the folders from the template collection of the building school of the Swiss Federal Polytechnic (today ETH Zurich), with journal clippings on sanatoriums, asylums, and prisons, appears like physical evidence for Foucault's future theses. As the folder demonstrates, at the end of the nineteenth century, these building types already belonged together as a matter of course.

Daniel Weiss From the gta Archives

3 Pfeghard & Haefeli, Queen Alexandra Sanatorium, Davos, 1906–1909; layout design for Sigfried Giedion: *Befreites Wohnen*, Zurich 1929; Bequest of Sigfried Giedion, gta Archives, ETH Zurich.

No. 65. Davos.

Until well into the twentieth century, the lung disease tuberculosis had one of the highest mortality rates among epidemics. Before the discovery of the *tubercle* bacillus and the development of a vaccine, doctors hoped that rest, healthy mountain air, and sunshine would cure the disease. High-altitude spas were developed all over the Alps in the second half of the nineteenth century, and the new type of sanatorium developed in close cooperation between physicians and architects. One of the pioneers was the Zurich office of Pfleghard & Haefeli. The Queen Alexandra Sanatorium in Davos, built between 1906 and 1909, features rooms with generous windows facing south and loggias in front, where patients were to lie in the open air for several hours a day as a therapy. Sigfried Giedion celebrated the building in his booklet *Befreites Wohnen* as an "anticipatory solution" with a view to "liberated living" in general.

4 Otto Rudolf
Salvisberg and Otto
Brechbühl: a home for
babies and mothers
at Elfenau in Berne,
1928–1930; Bequest of
Otto Rudolf Salvisberg,
gta Archives, ETH
Zurich.

Otto Rudolf Salvisberg
was one of the
leading hospital
construction specialists
in Switzerland around
1930. On the basis
of his successes in
competitions, he was
able to execute a series
of hospitals in a short
time. As a professor
at the architecture
department of ETH
Zurich, he lectured on
hospital construction
and repeatedly gave
his students the
topic of hospitals as a
design task. His own
hospital buildings each
followed a similar basic
scheme: elongated
structures accessed
by a central corridor
with south-facing
patient rooms opening
onto ribbon-shaped
balconies that ran along
the building's length.

KÖRBCHEN

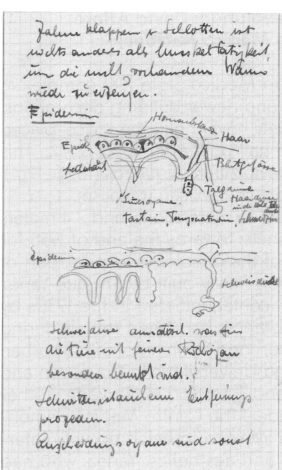

5 Hannibal Naef, lecture notes on the subject of building hygiene, ca. 1922; Bequest of Hannibal Naef, gta Archives, ETH Zurich.

Around 1900, the subject of building hygiene appeared for the first time in the curriculum of the building school of the Swiss Federal Polytechnic in Zurich (now ETH Zurich), and in 1903 it even became part of the final diploma. The lectures were given by the physician Otto Roth, who from 1894 held the newly created professorship for hygiene and bacteriology and advocated a broad concept of preventive health care, including accident prevention at work, sensible nutrition and sport, and the right to decent housing. Under his successor, Wilhelm von Gonzenbach, future Swiss modernist architects also came into contact with the ideas of the hygiene movement. Hannibal Naef's lecture notes on the subject of building hygiene have been preserved. The topics ranged from the structure and function of the human skin to personal hygiene and adequate clothing for different climates.

Medical Progress and Social Revolution: David Alfaro Siqueiros' Mural for the Centro Médico Nacional
Alex Winiger

Alex Winiger is a visual artist and archivist at the gta Archives, ETH Zurich.

1 Around the time state sponsorship of murals in the tradition of the "Mexican School" was abandoned, the Instituto de Investigaciones Estéticas of the National Autonomous University of Mexico launched a series of inquiries, performed by students within the framework of a seminar and published as "El muralismo, producto de la revolución Méxicana", *Crónicas* (1998–), http://www.revistas.unam.mx/index.php/cronicas/ (accessed January 3, 2021). This has contributed to a new generation of scholars in Mexico who, together with a growing number of specialists in the United States, have focused academic (and sometimes official) attention on this heritage. Nevertheless, many works or their original architectural context have disappeared.

fig. 1 (a-c) Centro Médico Siglo XXI, entrance hall with David Alfaro Siqueiros' painting, 2018 Source: Oscar Cázares, Mexico City

2 The genesis of Siqueiros's painting is retraced by Leticia López Orozco et al., "Siqueiros y la victoria de la medicina sobre el cáncer," *Crónicas* 10–11 (2010), 73–98. For Yáñez's work, including the Hospital de Oncología, see Rafael López Rangel, *Enrique Yáñez en la cultura arquitectónica mexicana* (Mexico City: Editorial Limusa, 1989). A complementary documentation of Siqueiros's work can be found at https://www.mural.ch (site maintained by the author, accessed April 8, 2021).

3 Original title: *Apología de la futura victoria de la ciencia médica contra el cáncer: Paralelismo histórico de la revolución científica y la revolución social.*

In 2004, while visiting the Centro Médico Siglo XXI complex in Mexico City in search of historic and newer building decorations, I discovered a large frieze, strangely hovering in the space, placed awkwardly in the main entrance hall built after 1990. **fig. 1 a-c** This was, I realized, a major work of David Alfaro Siqueiros (1896–1974), one of the so-called "tres grandes" of Mexican muralism. **1**

Siqueiros created this mural, 26 meters long and 2.4 meters high and painted on wooden panels, towards the end of 1958 for a foyer near the main entrance of the oncology hospital, part of the Centro Médico Nacional, then newly built by Enrique Yáñez de la Fuente. **2 fig. 2** The medical center, initiated in the 1930s by the Ministry of Health and Assistance, had been rebuilt during the 1950s in the Doctores neighborhood as an autonomous urban satellite. Together with the Ciudad Universitaria in Coyoacán and the Ministry of Communication and Transport in Narvarte—other *grands projets* of the same decade—the Centro Médico demonstrated the ambition of postwar Mexico to catch up with international technological progress and aesthetics. Yáñez, who had traveled in the Netherlands, France, and Germany during the 1930s, designed the masterplan of the compound in a rationalist manner, providing high-rise buildings for the wards, lower ones for research and teaching, and a huge cylinder (built by José Vil-

lagrán García) for congresses. The slab high-rise, dedicated to the treatment of cancer patients, was a concrete frame with two finely structured glass facades. The floor plans show an alignment of rooms along spinal corridors, forming a cross with lower annexes. The visitor accessed this building coming from an exterior U-drive to the waiting zone behind the main entrance: a rather low but quite deep space where Siqueiros' epic painting filled the back wall. The mural wrapped around two corners and was divided by three columns and perforated by a large passage to the treatment rooms.

The work, entitled *Advocacy for the Future Victory of Medical Science against Cancer: The Historical Parallel between the Scientific Revolution and the Social Revolution*, **3 fig. 3** shows a multi-figured, dynamic movement, generally from the right to the left. It is commonly divided into four segments: humanity's prehistory, the ancient world, the present, and the future. 4 The first part shows a mass of human beings struggling and suffering helplessly on a barren landscape, while one figure frees himself from the mass and jumps towards the foreground through skeletal remains. Antiquity is introduced with sharply contrasting priests in white. Behind the priests, the still-faceless humans now push forward towards the center of the painting, which arches over the passage door. In the center of the painting, a red flag

marks the Mexican Revolution of 1910 and the Constitution of 1917. From this turmoil a flame-like woman in an orange gown emerges, imploring a medical doctor dressed in white. The doctor is the first of a formation of medical personnel oriented towards the doorway. Alongside them stands the famous "Cobalt Bomb," 5 a radiation machine that had been introduced into medical practice a few years earlier. It seems about to engulf the recumbent body of a dark woman, perhaps the same figure who was previously addressing the medic. Towards the left, the machine is extended into a barrel, a fanciful elaboration of its real construction. This points at a monstrous, bony, and veiny being with blind eyes, followed by a second deformed organism with tentacles, ulcerations, and a gelatinous head. Carcasses around it illustrate its devastating work and link the end of the mural to the wasteland at the beginning. Above the barrel of the Cobalt Bomb, a row of men and women are marching to the left, implicitly joining the historical struggle. Their colors and order contrast with the brownish disorder of the mass of figures on the right.

The overall movement is one of pushing and pulling, with complex overlaps. The right-hand portion of the mural refers to the past, whereas the medical doctor (who, let us not forget, faces a doorway through which living patients and medical professionals pass) refers to the present. The portion on the left shows a future in the midst of being formed, and in its foreground we see another struggle of movements.

The barrel of the machine is ambiguous: it pierces the red organ next to the bony creature, but it can also be read as emanating from there. Seen this way, the therapeutic radiation unit can be understood as both a weapon against but also a product of, monsters: the monster of cancer tamed by the monster of nuclear fission. Siqueiros had created a mural called *Man Master Not Slave of Technology* in 1952, 6 where one hand growing out of the machine is held strongly by a second one. fig. 4 Whether he

4 Raquel Tibol, *Siqueiros: Vida y obra* (Mexico City: Departamento del Distrito Federal, Secretaría de Obras y Servicios, 1973), 152.

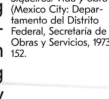

fig 2 Oncology Hospital, Mexico City, main facade, around 1958
Source: Rafael López Rangel, *Enrique Yáñez en la cultura arquitectónica mexicana* (Mexico City: Editorial Limusa, 1989), 181

5 The "Cobalt Bomb" primarily means a nuclear weapon designed to contaminate a maximal area. The term was also ambiguously used for medical radiation devices, more often in German than in English. See Nancy Z. Tausky, *Cultural Heritage Assessment: Buildings in the South Street Hospital Complex, London, Ontario* (London, Ont.: City of London, 2011). For the same use of the term, see López Orozco et al., "Siqueiros," 92.

6 Original title: *El hombre amo y no esclavo de la tecnología,* Instituto Politécnico Nacional (today: Escuela Nacional De Ciencias Biológicas), Mexico City.

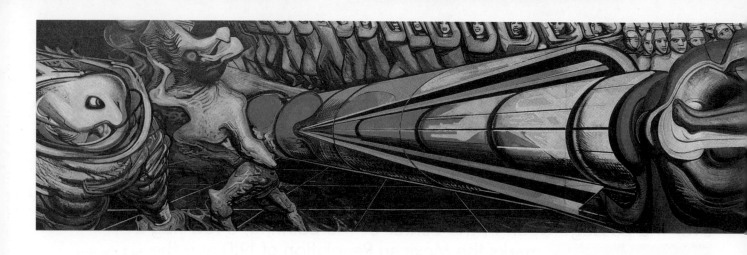

fig. 3 David Alfaro Siqueiros, *Apología de la futura victoria de la ciencia médica contra el cáncer: Paralelismo histórico de la revolución científica y la revolución social*, 1958, acrylics on plywood, ca. 2.35 × 30 m: Centro Médico Siglo XXI (main entrance), Aves. Cuautémoc and Dr. Morones Prieto, col. Doctores, Mexico City Source: Agustín Arteaga, Shifra M. Goldman, and Raquel Tibol, *Los murales de Siqueiros* (Mexico D.F.: CONACULTA/INBA, 1998), 258–260

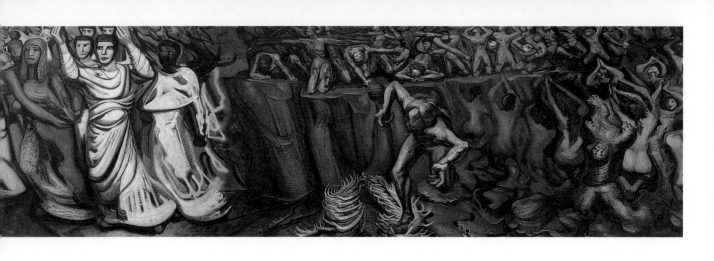

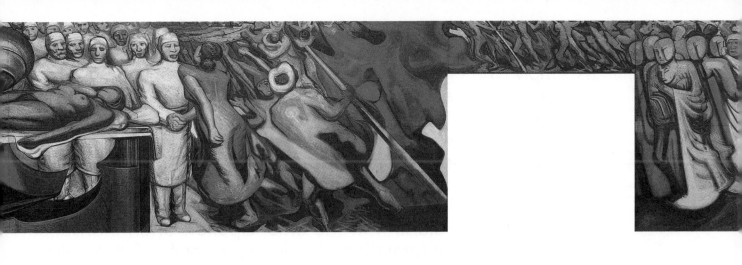

had a similar ambiguity in mind for the later hospital painting is not documented. Biographies of Siqueiros present the monsters as simply "the enemy," [7] but Siqueiros was obviously sensitive to ambivalent readings.

As his subtitle — *The Historical Parallel between the Scientific Revolution and the Social Revolution* — indicates, Siqueiros embedded medical progress in a historically determined dialectic. But he also interspersed it with personal inventions and myths. While in the beginning humanity is a uniform crowd in Siqueiros's painting, history starts with the emancipation of an individual from this mass. The formation of antique society that follows gives rise to social functions: individualized priests preside over a mass of humans, now differentiated by colors representing nationalities. In the intermediary phase preceding revolution, humanity is depicted as figures without individual features moving forward.

7 Tibol, *Siqueiros*, 152; Antonio Rodriguez, *Der Mensch in Flammen: Wandmalerei in Mexiko von den Anfängen bis zur Gegenwart* (Dresden: VEB Verlag der Kunst, 1967), 195. In these interpretations, the two monsters are characterized as the "social and physical tumors" or the "cancer of the human and of the social body, which humanity must extirpate."

fig. 4 David Alfaro Siqueiros, *El hombre amo y no esclavo de la tecnología* (detail), 1952, pyroxaline on aluminium, 4 × 18 m: National Polytechnic Institute, Plan de Ayala, col. Casco de San Tomás, Mexico City
Source: Bob Schalkwijk

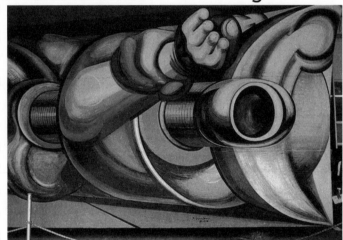

The revolution stage itself is populated by humans wearing headscarves, fezzes, or turbans, their faces brown. In this visualization, the impulse for revolution comes from the colonized nations, rather than the industrial workers. The woman addressing the medical doctor is a member of post-revolutionary society and has adopted its fiery color. Medical personnel are distinguished by the priestly white of their dresses, suppressing their national diversity, while their homogenized faces demonstrate the alliance of ethnicities and sexes in the effort for medical progress. The recumbent patient, deprived of individual features, is clearly characterized as a mestizo woman, recalling that a main goal of the Mexican Revolution was to benefit this oppressed group. The militants marching into the future wear the complete color spectrum: in order to conquer the monsters of disease and social deformation, all nations have to unite. The facial features of the people of the future, unlike those of the masses of the past, are distinguishable but also conform to an idealized norm. Individual tragedy and collective consolation are tied together: the sick have their part to play in the historical evolution of humankind, and historical evolution is in favor of the sick.

Nicknaming a therapeutic radiation machine the Cobalt Bomb (or the Cobalt Ray-Gun) indicates that winning the fight against cancer required an appropriate weapon. When Siqueiros's painter colleague Diego Rivera returned from cobalt therapy in the Soviet Union in 1956, his daughters, Lupe and Ruth, welcomed him with the following song: "He was cured with cobalt, which is used to make bombs, but will now be used to make men well." [8] Rivera, who originally had the commission to design the mural in the oncology center before Siqueiros, declared his intention to "paint an advocacy for medicine and for the medics who fight against cancer." [9] Despite his radiation therapy, Diego Rivera died soon afterwards, at the end of 1957. In early 1958, Siqueiros was appointed to paint a mural for the Medical Center two-and-a-half times the size of *Advocacy*. He called it *Death for Life*; [10] the painting was intended for the auditorium of the research department of the Anatomo-Clínicas, not a part of the hospital patients would have visited. [11] After investing two months of work in the project, the commission was cancelled, and Siqueiros

was instead asked to paint the mural Rivera was unable to undertake. One can assume that Siqueiros adapted elements of his drafts for *Death for Life* with Rivera's project for an *Advocacy* for those who fought cancer. [12]

Siqueiros was able to give monsters a face. While he characterized the patricides in the Ex-Aduana de Santo Domingo traditionally (but still inventively) as devils, he found the form for the invisible threat of cancer from randomly created spray-gun spots. [13] Visually, he needed the two creatures to draw the spectator's attention to the climax of his drama with the desired drive. According to his assistant and biographer, Philip Stein, Siqueiros chose his combative solution for the "dread" interior of the hospital after some hesitation. [14] The journalist Julio Scherer García (1926–2015) anticipated critical questions:

"Why, precisely in this room, speak of cancer, especially with brushes? Why mention this subject to the sick of the Cancer Section of the Medical Center? Why hammer away at the anguish of the sick? ... Is it not possible to imagine something that would distract the cancer victims from their terrible drama?" [15]

Siqueiros's militant attitude was inevitable—he was, after all, a committed revolutionary soldier. A cadet in the constitutionalist army of Venustiano Carranza during the Mexican Revolution, Siqueiros became a communist after his Paris sojourn in 1919 and joined the Republican Army in Spain in 1937. His political activism

8 Gladys March and Diego Rivera, *My Art, My Life: An Autobiography* (New York: Citadel Press, 1960; repr. New York: Dover Publications, 1991), 181. Citation refers to the Dover edition.

9 March and Rivera, *My Art, My Life*, 75.

10 Original title: *La muerte para la vida*.

11 López Orozco et al., "Siqueiros," 80. These drafts probably exist in the Sala de Arte Público Siqueiros in Polanco, Mexico City. The author could not investigate them as a consequence of COVID-19 restrictions.

fig. 5 David Alfaro Siqueiros, *La Marcha de la Humanidad en la Tierra y hacia el Cosmos*, 1965–1971, acrylic on asbestos cement mounted on iron frames with attached sculpted fiberglass elements, 2165 m²: Polyforum cultural Siqueiros, Avenida Insurgentes sur 701, col. Nápoles, Mexico City Source: MXCity

12 The complex genesis of Siqueiros' work is retraced in López Orozco et al., "Siqueiros," 78–81.

13 López Orozco et al., "Siqueiros," 84–85.

14 Philip Stein, *Siqueiros: His Life and Works* (New York: International Publishers, 1994), 248.

15 Julio Scherer García, "Siqueiros con la pistola en la mano," *Excelsior: Diorama de la Cultura*, January 11, 1959. Cited in Stein, *Siqueiros*, 248. The original article can be accessed at https://icaa.mfah.org/s/en/item/796090 (accessed January 9, 2021).

16 Stein, *Siqueiros*, 350.

17 David Alfaro Siqueiros, "Integración plástica," *David Alfaro Siqueiros* [printed supplement of vinyl record] (Mexico City: UNAM, 1967), 5.

18 From this resulted a manifesto called "Three Appeals for the Current Guidance of the New Generation of Painters and Sculptors" with a cubo-futurist flavor. See David Alfaro Siqueiros, "Tres llamamientos de orientación actual a los pintores y escultores de la nueva generación de América," *Vida americana* (May 1921), 2–3. The original Spanish version of the text is reprinted in Gilberto Mendonça Teles and Klaus Müller-Bergh, *Vanguardia Latinoamericana: Historia crítica y documentos. Tomo I México y América Central* (Madrid: Vervuert, 2000), 96–98. See also the English translation in Héctor Olea and Mari Carmen Ramírez, eds., *Inverted Utopias: Avant-garde Art in Latin America* (New Haven: Yale University Press, 2004), 458–59.

19 See, for example, David Alfaro Siqueiros, *Como se pinta un mural* (Mexico: Ediciones mexicanas, 1951; repr. La Habana: Editorial Arte y Literatura, 1985), 181. Citation refers to the Editorial Arte y Literatura edition. The artist explained the principle in a filmed interview in J. Martínez Gómez, *Mujeres para una Época: Angélica Arenal y David Alfaro Siqueiros* (Televisión Española, May 21, 1985), https://youtu.be/sF2GjnR34zo (accessed January 8, 2021).

20 Siqueiros, *Como se pinta un mural*, 195.

21 See, for example, the murals for the Ex-Aduana de Santo Domingo (1945–1966) and the La Raza Hospital (1951–1954).

brought him six years of detention in the infamous Lecumberri prison in Mexico City and years of exile. He was not a man afraid of confrontation, except when it came to his own sickness. His wife, Angélica Arenal, insisted upon his stoicism shortly after his death: "he was the enemy of doctors and clinics of the whole world. So he said, 'No, comrades, I feel very good.'" **16**

Siqueiros was also polemical in his views on the appropriate form of a mural:

"For me, a functionalist in war as in the arts, defense is offensive because it is counteroffensive; it implies mobility ad infinitum. ... [W]e functionalists defend a zone, fortify a zone, flush a zone with traps. ... [The functionalist's] defensive traffic touches totally and absolutely the whole platform of his zone, the whole platform of his problem, in any direction and interconnecting in a movement all possible lines and arabesques." **17**

This passage was informed by Siqueiros's military and avant-gardist past. Traveling to France, Italy, and Spain between 1919 and 1921 formed his artistic orientation between Cubism (Léger), Futurism (Carrà) and his admiration of the Renaissance (Masaccio). **18** In the early 1930s he started to experiment with the anticipation of multiple spectators' viewpoints, which he called "polyangularity." **19** He later added the deformation of the architectonic space to this. In a further step, he extended the surface by relief parts, which he called *"escultopintura."* **20** This escalation of his means of expression was accompanied by a shift in the work to use spray guns, synthetic paint like pyroxiline, vinyl acetate, and acrylics, as well as supports like plywood or asbestos panels—all culminating in his final *Gesamtkunstwerk*, the *Polyforum* (1966–1971). **21** **fig. 5**

In the case of the *Advocacy* mural, Siqueiros incorporated the architectural context in a simple and efficient way. **fig. 6 a-c** As the historical photographs and ground floor plan show, the phases of human development on the right hand side of the mural were framed by the columns. Siqueiros directed the movement over the doorway to the red flag at its left side. This produced an intersection where actual medical personnel entered the waiting room or rushed back into the service corridor, making visible the equation of the medics with the revolutionaries, as expressed in the subtitle of the work. The artist furthermore skillfully instrumentalized the meandering of the wall, ending the mural on a protruding short section. The monsters thereby appeared to jump into the

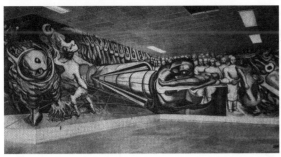

space, toward the visitor coming from the entrance, and thus immediately drew attention to themselves. They manifested the patient's fears: seen from the protruding corner's side, the barrel element was foreshortened, producing an immediate relation between the monsters and the recumbent patient in the machine. Entering the waiting bay and probably sitting down near the back wall, [22] the

visitor would become aware of the waving masses in their rainbow colors and then see a much longer barrel and more of the receding bony monster than of the attacking one. Siqueiros's "polyangularity" produced shifting focuses in this way, enhancing the threat of disease for the newcomer but comforting the waiting patient.

The subsequent course of history would in many ways

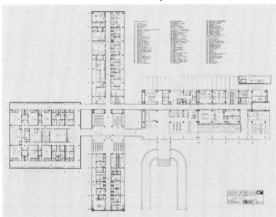

undermine Siqueiros' intentions. In 1961, due to the state's financial difficulties, the Medical Center was sold by the Ministry of Health to the Mexican Social Security Institute. [23] Siqueiros's message, an appeal to the country's whole population, was thereafter accessible only to the privileged insured. The terrible earthquake on September 19, 1985, destroyed many symbols of a thriving welfare state whose glory had already faded by that time. Yáñez' oncology hospital was torn down the same year. Siqueiros' painting fortunately survived, thanks in part to the fact that it was painted on a wooden support that could easily be removed from the walls. [24] The symbols of social progress that Siqueiros used in his imagery, however, lost their footing with the collapse of the existing socialism of the Soviet world shortly after. The panels were reinstalled in the entrance hall of the new Centro Médico Siglo XXI in 1997. The building complex, however, possesses little of the

fig. 6a Oncology Hospital with David Alfaro Siqueiros' painting (detail), ca. 1958
Source: Guillermo Zamora, Acervo Sala de Arte Público Siqueiros/ CONACULTA/INBA

22 The disposition of the seats can be seen in photographs by Desmond Rochfort captured in the 1970s. See Desmond Rochfort, *Mexican Muralists* (San Francisco: Chronicle Books, 1993), 213.

fig. 6b Oncology Hospital with David Alfaro Siqueiros' painting (detail), around 1958
Source: López Rangel, Enrique Yáñez, 184

fig. 6c Oncology Hospital, Mexico City, ground floor, ca. 1955. The position of Siqueiros' painting is marked in yellow
Source: Rafael López Rangel, *Enrique Yáñez en la cultura arquitectónica mexicana* (Mexico City: Editorial Limusa, 1989), 183

23 The Mexican Social Security Institute (IMSS) is a government institution funded by employees, employers, and the government that insures the employed of the private sector. Public employees are insured by the Institute for Social Security and Services for State Workers (ISSSTE). These organizations possess their own hospitals, accessible to their respective clientele.

24 Alejandro Horacio Morfín Faure, "Memorias de conservación extrema, septiembre de 1985," *Nierika* 4 (2013), http:// revistas.ibero.mx/arte/ uploads/volumenes/4/ pdf/Nierika_4-1.pdf (accessed January 9, 2021).

elegance of its predecessor. Siqueiros' work now hovers aloft in an atrium, interrupted by a balustrade and protruding into a passage. The work cannot be observed up close, and its spatial dynamism and close integration with the architecture are lost.

In 1974, Siqueiros succumbed to his own cancer. His home in Polanco, Mexico City, and his workshop in Cuernavaca became part of a donation to the state (*fideicomiso*), with the aim of encouraging and instructing the next generation of artists. By the time his wife, Angélica Arenal, died in 1989, the house and the archives were in a bad state. The Consejo Nacional para la Cultura y las Artes (since 2015 the Secretaría de Cultura) and the Instituto de Bellas Artes — two agencies which support a large share of Mexican cultural manifestations — transformed and professionalized the Sala de Arte Público Siqueiros into a museum and research facility, whereas its founders had rather imagined a workshop for artists and activists of the left. [25]

25 Itala Schmelz, "La Sala de Arte Público Siqueiros," *Crónicas* 8–9 (2005), 177–88.

A Room of One's Own
Jeanne Kisacky

Jeanne Kisacky has taught at Cornell University, Syracuse University, and Binghamton University.

At the 1916 American Hospital Association Convention in Philadelphia, Asa S. Bacon, the superintendent of the Presbyterian Hospital in Chicago, described a conversation about hospital design he had recently had with an unnamed architect, which ended with the architect first calling him "crazy" and then saying that he "needed a vacation." That conversation had been about Bacon's concern that hospitals were being designed "for the rich and the very poor" but not for the "great middle class." [1] Instead of the usual practice of building hospitals with large multi-bed wards for charity patients and luxurious private rooms for wealthy paying patients, Bacon proposed that "every patient should have a room by himself." [2] He described a modest, affordable room that provided comfort and privacy and which, if located in

DECEMBER, 1922   THE ARCHITECTURAL FORUM   PLATE 89

GENERAL VIEW FROM CENTRAL PARK
FIFTH AVENUE HOSPITAL, NEW YORK
YORK & SAWYER, ARCHITECTS
WILEY E. WOODBURY, M.D., CONSULTANT

an efficient, high-rise structure with centralized services, could also diminish cross-infections, streamline nursing, reduce service costs, and increase hospital efficiency. Crazy or not, this innovation would have transformed hospital practice.

Six years later, journalist Edwin A. Goewey praised the magnificent new ten-story Fifth Avenue Hospital designed by architects York & Sawyer and hospital consultant Wiley E. Woodbury as a new type of hospital, one for the modern age rather than the "stone age." [3] fig.1 Glowing articles celebrating it as the first all-single-bed-room hospital appeared in journals and newspapers from Nebraska to Melbourne, Australia. Except it was not the first; Bacon's ideas preceded it. So did the Henry Ford Hospital in Detroit and the all-single-bed-room skyscraper hospital designed for the Beth Israel Hospital in New York City. Why did the Fifth Avenue Hospital, and not the other projects, get all the attention?

Architectural designers and historians celebrate creativity and highlight innovative projects; this assumes that innovation is recognizable, attributable, and traceable. History, however, can also show that architectural innovation is rarely straightforward. How does precedence become established? Is having a novel

1 Asa S. Bacon, quoted in American Hospital Association, *Transactions of the American Hospital Association, Eighteenth Annual Conference, Held at Philadelphia, Pa. September 26th to 30th Inc.* (Philadelphia: American Hospital Association, 1916), 337. Bacon's comments were part of an extended discussion after presentations by other persons, and so no authorship was cited.

2 Bacon, in American Hospital Association, *Transactions*, 337.

fig.1 Fifth Avenue Hospital, New York City Source: *Architectural Forum* 37, no. 6 (December 1922), Plate 89

3 Edwin A. Goewey, "An Architect of Mercy," *Frank Leslie's Weekly*, October 16, 1920, 486.

idea enough? Is drawing it up enough? Is building it necessary? And what happens when the innovation is unrealized because of circumstances beyond the designer's control? This is the story of four innovative all-single-bed-room hospital projects designed and built in the first decades of the twentieth century, and the complex historical situations that contributed to the obscurity of three of them. Together, their history reveals just how difficult the questions of architectural innovation can become.

Bacon's proposal for a hospital with all-single-bed rooms created a stir at the 1916 American Hospital Association Convention and was reported widely among hospital administrators. Bacon published his ideas in articles in 1919 and 1920, with accompanying illustrations of the new room drawn by Chicago architect, Perry Swern, of Berlin, Swern & Randall. **4** **figs. 2 and 3** Swern also publicly presented the novel layout at the Wisconsin

4 Asa S. Bacon, "The New Efficient Hospital," *Presbyterian Hospital Bulletin* 39 (April 1919), 2–8; Asa S. Bacon, "Room Equipment in the Efficient Hospital," *Hospital Management* 8, no. 6 (January 1920), 34–36; Asa S. Bacon, "Efficient Hospitals," *Journal of the American Medical Association* 74, no. 2 (January 10, 1920), 123–26.

fig. 2 Perspective of a single-bed patient room
Source: Asa S. Bacon, "Room Equipment in the Efficient Hospital," *Hospital Management* 8, no. 6 (January 1920), 34–36, here 34

5 Perry W. Swern, "The Interior Arrangement of Hospitals," *Modern Hospital* 17, no. 2 (August 1921), 104–108.

6 Alden B. Mills, "Milestones in Hospital History: 1913–1938," *Modern Hospital* 51, no. 3 (September 1938), 144–64 (even pages only), here 148.

7 "Presbyterian Hospital, Chicago, Adds New Unit of 'Bacon Plan' Rooms," *Modern Hospital* 24, no. 3 (March 1925), 203–204, 241.

· THE TYPICAL ROOM ʀᴏʀ EFFICIENT HOSPITALS · BERLIN, SWERN & RANDALL ARCHITECTS ·

Hospital Association meeting in May 1921, and that talk was published with updated drawings in August 1921. **5** In professional hospital and medical circles, the all-single-bed-room hospital was linked to Bacon and even referred to as the "Bacon Plan" of hospital design. **6** Swern and Bacon then realized their ideas in an all-single-bed-room addition to the Presbyterian Hospital of Chicago, which was completed in 1925. **7**

Meanwhile, an all-single-bed-room addition to the Henry Ford Hospital in Detroit was built and operational by May 1921. It was a parallel development of the same solution to the same problem. Ford, a fan of self-sufficient citizens, did not want to build a charity for the destitute sick or a luxurious medical resort for the wealthy. He wanted to build a democratic institution in which every patient, rich or poor, would receive care in the same basic room, with the same comforts, from the same doctors, with the same diagnostic approach. [8] He had already established a revolutionary new medical and administrative organization for the existing hospital, one that treated it like a business, with full-time staff doctors and flat rates, and the new building design had to fit that new institutional model. [9]

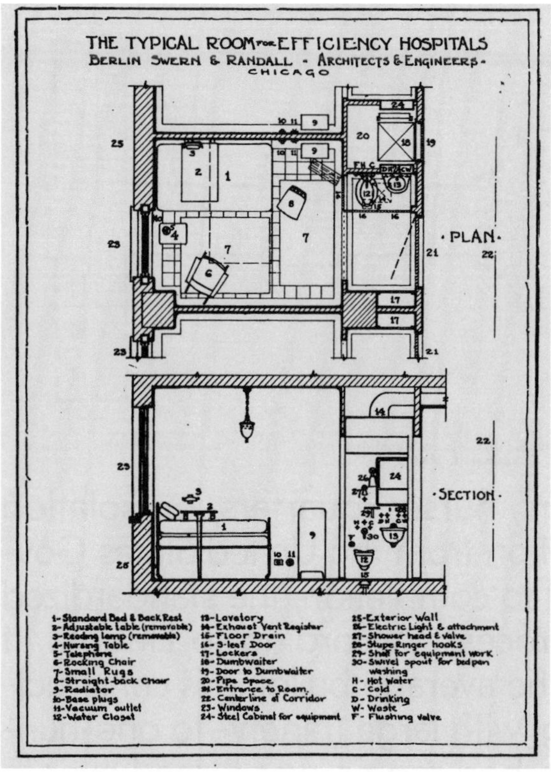

Instead of hiring hospital design specialists, Ford treated the hospital design as a functional problem requiring an entirely novel solution. He asked the doctor in charge of the existing hospital what the "unit" of design was for a hospital and was told it was the patient room. [10] In 1916, Ford assigned Ernest G. Liebold, his personal assistant, to manage the project. Liebold asked Albert Wood, a young Ford Company staff architect, what he knew about hospital design. Wood replied he had no hospital design experience but some hotel experience, and that a hospital was essentially "a hotel for sick people." [11] Liebold made Wood the architect for the new hospital, and the two of them spent six months visiting prominent hospitals and learning about their operation.

Upon their return, at Ford's request, Liebold and Wood's team created a full-scale model of the "unit" — the single-bed room — and reworked the layout and details until it was efficient, effective, and economical. [12] The resultant building design arranged the standardized patient room units (each with individual temperature controls and a private bathroom) into separate, independent nursing unit wings of thirty-six rooms. To save travel time, extensive modern building technologies (including silent call-systems, pneumatic tube delivery systems, telautographs, and dictation stations) connected the nursing units to a central diagnostic and administrative hub. [13] fig. 4

fig. 3 Plan and section of a single-bed patient room
Source: Asa S. Bacon, "Room Equipment in the Efficient Hospital," Hospital Management 8, no. 6 (January 1920), 34–36, here 35

8 William Atherton Du Puy, "Henry Ford's Pet Plans," Boston Sunday Globe, December 4, 1921, magazine section, 1.

9 Patricia Scollard Painter, Henry Ford Hospital: The First 75 Years (Ann Arbor, MI: Henry Ford Health System, 1997), 28–35.

10 Du Puy, "Henry Ford's Pet Plans"; "How a Hospital Was Built: Mr. Henry Ford and Amateurs," Gympie Times, November 9, 1918, 2.

11 Painter, Henry Ford Hospital, 37–38. Design of the Henry Ford Hospital was incorrectly attributed to Albert Kahn in Jeanne Kisacky, Rise of the Modern Hospital: An Architectural History of Health and Healing (Pittsburgh: University of Pittsburgh Press, 2017), 266 and 281.

12 "How a Hospital Was Built"; Painter, Henry Ford Hospital, 39.

13 D. D. Martin, "Henry Ford Hospital in Time of Peace," Modern Hospital 14, no. 4 (April 1920), 266–70.

Construction was beginning when the United States declared war on Germany on April 6, 1917. Ford offered to lease the building upon completion to the United States Army for use as a military hospital for one dollar per year. The army accepted but "desired that the wards should not be completed as private rooms," except

fig. 4 D. D. Martin, "Henry Ford Hospital in Time of Peace," *Modern Hospital* 14, no. 4 (April 1920), 266–70, here 268

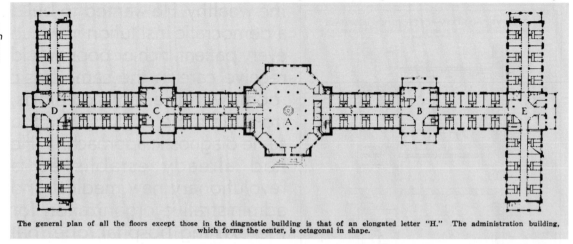

The general plan of all the floors except those in the diagnostic building is that of an elongated letter "H." The administration building, which forms the center, is octagonal in shape.

14 Alexander T. Cooper, "The Henry Ford Hospital in Time of War: U.S. Army General Hospital No. 36," *Modern Hospital* 14, no. 4 (April 1920), 259–66, here 259.

15 "Ford to Help Sick," *Sunday Oregonian,* July 7, 1918, sections 4, 8.

for the areas reserved for officers, nurses' quarters, or isolation wards. 14 With extensive cooperation from the United States Government, Ford rushed the hospital to completion; the standardized layout further streamlined the process. According to Liebold, it was "built faster in war time than the average building is constructed in peace time." 15 The building, with large (ninety- to one-hundred-bed) wards instead of single-bed rooms, was turned over to the Army on September 16, 1918. figs. 5 and 6 The Army returned the building to civilian use in November 1919, but extensive renovation was needed to convert the building to its original all-single-bed room designs. It reopened on May 31, 1921.

One drawback to the novel plan was its cost — the multiplication of private bathrooms, utilities, and partitions made all-single-bed-room hospitals far more expensive to build than an

fig. 5 Exterior view of US Army General Hospital No. 36/Henry Ford Hospital Source: Alexander T. Cooper, "The Henry Ford Hospital in Time of War: U.S. Army General Hospital No. 36," *Modern Hospital* 14, no. 4 (April 1920), 259–66, here 260

16 Cooper, "The Henry Ford Hospital," 259.

open-ward building. Ford had personally bankrolled his hospital project. (Detroiters called it the "million-dollar hospital". 16) For less well-funded hospitals, like the Beth Israel Hospital in New York City, then a small neighborhood hospital (founded, funded, run by, and largely providing care to Jewish immigrants), the initial high con-

A general view of the main building of Army General Hospital No. 36, Detroit, Mich., characterized as "one of the finest of the Army hospitals" by Surgeon General Ireland. This was formerly the Henry Ford Hospital, built by the automobile magnate.

struction costs proved difficult. Planning for a new Beth Israel Hospital building with a traditional layout of multi-bed wards and luxurious private rooms began in late 1915. 17 By early 1916, with $330,00 in the building fund, the building committee

17 Beth Israel Hospital, Board of Directors Minutes, February 29, 1916, Beth Israel Hospital Archives.

hired architect Louis Allen Abramson and tasked the hospital superintendent, Louis J. Frank, with assisting Abramson in developing functional, efficient hospital plans. [18] In early 1917, Frank and Abramson traveled to see hospital buildings across the country, but wartime limitations on construction kept the project on hold. [19]

By March 1919, Abramson finished his preliminary building plans for a hospital with wards and private rooms, but Frank took months to review them (despite complaints from Abramson and prodding by building committee member Isaac L. Phillips). [20] Frank was doing more than reviewing the building plans as drawn, he was reconceptualizing the basic layout for patient rooms. In early May he proposed a new layout with no wards but all-single-bed rooms, each with private utilities and bathrooms. [21] Frank was aware of the novelty of the project:

"I can state without any fear of successful contradiction that the new hospital, if our present ideas will be carried out will be a pattern for all hospitals. People will come to us from all over the world to study our methods. No hospital will be built hereafter except our way. No patient will want to go to any other kind of a hospital." [22]

The building committee agreed, and asked Abramson to redesign the project according to the new, single-bed-room plan.

By October 1919, Abramson had finished the revised plans for an all-single-bed-room hospital, but delays continued. Frank wanted to make the design a more "democratic process" by involving doctors and nurses, but this took time; [23] plan review stretched into December. Persons in control of the funding opposed the single-bed-room design as an untried and therefore risky plan and withheld financial approval for months. [24] The total building costs quickly exceeded the available funds, and new fundraising proved ineffective. Demolition began in May 1920, and construction began soon after. Without money to pay the contractors, the work proceeded irregularly.

News of the well-funded Fifth Avenue Hospital's "wardless" approach to hospital design began to appear after June 1920, when architects York & Sawyer filed plans at the New York City building department. [25] In late September 1920, Woodbury, the hospital superintendent and consultant on the project design, gave a presentation on the new building and its innovations

18 Beth Israel Hospital, Board of Directors Minutes, 1916.

19 Louis J. Frank to Medical Board, in Beth Israel Hospital, Board of Directors Minutes, April 6, 1917 and April 15, 1917, Beth Israel Hospital Archives.

20 Beth Israel Hospital, Louis J. Frank Papers, March 16, 1919; March 21, 1919, April 10, 1919; April 11, 1919, Beth Israel Hospital Archives.

21 Beth Israel Hospital, Building Committee Minutes, May 8, 1919, Beth Israel Hospital Archives.

22 Beth Israel Hospital, Board of Directors Minutes, March 16, 1919, Beth Israel Hospital Archives.

23 Beth Israel Hospital, Medical Board Minutes, October 10, 1919, Beth Israel Hospital Archives.

24 Beth Israel Hospital, Building Committee Minutes, September 26, 1921, Beth Israel Hospital Archives.

fig. 6 US Army General Hospital No. 36, Detroit, interior view of ward. The wards were converted to all-single-bed rooms for civilian use.

25 "New 5th Avenue Hospital," *New York Times*, June 12, 1920, 15.

26 New Hospital for N.Y. to Be Unique," *New Castle News*, September 29, 1920, 5.

27 Goewey, "An Architect of Mercy;" Frederic J. Haskin, "The Haskin Letter: The Passing of the Ward," *Perth Amboy Evening News*, December 20, 1920, 4.

28 Wiley E. Woodbury, York & Sawyer, Architects, "The Fifth Avenue Hospital and Laura Franklin Free Hospital for Children, New York City," *Architectural Review* 11 [original series vol. 27], no. 5 (November 1920), 129–40; York & Sawyer, "The Fifth Avenue Hospital, New York," *Architecture and Building* 54, no. 9 (September 1922), 86–88 (and plates).

fig.7 Early plan of Fifth Avenue Hospital Source: *Architecture and Building* 54, no. 9 (September 1922), Plate 145

29 Beth Israel Hospital, Louis J. Frank Papers, August 16, 1921, Beth Israel Hospital Archives.

30 Louis J. Frank, "Planning a Hospital Synthetically," *Modern Hospital* 17, no. 2 (August 1921), 100–103.

31 Beth Israel Hospital, Board of Directors Minutes, October 16, 1921, Beth Israel Hospital Archives; "A New Sort of Hospital," *Literary Digest* 71 (October 15, 1921), 20–21; "The Fifth Avenue Hospital of New York," *Science* 54, no. 1400 (October 28, 1921), 402–3; "Old Hamilton Square," *New York Times*, November 6, 1921, Section 7, 7; "A Hospital without Wards," *Warwick Daily News*, January 7, 1922, 5.

32 Russell B. Porter, "The Fifth Avenue Hospital," *New York Times*, November 19, 1922, Section T, 71.

33 Beth Israel Opens with 40 Patients," *New York Times*, March 13, 1929, 20.

at the Union League Club, a private men's club with members who promoted progressive projects. **26** The story Woodbury told captured the imagination of a number of listeners, many of whom had political clout, money, and media connections. Articles on Woodbury and the "wardless" Fifth Avenue Hospital soon appeared in multiple newspaper articles and even in *Frank Leslie's Weekly*. **27** The popular press credited Woodbury with the innovations, but articles in the professional architectural periodicals also gave York & Sawyer their due. **28**

Despite the attention given to the Fifth Avenue Hospital project, as late as August 1921 Frank still believed that the new Beth Israel Hospital building would be "the first of its kind," and that "pilgrimages will be made to our Institution from all over the world." **29** Frank's article in the August 1921 issue of *Modern Hospital* described the innovative Beth Israel Hospital plan, but it was too little, too late. **30** On October 16, with funding uncertainties still

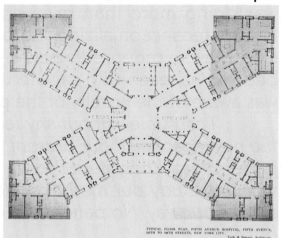

TYPICAL FLOOR PLAN, FIFTH AVENUE HOSPITAL, FIFTH AVENUE, 105TH TO 106TH STREETS, NEW YORK CITY
York & Sawyer, Architects.

holding up construction of the Beth Israel Hospital and media attention focused on the Fifth Avenue Hospital, Frank admitted that his project had been "scooped." **31** When the Fifth Avenue Hospital opened in September 1922, it was already widely known as the first hospital with all-single-bed rooms. **32 fig.7**

It took eight more years of delays, redesigns, funding shortages, and disputes between the client, the contractors, the architect, and the construction manager before the completed Beth Israel Hospital opened on March 12, 1929. **fig.8** The *New York Times* did print a favorable article that noted its design was "a sharp departure from the conventional type of hospital. There are no wards, each patient having an individual room, regardless of financial status." **33** By then, this was old news.

Tracing formal innovation implies a linear, progressive development which suggests to the practitioner that the path to success is paved with a discernible sequence of incremental formal innovations. But architectural form develops across years and through complex circumstances. Clearly, a novel design idea is not sufficient, or Bacon would be better remembered. Similarly, favorable political circumstances that permit the realization of the design are important; otherwise, the Henry Ford Hospital might have been more widely celebrated. Without smooth execution of construction—involving funders, contractors, designers, clients, and regulatory agencies—innovative projects like Frank and Abramson's Beth Israel Hospital can languish in obscurity. Publicity vaulted the Fifth Avenue Hospital to its notoriety, but it shone a fickle and unpredictable light on the complicated truth of the historical moment.

Indeed, the history of these four projects prove innovation to be a diffuse, perhaps even unreliable, measure of architectural worth for any individual project. Architectural change happens in a messy continuity that can extend across decades, not just years. In a longer historical view, even Asa Bacon was not the first to advocate an all-single-bed-room hospital. From the 1870s to the 1910s, designers of isolation wards advocated all-single-bed-room designs, not as a means of democratizing and privileging patient experience but as a means of disease prevention. [34] By the 1910s, the King's Daughters' Hospital in Temple, Texas adopted the practice of assigning every patient to a single-bed room but implemented it within an existing multi-bed ward building rather than a brand new design. [35] This begs the question of whether formal or functional innovation should take precedence in charting innovations into a single historical narrative.

This brief history highlights expectations that fueled innovation in hospital layouts and what designers hoped they and hostpital users would gain from that innovation. This focuses historical attention on process as well as formal product and reveals how and why innovation was made, not just what was done. If architectural projects (past and present) can be considered intentional efforts to effect change, history might offer more than a means of creating a timetable of new building forms. It could offer a means of understanding the motivations behind a desired formal change, assessing the architectural strategies undertaken to effect that change, and more importantly, of evaluating the results (both expected and unexpected) of the innovations. It might trace the "science" underlying the "art."

In the end, the all-single-bed-room hospital did not prove to be a lasting turning point in 1920s hospital design. As the prosperity of the Roaring Twenties gave way to the economic

A striking evidence of the skyscraper tendency in hospitals is the new Beth Israel Hospital being erected in New York, which with its seventeen stories may lay claim to the title of the "world's tallest hospital."

fig. 8 Sketch of the Beth Israel Hospital Project
Source: S. S. Goldwater, "Hospital Planning and Construction in 1922," *Modern Hospital* 20, no. 1 (January 1923), 1–4, here 2

34 Henry Greenway, "A New Mode of Hospital Construction," *British Medical Journal* 1, no. 593 (May 11, 1872), 495–97; John Shaw Billings, *Description of the Johns Hopkins Hospital* (Baltimore: Isaac Friedenwald, 1890).

35 George S. McReynolds, "'Efficient Hospitals': Success of Private Room Plan at Temple, Texas," *Journal of the American Medical Association* 74, no. 7 (February 14, 1920), 479.

hardship of the Great Depression, even modestly priced private rooms lay vacant and multi-bed wards overflowed. After the 1930s, payments for hospital stays were increasingly made by insurance plans rather than individuals; most insurance plans treated single-bed rooms as expensive luxuries and only reimbursed claimants for the cost of a semi-private (two-bed) room. To remain economically viable, hospital designs of the latter half of the twentieth century continued to include a few wards, some private rooms, and an ever-increasing share of two-bed rooms. Interest in single-bed rooms for all patients has again rekindled in the last two decades, this time as a means of infection control. **36** In the anticipated aftermath of the COVID-19 pandemic, it is likely that this interest will become policy. Yet for that policy to be effective, all-single-bed room designs will have to be made practical, affordable, and preferable.

36 The American Institute of Architects Academy of Architecture for Health, Facility Guidelines Institute, and US Department of Health and Human Services, *Guidelines for Design and Construction of Hospital and Health Care Facilities*, 2001 ed. (Washington, DC: The American Institute of Architects, 2006), 40.

Separate and Together: The General Hospital and the Twentieth-Century City
Annmarie Adams and David Theodore

Annmarie Adams and **David Theodore** are faculty members at the Peter Guo-hua Fu School of Architecture, McGill University, Montreal.

"Our project is more of an urban intervention than a hospital," said Basel-based architect Emanuel Christ. He was talking to an online audience in August 2020 about Kernareal USZ, his firm Christ & Gantenbein's conceptual design for University Hospital Zurich. fig.1a,b The first two of five planned buildings are set to open in 2027 as part of a master plan for the city's downtown university district. "It's an urban intervention that happens to be a hospital, not a hospital that's an urban intervention." [1] Christ draws an attractive image but, like many architectural propositions in the modern hospital era, such comments raise a complex question about the integrity of healthcare architecture: where exactly is the threshold between city and hospital? [2]

The Zurich hospital architects want us to understand their project as less like a hospital and more like a city: "we are not building a hospital!" insists Christ's partner, Christoph Gantenbein. "Of course there are operating theaters and similar facilities. But in terms of quantity, that's a small part. There

are also patient rooms, offices, laboratories, restaurants, and shops. So we didn't develop a building, but a neighborhood." [3] It makes sense to conceive of the hospital as an intervention in an urban district that just happens to house a hospital when set against the multiple activities that make up hospital life. Cities and hospitals tend to grow in similar ways: in planned and unplanned spurts that create layered, overlapping structures and activities. Even though we live in the midst of a movement towards patient- or family-centered

care, hospitals today are not focused on the patient, and, consequently, the patient room is not the key element in hospital architecture.

Reflection on the ideal relationship of the general hospital and the city has created a long-standing discourse involving architects, planners, and medical authorities. They debate whether hospital life and medical care thrive best when tightly coupled to city life or through keeping city and hospital physically distinct. Christ & Gantenbein's desire to fuse a 330-bed healthcare institution with its surroundings illustrates one pole of this debate on separation versus integration. "It's the opposite of the Forbidden City," says Christ,

1 Zoom meeting of Annmarie Adams, Emanuel Christ, and Irina Davidovici, *gta Invites*, August 19, 2020. See Zurich University Hospital, https://www.christgantenbein.com/projects/zurich-university-hospital-usz (accessed March 17, 2021).

2 This paper draws from David Theodore, "The Hospital City ca. 1970," American Association for the History of Medicine annual meeting, Los Angeles, CA, May 10–13, 2018. We are grateful to Cigdem Talu for assistance.

3 This is a rough equivalent from Google Translate of the following source: https://architekturbasel.ch/christ-gantenbein-und-herzog-de-meuron-basler-bauen-zuerich/ (accessed March 17, 2021).

fig.1 a, b Visualization and site plan by Christ & Gantenbein, University Hospital Zurich Source: https://afasiaarchzine.com/2019/03/christ-gantenbein-48/christ-gantenbein-university-hospital-extension-zurich-afasia-4–2/ (accessed April 8, 2021)

4 Zoom meeting, Adams, Christ, and Davidovici, August 19, 2020.

5 Hermann H. Field, "Application of Comprehensive Planning to the Urban Teaching Medical Center," Part Two, *Hospitals* 39, no. 22 (November 16, 1965), 67–72, here 72.

6 Linda Luxon, "Infrastructure: The Key to Healthcare Improvement," *Future Hospital Journal* 2, no. 1 (February 2015), 4–7.

7 Lisa Smith, et al., "The Impact of Hospital Visiting Hour Policies on Pediatric and Adult Patients and Their Visitors," *Joanna Briggs Institute Library of Systematic Reviews* 7, no. 2 (2009), 38–79.

8 R. A. Kearns and J. R. Barnett, "To Boldly Go? Place, Metaphor, and the Marketing of Auckland's Starship Hospital," *Environment and Planning D: Society and Space* 17, no. 2 (April 1999), 201–26.

9 We are indebted to excellent work by others on hospital architecture, especially by Adrian Forty, Philip Goad, Jeanne Kisacky, Cameron Logan, David C. Sloane, Christine Stevenson, Leslie Topp, Stephen Verderber, Julie Willis, and Carla Yanni.

10 Annmarie Adams, "Modernism and Medicine: The Hospitals of Stevens and Lee, 1916–1932," *Journal of the Society of Architectural Historians* 58, no. 1 (March 1999), 42–61; David Theodore, "Sound Medicine: Studying the Acoustic Environment of the Modern Hospital, 1870–1970," *Journal of Architecture* 23, no. 6 (2018), 986–1002.

11 Rajendra Kale, "Parking-Centered Health Care," *Canadian Medical Association Journal* 184, no. 1 (January 10, 2012), 11; Annmarie Adams, et al., "Kids in the Atrium: Comparing Architectural Intentions and Children's Experiences in a Pediatric Hospital Lobby," *Social Science & Medicine* 70, no. 5 (March 2010), 658–67; David Theodore, "Feeling Foreign: What Happens When a Hospital Looks Just Like a Shopping Mall," in Giovanni Borasi, ed., *Journeys: How Travelling Fruit, Ideas and Buildings Rearrange our Environment* (Montreal: Canadian Centre for Architecture, 2010), 215–21.

evoking the exclusivity of Beijing's famous imperial residence to emphasize the openness and visibility of his firm's plans for the hospital site in central Zurich. **4** In 1965, influential hospital planner Hermann H. Field wrote that "one of the most obvious violations in design is the usual disregard by the hospital of its surroundings. Few building types have so consistently developed at variance with everything around them." **5** Integrating hospitals in city centers, planners claimed, expedites links to transportation, technology, and expertise. **6** Easy access to hospitals means more visitors for patients. **7** And most importantly, placing hospitals downtown connected to other buildings makes them part of everyday life and can even normalize sickness. **8** If hospital and city overlap, that is, going for medical treatment becomes like going to the bank, or akin to how city dwellers might go to a university hospital to attend a public lecture.

In this paper we explore the relationships between modern hospital architecture and the twentieth-century city. In urban general hospitals in Europe, North America, and Australia, design has kept the hospital and city both separate and integrated. **9** On the one hand, good architecture can help hold undesirable aspects of urban life at bay, working alongside security agents and surveillance technologies to keep people and crime out of hospitals. Likewise, highly sophisticated ventilation systems and wall sections can separate hospital air from city air and hospital sounds from city sounds. **10** On the other hand, architects also fashion networks of tunnels, bridges, atria, and parking lots to connect hospital life back to the city, deliberately imbricating city streets and hospital walls. Such architectural connectors entice citizens to visit the hospital. If bad food and expensive parking can keep people away from hospital sites and segregate hospital activities from downtown, then hospital lobbies, especially those with atria, can look and function like shopping malls, attracting non-medical visitors and encouraging them to linger and consume, creating familiar surroundings for suburban dwellers. **11**

Yet architects also deploy many arguments for keeping hospitals separate from the city. As do other institutions where people both work and sleep, hospitals look inward and benefit from distinct architectural boundaries. [12] Since the nineteenth century, architects have organized mental asylums, prisons, military barracks, boarding schools, universities, holiday retreats, and hospitals behind gated walls, as campuses, or as sculptural towers—sometimes all three. A twentieth-century example of separation in remarkably pure form is Tony Garnier's Hôpital Grange-Blanche (1913–1933, now Hôpital Edouard Herriot), arranged on the east edge of Lyon as distributed barracks strictly isolated from each other (discussed in more detail below). [13] And even as Christ & Gantenbein's plans progress, authorities are simultaneously planning "an almost autonomous hospital for highly specialized medicine," independent from its surroundings, the historic buildings of ETH Zurich and the University of Zurich, and the university hospital's larger institutional footprint. [14]

In short, throughout the last 120 years, architects and administrators have proposed designs that both separate hospitals and cities and bring them together. These dual impulses have accompanied the modern hospital since its invention at the end of the nineteenth century. At the time, hospital planners looked to build away from the congestion and pollution of the industrializing city; the desire to maximize clean, natural ventilation permeated every design decision. [15] fig.2 With the propagation of the pavilion plan, a type that flourished well into the 1930s, hospital architects and planners sometimes seized vast sites on the edges of cities. Pavilion-plan hospitals were contained by walls which marked the all-important boundary between sickness and the city. They comprised multiple separate pavilions linked by covered walkways, tunnels, or bridges. Inside, architects stipulated open or so-called Nightingale wards, typically occupied by thirty-two to thirty-six patients. To prevent or reduce the spread of infection, patient beds were separated by strong drafts of fresh air brought in through windows and ventilation systems. [16]

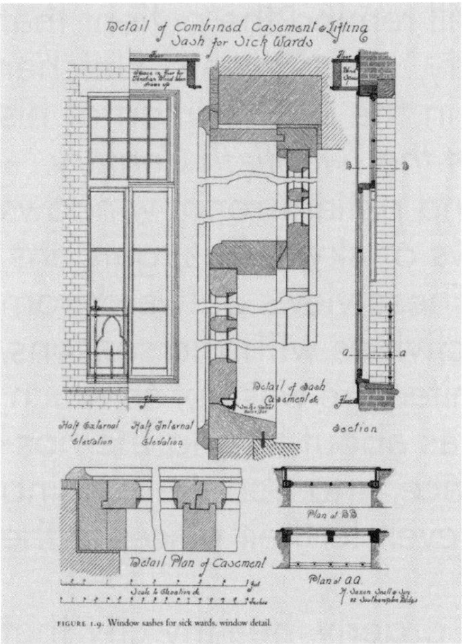

While hospitals are often physically removed from the city, they are also planned like the city, with functional zoning for personnel and modern transportation systems for supplies. Early city-inspired hospitals were self-contained communities, with food, laundry, and other services managed on-site. These

FIGURE 1.9. Window sashes for sick wards: window detail.

12 Charles Rosenberg, "Inward Vision & Outward Glance: The Shaping of the American Hospital, 1880–1914," *Bulletin of the History of Medicine* 53, no. 3 (Fall 1979), 346–91.

13 For an influential sociology of such custodial institutions, see Erving Goffman, *Asylums: Essays on the Social Situation of Mental Patients and Other Inmates* (Harmondsworth: Penguin, 1961).

14 "University Hospital Zurich, New Building Campus MITTE1," https://www.dreso.ch/en-CH/projects/university-hospital-zurich-new-building-campus-mitte1/ (accessed March 17, 2021).

fig.2 Large-scale window details Source: Henry Saxon Snell, *Charitable and Parochial Establishments* (London: B.T. Batsford, 1881), 103

15 Annmarie Adams, *Medicine by Design: The Architect and the Modern Hospital* (Minneapolis: University of Minnesota Press, 2007), 9–14.

16 Annmarie Adams, "Architecture that Breathes," *Harvard Design Magazine* 40 (Spring and Summer 2015), 14–19.

hospitals had gates, driveways, and centralized, carefully monitored entrances, alerting citizens to the distinctiveness of the hospital grounds. Patients and supplies were wheeled through hospitals, still iconic of hospital life today. Particularly large institutions might even have had interior trains. fig.3 Nurses, doctors in training, and hospital staff lived on-site, in accommodation embedded in hospital pavilions or in specially designed residences. 17 Multi-purpose, non-medical spaces echoed those in city centers. Hospitals featured religious rooms, chapels, temples, and synagogues, and had elaborate theaters and other rooms for entertainment. Simultaneously, hospital landscapes simulated nature-based places, featuring picturesque ornamental gardens, and wooded areas, designed with special pathways for patients. Sports fields provided opportunities for exercise, team building, and leisure. Long walks, the enjoyment of gardens and flowers, team sports, and even holiday-centered parades were seen as curative—that is, it was therapeutic to get patients out of bed to socialize and exercise within a strictly monitored landscape modeled on non-medical rural and recreational precedents. 18

The pavilion-plan hospital looked beyond itself. "An outlook that while distant from industries may still remind the patient that he is part of the world's life and activity," said Edward Fletcher Stevens, hospital architect and expert, in the 1928 edition of his influential book, The American Hospital of the Twentieth Century. 19 Roof-top terraces, fresh-air balconies, and patient-room windows provided carefully choreographed views of sky, lawns, gardens, woods, people, and buildings outside. These views outward from hospital interiors connected hospital activities with the seasons, climate, daylight, and stars. Hospital architecture was not so much, then, about shutting off the city as it was about linking the hospital with larger systems of time and place, and about engaging patients' senses with their surroundings, even to their places in the larger universe. 20

The pavilion plan established an orderly, healthy city that countered the congestion and unhygienic crowding common in rapid urbanization. 21 Hôpital Grange-Blanche is a good example. The plan of Garnier's hospital is composed of repeating, U-shaped, south-facing pavilions, each accommodating a medical specialty, connected underground by a network of tunnels. fig.4 The hospital was organized as a rational, grid-based city, an idealization held aloft by Garnier's stark vision of urban order. Its power derived from its adjacency to the disorderly, industrializing city: a bold vision of what a city could be next to what a city really was.

Changes in urbanism and changes in medicine itself quickly influenced the relations of city and hospital. The pace of urbanization

17 Annmarie Adams, "Rooms of Their Own: The Nurses' Residences at Montréal's Royal Victoria Hospital," Material History Review 40 (Fall 1994), 29–41.

18 Clare Hickman, Therapeutic Landscapes: A History of English Hospital Gardens Since 1800 (Manchester: Manchester University Press, 2013).

19 Edward Fletcher Stevens, The American Hospital of the Twentieth Century, 2nd, rev. ed. (New York: Dodge, 1928), 15.

20 Architects of Stevens' generation traveled widely, acquiring expertise by visiting hospitals that showcased design informed by medical theories. See Cameron Logan and Julie Willis, "International Travel as Medical Research: Architecture and the Modern Hospital," Health and History 12, no. 2 (2010), 116–33.

21 For a general history of the pavilion plan, see Jeremy Taylor, The Architect and the Pavilion Hospital: Dialogue and Design Creativity in England, 1850–1914 (London: Leicester University Press, 1997).

fig.3 Train for patient transport, Longue Pointe Asylum, Montreal, QC, 1911, VIEW-11277 Photographer: Wm. Notman & Son/Source: McCord Museum, Montreal

and industrialization meant that hospitals set up far from the urban core eventually became surrounded by the growing city. Crowding and densification meant hospitals adjoined other building types, such as office buildings. When around the First World War hospitals began to boast surgery and trauma care, surgical theaters became visible on hospital exteriors, advertising the institution's modernity through massing and form. **22** By the advent of a hospital building boom after the Second World War, general hospitals dealt primarily with chronic disease, not contagious disease, obviating the need for separating the sick from city life. Throughout the nineteenth and twentieth centuries, hospitals rejected patients with infectious diseases. One of the reasons for the development of specialist hospitals, such as tuberculosis sanatoriums, was to safeguard patients in the hospital from other conditions. At the same time, the general hospital became the primary location for birth and death, not just for the urban poor but for all citizens. **23** These new medical issues meant that hospitals should be built close to where people worked (and accidents occurred).

In the postwar period, hospital authorities searched for new ways to integrate the institution into the city. Influential planners, architects, and consultants advocated parallels between hospital planning and urban planning. **24** Lord Richard Llewelyn-Davies, who planned both hospitals and cities in postwar England, argued that "the structure of the health service from the doctor up to the regional medical center should be considered a major element in the arrangements of cities." **25** The impetus for designing that interface was a new infusion of state funding into healthcare systems across the West. The idea was that providing access to hospital medicine was fundamental to modern government, so a first response was increasing the number of hospitals outside cities. Both the Hill-Burton Act of 1946 in the United States and the founding of the National Health Service in Great Britain two years later led to an era of self-conscious hospital design. **26** The accessibility of health services came to be gauged through the number of hospital beds in particular regions; the Hill-Burton Act famously settled on the ratio of four and a half beds per thousand inhabitants.

fig. 4 Plan of Hôpital Grange-Blanche, Lyon, France, by Tony Garnier, 1913–1933
Source: Catherine Fermand, *Les Hôpitaux et les Cliniques: Architecture de la Santé* (Paris: Le Moniteur, 2000), 26

22 Annmarie Adams, "Surgery and Architecture: Spaces for Operating," in Thomas Schlich, ed., *Palgrave Handbook of the History of Surgery* (London: Palgrave Macmillan, 2018), 261–81, here 266.

23 Judith Walzer Leavitt, *Brought to Bed: Childbearing in America 1750–1950* (New York: Oxford University Press, 1986).

24 Jonathan Hughes, "Hospital City," *Architectural History* 40 (1997), 266–88.

25 Lord Llewelyn-Davies, "Facilities and Equipment for Health Services: Needed Research," *Milbank Memorial Fund Quarterly* 44, no. 3, Supplement (July 1966), 249–72, here 264.

26 Joy Knoblauch, "The Work of Diagrams: From Factory to Hospital in Postwar America," *Manifest* 1 (October 2013), 154–63; Alistair Fair, "'Modernization of Our Hospital System': The National Health Service, the Hospital Plan, and the 'Harness' Programme, 1962–77," *Twentieth Century British History* 29, no. 4 (December 2018), 547–75.

Auto-mobility was key. Twentieth-century hospital designers took on the challenge of integrating car culture into hospital life. The cover of *Modern Hospital* in 1966 featured the "Drive-in Hospital," a competition-winning design concept for the University of Cologne Medical Center, a few minutes' drive from the city center. fig.5 It is a diagrammatic drawing of the proposed vertical relationships between the city and hospital activities, showing an underground reception area for automobiles and ambulances. The dependence on the automobile is important enough to call it a drive-in, but the architects were not suggesting that patients were treated without leaving their cars. It was merely a way to celebrate that hospital planners were incorporating the patterns of car use in the city—going to the hospital could be promoted as an everyday experience like ordering a hamburger at a drive-in restaurant.

McMaster University Medical Centre, which opened in 1972 in Hamilton, Canada, illustrates the equivocation between integration and separation in hospital planning. McMaster's move from hospital to health sciences center was a fundamental change in institutional self-imaging. Here the car was relegated to the parking lot, yet the building nevertheless evokes the urban utopianism of the 1970s. [27] fig.6 Flexible and infinitely expandable, low-rise, and massive, the design by Craig, Zeidler & Strong was an architectural response to the issue of medical and technological change: we never know what is ahead. [28] Instead of walls, gates, and separate pavilions for separate medical specialties, the Toronto-based architects engaged a long-span superstructure. The use of interstitial space, designating an entire floor to house mechanical equipment between patient floors, allowed floor layouts that were unrestricted by the placement of structure and mechanical equipment. Different medical specialties such as surgery, pathology, and obstetrics could occupy plug-in, interchangeable units. Like Garnier's hospital from six decades earlier, it provided a stark contrast to the adjacent city but this time through its massive scale and integration of patient care, research, and teaching.

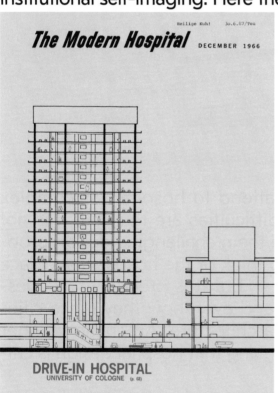

The Modern Hospital DECEMBER 1966

DRIVE-IN HOSPITAL
UNIVERSITY OF COLOGNE (p. 68)

fig.5 Drive-in hospital designed by Heinle, Wischer und Partner, Freie Architekte Source: Cover of *Modern Hospital* 107 (December 1966)

27 Thomas Strickland, "Passive and Active: Public Spaces at the McMaster Health Sciences Centre, 1972," in Sarah Schrank and Didem Ekici, eds., *Modern Architecture and the Body* (London: Routledge, 2016), 203–23.

28 See John Weeks and Gordon Best, "Design Strategy for Flexible Health Science Facilities," *Health Services Research* 5, no. 3 (Fall 1970), 263–84, and Daniel M. Abramson, *Obsolescence: An Architectural History* (Chicago: University of Chicago Press, 2016), 61–78.

fig.6 John Evans and architect Eberhard Zeidler with model for McMaster University Health Sciences Centre, 1969
Photographer: Tom Boschler/Source: Health Sciences Archives, McMaster University, Hamilton

29 David Theodore, "Better Design, Better Hospitals," *Canadian Medical Association Journal* 188, no. 12 (September 2016), 902–3.

It is important for architects to attend to hospitals as complex urban questions: the technical difficulties are real, but it is not their medical functions that make them challenging design problems. We might all be tempted to think of the hospital as a place laser-focused on medical care. 29 But it is precisely the question of how they fit into cities—and even how they make cities better—that motivates hospital architecture. American planner Hermann H. Field went further, arguing that hospital design is critical to improving city life:

"Furthermore, the day has passed when the institution can afford to be an island to itself with its back turned to its surrounding community. Fulfillment of its service, teaching and research goals will increasingly cast it in the role of partner in revitalizing our cities and making them healthier and better places to live in. Thus, the institutional planning process should not only be oriented inward, but equally to the complex interface area as it looks out from itself." 30

30 Hermann H. Field, "Organizing the Planning Process," *Annals of the New York Academy of Sciences* 128, no. 2 (September 1965), 670–78, here 670.

This year, the relationships of hospital and city have been challenged by the need to use hospitals, and especially their intensive care facilities, to deal with the COVID-19 pandemic. While public health authorities suggest contagious patients should be separated from communities, separating hospital workers and visitors from the rest of the city has proven less viable. Overall, the pandemic raises questions about the efficacy of hospital buildings at all: personal protective equipment is more effective at arresting the spread of the coronavirus inside the hospital than traditional architectural modes of separating humans such as rooms, corridors, walls, doors, curtains, and ventilation. [31] Now healthcare workers and visitors seal themselves off from patients with masks, shields, gowns, and shoe protectors, all specially designed to minimize contact and the sharing of droplets or air that might contain the deadly virus. The new protective space is medical clothing, not architecture. Medical and non-medical spaces, separate and together, are once again tested and contested.

[31] Kasey Grewe, "Headlines Don't Capture the Horror We Saw: I Chronicled What COVID-19 Did to a Hospital; America Must Not Let Down its Guard," Atlantic, December 6, 2020, https://www.theatlantic.com/ideas/archive/2020/12/new-york-doctors-know-how-bad-pandemic-can-get/617302/ (accessed December 12, 2020).

H: Hospital-as-City — The Healthcare Architecture of Herzog & de Meuron
Irina Davidovici

Irina Davidovici is a senior researcher, lecturer, and leads the doctoral programme at the Institute for the History and Theory of Architecture (gta), ETH Zurich.

"H" stands for hospital. A rectilinear sign, pointing at once in four directions, it indicates a kind of systematic, non-hierarchical accessibility. The modern institution of the hospital calls a truce on race, gender, and social class. It brackets most human lives at both ends, whatever their circumstances. In it, the membranes between individual and society, between the body and the body politic, thin out.

"H" embodies clinical efficiency. The institution of the hospital involves strict routines that depersonalize individuals, confining them to a hierarchy of doctors, staff, patients, and visitors. Like the institutions of the army, prison, or monastery, the hospital diminishes the external components that make up one's identity. Family, despite all efforts, becomes remote; property, beyond a point, demonstrably irrelevant. At the same time, the temporary release from one's own obligations and the suspension of everyday life, however dramatic, allow space for reflection, for reckoning with oneself. A different set of codes takes over. The long corridors smelling of antiseptic, the relentlessly single beds, the ubiquity of white uniforms instill a universality amongst hospitals as much as a distinct barrier between those inside and outside of them.

On the outside, however, hospitals differ greatly. Once stripped of iconographic pointers such as ambulances and signage, hospitals become vaguely, anonymously institutional, replicating other Western architectural types — from the convent and the palace to the penitentiary, the garden pavilion, the office building, and the mall. Each of these types' geographical, political, and social environments imply a different kind of engagement with the public realm. There is no clear correspondence between hospitals' appearance and their use — which only becomes unambiguous once we are inside. As a result, their variegated architectures embody a set of shape-shifting perspectives upon the role of healthcare in public life. Their external appearance and attitude towards their surroundings betray not only their actual age but also the predominant ideologies regarding public health at the time of their design.

Herzog & de Meuron's hospital projects represent the latest development of an architectural genre that has been recently stagnating. In the last few decades, the design of healthcare facilities has become encumbered by programmatic complexity, onerous building standards, high liability, and intense commodification. The result is that nowadays hospitals are, almost exclusively, the product of corporate expertise. [1] So, when healthcare

1 Annmarie Adams, "Decoding Modern Hospitals: An Architectural History," in "Design for Health: Sustainable Approaches to Therapeutic Architecture," special issue, Architectural Design 87, no. 2 (March/April 2017), 16–23, here 18.

architectural historian Annmarie Adams hailed the new projects of Herzog & de Meuron as a "recoding" of the modern hospital, she recognized that hospital innovation was coming from outside the narrow specialization of healthcare design—and from an unexpected direction. ₂

2 Adams, "Decoding Modern Hospitals," 23.

The forays into the healthcare domain by Herzog & de Meuron, a global, Pritzker-Prize winning practice mainly associated with landmark large-scale cultural venues, such as the Tate Modern in London (1994–2016) and the Elbphilharmonie in Hamburg (2001–2016), might come as a surprise. Still, Herzog

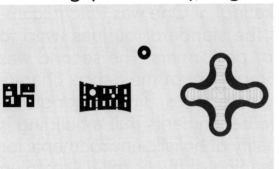

& de Meuron's claims upon this restricted market are fully consistent with the strategies that have historically propelled their development. Their projects question conventions and typological norms, their success leading, eventually, to the formation of new conventions and new norms. Considering archi-

Fig.1 Scale comparison between the plans of (left to right) REHAB Basel, the Kinderspital (the Children's Hospital) in Zurich, and Nyt Hospital Nordsjælland in Hillerød Source: Herzog & de Meuron Architekten

tecture's reorientation towards issues of societal, urban, and, ever more explicitly, biopolitical relevance, Herzog & de Meuron's new healthcare projects signal a shift in the mainstream architecture of hospitals. Their "recoding" of the hospital occurs through a multi-layered engagement with its parallel histories: the history of the hospital as a building type, its architectural history as a genealogy of notable projects mixing utopia and pragmatism, and, finally, the history of urban planning, itself profoundly shaped by the projection of healthcare concerns upon the public and private spaces of the city. In the case of Herzog & de Meuron buildings, these interpenetrating histories are accompanied by the self-referential, consistent history of their own portfolio. Over four decades of activity, the office has constructed its own culture in which projects, details, and strategies inform each other as part of a collective research in the formal, material, programmatic, and symbolic qualities of architecture.

How these projects talk to each other is apparent in Herzog & de Meuron's healthcare projects, two of which are currently approaching completion in Switzerland and Denmark. Both the commissions for Zurich's Kinderspital (the Children's Hospital), and the New North Zealand Hospital in Hillerød (NHN), Denmark, were awarded in competitions in 2011 to 2012 and 2013 to 2015, respectively. While responding to specific briefs that impart strong characteristics, the two hospitals share a number of spatial and material strategies. Furthermore, both stem from the earlier, radical prototype of the REHAB Rehabilitation Centre for Spinal Cord and Brain Injuries in Basel, Switzerland, won in competition in 1998 and completed in 2002. **fig.1** Their discussion here, together and apart, proposes a multifaceted understanding of emerging notions of healthcare in Herzog & de Meuron's architecture.

A Shared Language

In a recent lecture at the Institute for the History and Theory of Architecture (gta) at ETH Zurich, Christine Binswanger, Herzog & de Meuron's Senior Partner in charge of the Kinderspital project, elaborated upon the practice's notion of healthcare by borrowing two terms from competitive ice skating. [3] One was *Pflicht* (compulsory exercise), understood as the standard routines used to demonstrate the technical level of performers. The second was *Kür* (free skating), the freestyle component of the dance, characterized by creativity and flair. With these terms, Binswanger distinguished between the performative benchmarks that a building is obliged to fulfill and the added quality of holistic environments for care. [4] The former ensured the planning of the hospital according to norms of flexibility, functionality, rationality, and modularity—values fulfilled by any working hospital and solidly grasped by corporate design expertise. The latter freestyle component is both more compelling and difficult to define. What distinguishes the Herzog & de Meuron hospitals from the standard offerings is a question of atmosphere and approach. In concrete terms, these result from the direct connection to nature, the introduction of daylight and architectural signposting to allow intuitive wayfinding, and the tactile, domestic materiality of timber claddings inside and out. Through the adoption of these elements, Herzog & de Meuron hospitals are positioned as more than *machines à guerir*, providing a more integrated notion of care than the curative technologies of medical science.

For over a century, the existing Children's Hospital in Zurich has operated from the central, leafy neighborhood of Hottingen. The residential location has rendered the hospital perplexingly hard to access, causing worried parents to ask passers-by for directions, and ambulances to negotiate their way through quiet, narrow streets. Hence the move to Zurich-Lengg, to an established yet dispersed healthcare campus on the city outskirts, with various clinics and outpatient buildings separated by swathes of countryside. Allowing for much-needed modernization, expansion, and access improvement, the new pediatrics ensemble consists of two complementary buildings: the acute hospital—a ground-hugging, horizontal volume—and a laboratory and teaching building housed nearby in a white cylindrical tower. In an otherwise indifferent, low-density suburban context, the new acute hospital

3 Christine Binswanger, *gta Invites: Healthcare,* May 5, 2020, https://youtu.be/pgz3MxrscfY (accessed December 31, 2020).

4 Binswanger, *gta Invites.*

faces the imposing Psychiatric University Clinic Burghölzli of 1869, designed by Johann Caspar Wolf. This notable neighbor is acknowledged in the main entrance elevation of the hospital, gently curved to facilitate access and emphasize encounters across an open public space, akin to an urban proscenium. **fig.2** In contrast to the severe, neoclassical, stone-clad Burghölzli Clinic, visitors access the Children's Hospital through a long, concave screen of continuous verandas veiled by generously spaced timber elements and vegetation.

Placed along a public transport route, the laboratory building signposts the way to the hospital. On a compact round footprint, the laboratory rises seven floors above ground and one under, an ivory tower delivered in an elegant, non-committal modernist idiom. This research and teaching venue borrows from the paramedical appearance of a 1930s sanatorium, with continuous

circular balconies around the perimeter. Opening outwards toward the collective terraces, the laboratories and perimetral offices are organized inward around a central, skylit atrium. The sunken ground floor, open to the public and to views of the landscape, is conceived as an agora of semi-circular amphitheaters that can be used formally or informally, separately or together.

Fig. 2 Herzog & de Meuron, Kinderspital (University Children's Hospital), Zurich, Switzerland (planned completion 2022). Visualization of entrance facade
Source: Herzog & de Meuron Architekten

The unified volume of the pediatric hospital rises three stories above ground, but the recessed structure of the top floor makes it seem more like two (with two underground additional floors for services and parking). On the top floor, the wards, consisting of one- or two-bed rooms, are arranged in rows around the perimeter. Each room has its own pitched roof and strongly projecting eaves that give the impression of a row of small houses or holiday cabins, incongruously and humorously raised atop the horizontal building. The hospital reassures visitors of all ages with its carefully crafted informal appearance. Its emphasis on domestic scale and the variety built into the curved facade put incoming patients and visitors at ease, acting as a foil to the program within.

Behind this casually trimmed, green, almost recreational appearance are grouped fifty state-of-the-art departments with two hundred beds. As a functional apparatus, the hospital is impeccably organized. The main prerogative of its planning is flexibility, with fifty-six functional units that can be rearranged, combined, or strictly compartmentalized as the need arises. Fixed and structural elements are kept to a minimum. The concrete columns, service and vertical circulation shafts, and glazed lightwells around planted courtyards and lightwells are the only fixed components of the system. fig.3 The rest can be moved around and replanned as demanded by evolving medical expertise. The principal components of the brief — outpatient clinics on the ground floor, offices and treatment areas on the first floor, and bed wards around the perimeter of the top floor — are spread out around a central spine circulation. On each floor, this public circulation expands and contracts along a succession of four circular glazed courtyards, of different sizes and characters, which facilitate wayfinding.

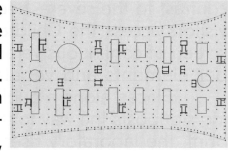

Fig. 3 Herzog & de Meuron, Kinderspital (University Children's Hospital), Zurich, Switzerland (planned completion 2022): plan showing fixed elements of cores, columns, courtyards and facades
Source: Herzog & de Meuron Architekten

While the larger scale, greater complexity, and rural location of the Nyt Hospital Nordsjælland in Hillerød demanded a different approach, both projects are bound to the initial premise of the hospital as a mat-like, horizontally expanded system, humanized and revitalized by views towards nature and the manipulation of daylight. The Nyt Hospital Nordsjælland is located in a flat natural landscape, forty kilometers northwest of Copenhagen, in the lowland countryside. Lacking a built context — the hospital is itself intended as a catalyst for urbanization — the plan is based on the ideal diagram of a square *hortus conclusus*. Its dimensions, around 300 meters across, resulted from the decision that each single-bed room should have its own view towards landscape, be it oriented to the outside or to the the internal garden. The midpoints of the imaginary square, where the vertical circulation nodes were located, were then squeezed together, bringing them within operational distance of each other. fig.4 This deliberate deformation resulted in the fluid, four-leaf-clover shape of the plan, enclosing at its center a large garden raised one level above entry. The top two floors, housing the wards, are built on top of this garden level. fig.5 They consist of a continuous perimeter of patient rooms and service stations, a serpentine figure varying between approximately 20 and 40 meters in depth. This two-story residential superstructure houses over 450 beds in individual rooms, all with landscape views. Lit from the sides or from above via light wells, the two floors under this garden level are filled in with a complex built fabric. The plan can be read

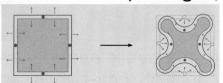

Fig. 4. Herzog & de Meuron, Nyt Hospital Nordsjælland, Hillerød, Denmark: diagram showing the origin of formal concept
Source: Herzog & de Meuron Architekten

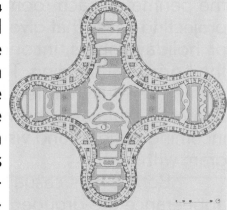

Fig. 5 Herzog & de Meuron, Nyt Hospital Nordsjælland, Hillerød, Denmark: plan of level two, showing wards and raised inner garden
Source: Herzog & de Meuron Architekten

as a field of fixed structural elements, articulated by an irregular grid of square and rectangular light wells which define two main axes. This grounded substructure comprises three levels: an entirely subterranean service floor; an intermediate lower level housing the intensive care, emergency, surgery and diagnostic rooms (with an additional hundred beds); and above them, at ground level, a main entrance offering access to various therapy departments, outpatient clinics, and the canteen.

Thanks to the undulating topography, both the main entrance and raised garden levels retain a feeling of connection to the ground. Two different landscaping schemes — for the forest park at the approach to the hospital and the raised garden — distinguish the two spatial conditions. The curving facades draw up their own horizon. Windows and balconies are placed behind a loose, yet visually unifying, screen of timber elements. Viewed from the internal garden, the meandering ward wings recede and protrude to appear rather as separate, manageably scaled pavilions. **fig.6** The primacy of this inner garden is based on research linking faster healing to access to natural environments, and recovering patients are actively encouraged to spend time outside. The extensive glazed circulations, with views to gardens on one or both sides, build up experiential parallels with the Louisiana Museum of Modern Art in Humlebaek, a popular destination on the coast, 20 kilometers to the east. **fig.7**

Fig.6 Herzog & de Meuron, Nyt Hospital Nordsjælland, Hillerød, Denmark (planned completion 2024): visualization of raised inner courtyard Source: Herzog & de Meuron Architekten

Fig.7. Herzog & de Meuron, Nyt Hospital Nordsjælland, Hillerød, Denmark (planned completion 2024): visualization of central lobby area Source: Herzog & de Meuron Architekten

Recoding the Hospital

How these projects "recode" the modern hospital becomes apparent from their critique of mainstream healthcare architecture. The architects observed that "the conventional layout of hospital buildings … may give patients the impression that they are being shifted back and forth between departments that are separate and distinct and do not work together." [5] In contrast, the large horizontal shape of the Children's Hospital seeks to highlight "the holistic nature of the building" — and, by implication, of care. [6] Rather than responding to the shape of the building plot, the volume was the result of a deliberate decision to maximize the building footprint and keep it low, unimposing, and casual, while

5 "377 Kinderspital Zürich, Herzog & de Meuron," https://www. herzogdemeuron.com/ index/focus/940-focus-hospitals/hospitals.html (accessed December 31, 2020).

6 "377 Kinderspital Zürich, Herzog & de Meuron."

keeping it volumetrically unified. A similar principle was applied at the hospital in Hillerød, whose horizontality and curved forms were considered as an addition to the natural landscape. The architects have argued that "a horizontal building is an appropriate building typology for a hospital, because this fosters exchange: across the various departments, the employees work on a shared goal: the healing of the ailing human being." [7]

In the history of hospitals as a type, this overall aim has often been overshadowed by the priority of procedural efficiency. From the ritual space of medieval cross-ward hospices, in which altars were placed at each junction so that all inmates could hear Mass, the modern hospital emerged through a process of secularization and rationalization. [8] During the Enlightenment, the hospital was re-imagined as what Sven-Olov Wallenstein calls "a biopolitical machine," [9] articulated through principles of isolation (of germs and contagious bodies) and flow (of air, views, and medical staff). Whether as a circular panopticon (Belleville Hospital, Antoine Petit, 1774) or as a system of modular pavilions (as prototyped by Bernard Poyet in 1788), modern hospitals envisaged treatment through means of control and surveillance, assuming the full

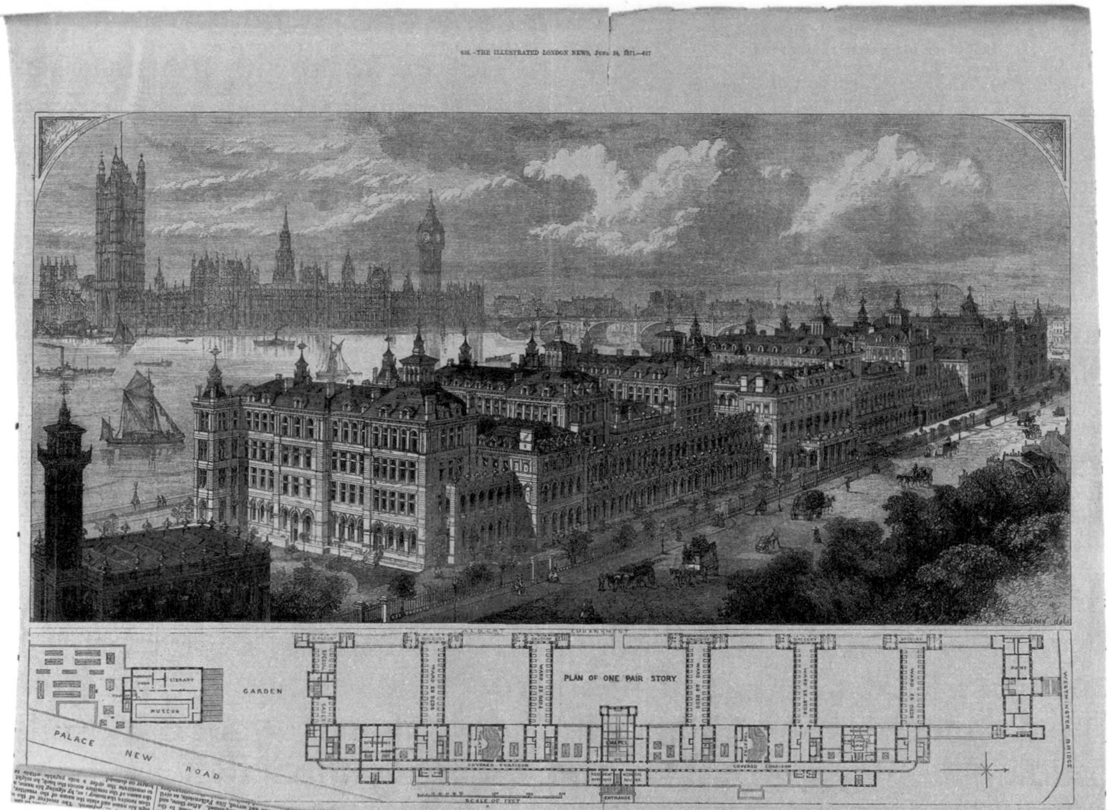

7 "416 New North Zealand Hospital, Herzog & de Meuron," https://www.herzogdemeuron.com/index/focus/940-focus-hospitals/texts.html (accessed December 31, 2020).

8 MASS Design Group, "Afflicted Form: A History of the Hospital," in "Well, Well, Well," special issue, *Harvard Design Magazine* 40 (Spring/Summer 2015), 168–176, here 171.

9 Sven-Olov Wallenstein, *Biopolitics and the Emergence of Modern Architecture* (New York: Princeton Architectural Press, 2008), 39.

fig. 8 St. Thomas' Hospital by Henry Currey, Lambeth, with Westminster in the background, plan and scale beneath. Wood engraver: Thomas Sulman/Source: *London Illustrated News*, June 24, 1871, 616–17; Wellcome Trust Collection

10 See Michel Foucault et al., eds., *Les Machines à guérir: aux origines de l'hôpital moderne* (Brussels: Pierre Mardaga, 1979), 32.

11 Blandine Barret-Kriegel, "L'hôpital comme équipement," in Foucault et al., *Les Machines à guérir*, 19–30.

compliance of sick bodies. [10] Gradually, hospitals morphed into complex systems of care and management, incorporating and giving form to the technological and scientific discoveries of their own time. [11] The pavilion type, characterized by the distribution of volumetrically distinct, ventilated wards extending perpendicularly from a common circulation spine, **fig. 8** found its natural successor in the twentieth-century mat-hospitals. [12] As pointed out by global design collective MASS, mat-hospitals were predicated on the assumption that "to design a hospital is to design a system." [13] As a container of increasingly sophisticated medical expertise and equipment, the hospital's inner workings became more opaque, calling for a collective trust in its healing powers centered around "heroic" doctors. Consequently, the popular image of the mid-century hospital became based on the "growing cultural perception of medicine as a miraculous system, capable of curing previously intractable health problems." [14] Paradoxically, processes of scientific rationalization and specialization caused hospitals to demand leaps of faith that recalled those required by the pagan and Christian institutions that lay at their origins. Consistent with this imagery was the suspension of individual agency imposed by the hospital. Within the hospital, individual patients became passive (believing) bodies, and their history became exclusively a medical one.

If, in the postwar decades, the hospital's image shifted from an instrumental healing machine to an efficiently run business, it changed again in the 1980s with the prevailing theory of "patient-centered care," which demanded a less institutional public image and emphasized accessibility. This doctrine was itself propelled through the convergence of two factors: on the one hand a competitive healthcare industry, compelled to regard the patient as a consumer; on the other, the influence of evidence-based research focused on the healing properties of architecture, as exemplified by Roger S. Ulrich's 1984 article, transparently titled "View through a Window May Influence Recovery from Surgery." [15] The combination of experiential, environmental, and market considerations explains the emergence of "mall hospitals" organized around multi-level, naturally lit atria, hiding illness and institutionalized care beneath the veneers of commerce, leisure, and spectacle. [16] Their technical counterpoint was the development of interstitial floors, in which equipment and mechanical systems were concentrated out of sight. Like commercial precincts and large office complexes, mall hospitals reserved their spectacle for the interior, while projecting a relative indifference towards the surrounding public realm.

Even this briefest overview presents the history of hospital typologies as one of accretion rather than selective evolution. Various configurations overlap, submerge, and reoccur in accordance with predominant trends and organizational diagrams, technical developments, and biopolitical agendas. While defining its unmistakable institutional interiors, the hospital has failed to develop an external appearance exclusively of its own. Depending on context,

12 For natural ventilation principles in the planning of the pavilion hospital, see Annmarie Adams, "Architecture That Breathes," in "Well, Well, Well," 14–19.

13 MASS Design Group, "Afflicted Form," 174.

14 MASS Design Group, "Afflicted Form," 173. See also Adams, "Decoding Modern Hospitals," 18.

15 R. S. Ulrich, "View through a Window May Influence Recovery from Surgery," Science, April 27, 1984, 420–21, https://doi.org/10.1126/science.6143402 (accessed January 2, 2021).

16 Adams, "Decoding Modern Hospitals," 19.

hospitals have consistently borrowed from other building types: from military barracks and penitentiaries to palaces, parkland pavilions and office towers. In that respect, the urban remit of hospital design has remained open, as long as the interior conforms to organizational diagrams of increasing complexity. The importance of programmatic adjacencies has led to a cumulative image of the hospital based on the practical extrusion of functional diagrams. [17] In recent decades, increasingly challenged by evolving medical, constructional, and servicing systems, and subject to complex building and environmental standards, hospital

17 Binswanger, *gta Invites*.

Fig. 9 Herzog & de Meuron, Day Clinic Extension, REHAB Centre for Spinal Cord and Brain Injuries, Basel, Switzerland (1998–2002). Photographer: Katalin Deér/Source: Herzog & de Meuron Architekten

architecture has become the preserve of a restricted design expertise. Contemporary hospitals have become "introverted, offering relatively little to their urban contexts ... bogged down by complex standards and stymied by pressures to justify design decisions through evidence-based research." [18] The rise of the hospital design has not been kind on the quality of the architecture, which has emphasized *Pflicht* at the expense of *Kür*—all compulsory routine with little scope for freestyle.

18 Adams, "Decoding Modern Hospitals," 18.

Against this wider context, Herzog & de Meuron's recent healthcare projects set up an agenda of differentiation: they are primarily meant to "neither look nor feel like hospitals." [19] On the one hand, they resist the institutional introversion of hospitals, the labyrinthine blind corridors of perplexing monotony, the unequivocal separation between the space of illness and the nominal normalcy of the outside. By contrast, the Children's Hospital and Nyt Hospital do everything to obliterate this distinction. Openness towards external views and the carefully varied landscaping

19 Herzog & de Meuron, "New Hospital for UCSF," July 7, 2020, https://www.herzogdemeuron.com/index/news/2020/547-new-hospital-for-ucsf.html (accessed October 20, 2020).

of internal courtyards bring in daylight, facilitate orientation, soothe, and distract. All procedures are intended to assist healing and alleviate alienation. By avoiding the formal replication of medical processes, as when the hospital becomes a volumetric extrusion of its functions, these buildings offer a coherent, unified set of experiences. **fig. 9**

In other words, Herzog & de Meuron "recode" the contemporary hospital—to continue using Adams' notion—by critiquing the accretive nature of the hospital as diagram and by rethinking buildings where each department is formally articulated as a separate entity. While seemingly informed by the horizontal typology of the mat-hospital, the projects reject its fundamental premise of a serviced spatial matrix for potentially infinite expansion. Instead, Herzog & de Meuron's hospitals trace definite, site-specific figures within fixed boundaries. By keeping immovable structural elements to a minimum, the plans allow for a redistributive logic of adjacencies within one unified, clearly defined figure. Their interiors can be inhabited, or hollowed out and reconfigured as required, around the fixed elements of the structure, perimeter, and lightwells. Instead of a system, the hospital is envisaged as an environment.

A Semantic Family

This "recoding" is also, partly, an unintended consequence of—put bluntly—being Herzog & de Meuron buildings. Rather than referencing the history of modern hospitals, these projects are shaped by the culture of Herzog & de Meuron as an office, and conceived in relation to internal precedent. In particular, the Children's Hospital and the Nyt Hospital Nordsjælland are built upon the conceptual, formal, and material strategies articulated for the practice's earliest healthcare commission, the REHAB clinic in Basel, completed in 2002. [20] A clinic for neurorehabilitation and paraplegic care, REHAB caters to mid- and long-term recovery processes, assisting the patients' acclimatization to their new condition. With patients staying an average of two months or, in some cases, up to eighteen months, REHAB straddles a fine line between medical clinic and transit house. [21] The day clinic pavilion recently added onto the roof terrace, where patients spend time between therapies, attests to the building's domestic aspects. The delicate nature of the recovery process was also reflected in the 1998 competition brief, which demanded that REHAB should not look like a hospital. This condition set in motion Herzog & de Meuron's long-term research into healing environments: research opposed to the stereotype of the hospital as "elevators and indoor corridors flanked by countless doors leading to rooms or

20 "165 REHAB Basel, Centre for Spinal Cord and Brain Injuries, Herzog & de Meuron," https://www.herzogdemeuron.com/index/projects/complete-works/151-175/165-rehab-centre-for-spinal-cord-and-brain-injuries.html (accessed November 23, 2020).

21 Jason Frantzen, "416 New North Zealand Hospital," 2018, https://www.herzogdemeuron.com/index/focus/940-focus-hospitals/videos.html (accessed November 23, 2020).

22 "165 REHAB Basel."

examination rooms, a waiting lounge at the end of the hall or next to the elevator." 22 The REHAB centre, in contrast, is a building on two levels, neatly aligned within a rectangular shape, in which courtyards of different shapes and characters were carved out as a way to guide fresh air and natural light within the deep plan. Individualized by their unique shape and landscaping, the courtyards also served as route-finding markers. The alternative presented by REHAB has been scaled up at the Children's Hospital and Hillerød, where courtyards structure the public routes, bring light into the deep plan, subliminally guide visitors, and mark the more public places such as reception desks and waiting areas. The three projects share a concern with emphasizing relations to, and connections between, interior and exterior. If conventional hospitals are introverted, these, by contrast, open views and offer access to their surroundings, encouraging patients to walk outside as part of the recovery process.

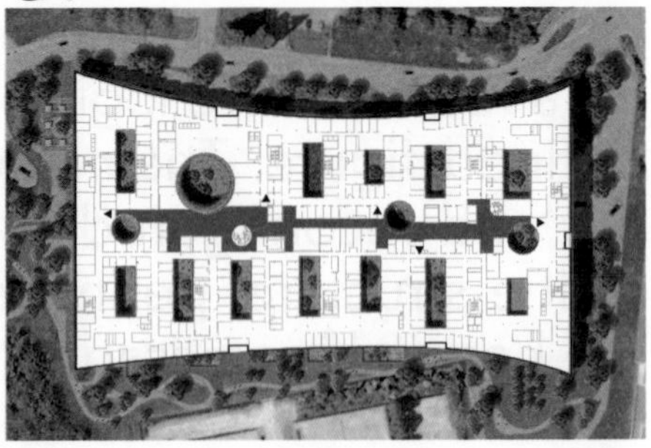

Fig. 10 Herzog & de Meuron, Kinderspital (University Children's Hospital), Zurich, Switzerland: ground floor plan highlighting the central circulation spine and main entrances Source: Herzog & de Meuron Architekten

Resistance to the machine aesthetic of early twenty-first century hospitals, and access to nature as an aspect of healing, are central to the projects' material strategy. By using timber — a lot of it — on the inside and outside of buildings, the architects defy the conventions of hospital architecture, deliberately undermining its institutional gravitas. Careful research has been put into injecting domestic references and scales into the design of hospital rooms, while for hygienic and maintenance reasons timber is only used in certain areas and with specific finishes. On the facades, the timber elements are spaced out to act as semi-open screens.

Fig. 11 Collage by Herzog & de Meuron showing pedestrian area in Niederdorf, Altstadt Zurich, equivalent to the central circulation spine of the Kinderspital Source: Herzog & de Meuron Architekten

In a further rebuke to the machine aesthetic, the detailing of columns and claddings invokes manual craft. The fine-grained texture of repetitive elements serves as a counterpoint to the continuous, expansive surfaces that result from their massing, and anchor the buildings in their natural, suburban locations.

The tactical use of courtyards, timber, planting, landscaping, and natural light are part of a more encompassing strategy to conceive the hospital as a city in miniature with streets, squares, and parks. The analogy itself is not new: the inevitably complex planning of any large hospital invites comparisons with urban fabric. 23 These architects take the metaphor to another level, working through its consequences in order to generate a family of new hospital environments. Urban imagery suffuses their project descriptions and presentations. The REHAB clinic was

23 This comparison is explored at length in another essay in this collection, Annmarie Adams and David Theodore, "Separate and Together: The General Hospital and the Twentieth-Century City."

conceived as a "multifunctional, diversified building, almost like a small town with streets, plazas, gardens, public facilities, and more secluded residential quarters." [24] Through a leap in scale, the plans of the Nyt Hospital Nordsjælland in bring the urban into play through the strict control exercised over internal routes of a hallucinatory complexity: "the hospital functions like a city. A network of internal public streets and service shortcuts link the most crucial functions." [25] In a similar spirit, the Children's Hospital "follows an urban grid with streets, intersections, and squares," in which "the functions or departments correspond to neighborhoods," and "every floor has a main street." [26] This last statement has been applied *ad litteram* in its design. On each floor, the hospital's front-of-house areas are planned along a circulation spine (referred to by the architects as a "main street") that can be spatially compared to a 200-meter section of the Niederdorfstrasse, the main thoroughfare in Zurich's medieval center, a relatively straight street opening into plazas. fig. 10 Not coincidentally, this location is near Zähringerplatz, where Zurich's earliest hospital, the Predigerkloster, operated from the thirteenth to late nineteenth centuries. fig. 11 [27]

Within Herzog & de Meuron's overall oeuvre, the city-in-a-building metaphor has been repeatedly deployed, and by no means restricted to healthcare. [28] This analogy becomes manifest in the inversion, or at least demonstrative ambivalence, of interior and exterior conditions in projects with complex programs. The building-as-city has an interior constructed out of elements associated with exterior facades; streets are cajoled inside to become public interiors, and interior foyers are presented as the public space of a miniature city. This cross-strategy was first articulated for the earliest phase of the Tate Modern renovation (competition 1994–1995, completion 2000), where the wide ramp descending into the Turbine Hall became a grand, sloping urban forum. (Similarly to the mall hospitals, the Tate became the prototype of a mall-museum: simultaneously one of London's most popular public interiors, a novel site for art experimentation, and a prototypical venue of cultural consumption.) [29] Another

24 "165 REHAB Basel."

25 "416 New North Zealand Hospital."

26 "377 Kinderspital Zürich."

27 Lorenzo Käser, "Illustrierte Geschichte des Züricher Cantonsspitals und der medizinischen Poliklinik: Nebst medizinischen, topographischen und kulturellen Nebenwirkungen," *Quartierverein Fluntern*, April 22, 2019, http://www.zuerich-fluntern.ch/index.php?nav=92 (accessed November 23, 2020).

28 The image of the city is fully assimilated in their work. Earlier in their career, Jacques Herzog and Pierre de Meuron described the "abrupt" urban transitions of their native Basel as their "home feeling." Alejandro Zaera, "Continuities: Interview with Herzog & de Meuron," *el croquis* 60 (1993), 6–23, here 13. In the wider context of the discourse on the city, Herzog & de Meuron have openly acknowledged this experiential condition of density and heterogeneity as having a bearing upon their approach.

29 The Tate Modern can be approached as an art venue, but it is inevitably a nexus for other modes of recreation, replete with shops, cafés, viewing platforms, and public meeting places. Like the mall hospitals, it can be inscribed into a wider tendency to blur the boundaries between functions and overlap them in the attempt to attract the greatest possible number of consumers into one place. This ambivalence was lamented in Herzog's recent open "Letter from Basel" to David Chipperfield: "Tate Modern's Turbine Hall was an innovation, inviting not only a different audience but also a new kind of art production and presentation that transcends the traditional format of an exhibition space. ... But it was also an ideal platform for the emergence of a dire development in art: its radical commercialization." Jacques Herzog, Herzog & de Meuron, Letter from Basel, August 2020, originally published in *Domus* 1050 (October 2020), https://www.herzogdemeuron.com/index/focus/letter-from-basel/letter-from-basel.html (accessed January 2, 2021) example of in-house cross-referencing becomes apparent in the formal and intellectual parallels between the Children's Hospital and the Laban Dance Centre in London (competition 1997, completion 2003). The hospital borrows from the ballet school both the shape of the plan and the concept of the building as a container of "cityscapes." [30]

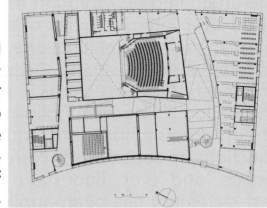

Herzog & de Meuron refrain from explicitly drawing upon historical precedent, particularly when it is authored. But as T. S. Eliot wrote, "no poet, no artist of any art, has his complete meaning alone." [31] At their junction with the historical fabric of the city, the coherent inner trajectory of their buildings can no longer resist all external influences. While the hallucinatory complexity of Herzog & de Meuron's plans collapses the systemic nature of hospital organograms, it also invites parallels with John Soane's additive works for the Bank of England (1790—1805), which completed a vast, deep urban block on the City of London's Threadneedle Street. Adding to a heterogeneous ensemble of buildings dating back to 1694, Soane unified them by means of a gigantic blind wall, which redefined the boundaries of the plot. Within the confines of this enclosure, he created a spatial chainmail of public and private offices,

bank halls, libraries, and secret vaults. This enfilade, punctuated by courtyards, was lit by vertical shafts of natural light, brought into the depth of the plan by means of an elaborate roofscape of domes, raised lanterns, and Diocletian windows. Akin to a laboratory of architectural inventiveness, the bank's natural lighting

30 "160 Laban Dance Centre, Herzog & de Meuron," https://www.herzogde-meuron.com/index/projects/complete-works/151-175/160-laban-dance-centre.html (accessed November 23, 2020).

Fig. 12 Herzog & de Meuron. Laban Dance Centre London, UK (1998-2003). Lower level plan with a topography of street-like ramps
Source: Herzog & de Meuron Architekten

31 T. S. Eliot, "Tradition and the Individual Talent" (1919), *Perspecta* 19 (1982), 36—42, here 37.

Fig. 13 Joseph Michael Gandy, *A Bird's-eye View of the Bank of England*, watercolour, 1830
Source: Sir John Soane's Museum, London

was intended to imbue even everyday business transactions with an aura of *"lumière mystérieuse,"* as noted by Nicholas Le Camus de Mézières. [32] The intention was to invoke a mood, to let arise in the beholder sensations and emotions that had little to do with the practical use of the building. A similar intention is contoured in the deep plans of Herzog & de Meuron's hospitals, similarly landlocked by immovable contours that nevertheless allow growth, change, densification, and diversification within their fixed perimeter. This is not to say that the connection proposed here was ever concrete, or that Soane's lost masterpiece acted as a conscious or a subliminal model to Herzog & de Meuron's current buildings. It is, rather, the accidental closeness of projects responding, more than two hundred years apart, to similarly restrictive circumstances with a combination of plan efficiency and impractical beauty.

Within the general "building-as-city" paradigm, the "hospital-as-city" metaphor is particularly potent. The relation between wellbeing and architecture, between healthcare and the urban territory, has long shaped the discipline of planning buildings and cities. In the 1970s, Michel Foucault connected the emergence of the modern hospital during the eighteenth century with the medicalization of urban space in city planning. More recently, Beatriz Colomina has once again placed medicine at the center of architectural endeavor, hypothesizing bodily illness as "the engine of modern architecture." [33] What we witness in the projects described above is a different, but not entirely unrelated, phenomenon. It is a willingness—albeit lucidly located in the logics of global cultural currency—to inscribe hospital buildings simultaneously into medical protocol and architectural canon. The aim is to provide not only a building, a room, a bed, and specialized treatment for each ailing body, but also to stage and enhance the environment in which healing may occur. According to this ambition, the "H" no longer stands merely for "hospital", but rather, for a holistic understanding of care.

32 Nicholas Le Camus de Mézières, quoted in David Watkin, ed., *Sir John Soane: The Royal Academy Lectures* (Cambridge: Cambridge University Press, 2000), fn. 9, 176–198, here 184.

33 Beatriz Colomina, *X-Ray Architecture* (Zurich: Lars Müller, 2019), 11.

Airborne Infection and Breathing Walls
Didem Ekici

Variations on miasma theory dominated medical discourse throughout most of the nineteenth century, which witnessed six cholera pandemics and long-standing epidemic threats such as tuberculosis. Some versions of the theory held that epidemics were caused by noxious gas emanating from rotting organic matter; others related miasma to specific kinds of climate. The miasma was imagined existing in the foul-smelling air of streets as well as domestic spaces in the nineteenth-century city. Some physicians warned that the vitiated air in badly ventilated, packed rooms in overcrowded housing was more deadly than the foul air outdoors. As the American physician Lewis Leeds proclaimed in a public lecture in 1866, "it is not in the external atmosphere that we must look for the greatest impurities, but it is in our own houses that the blighting, withering curse of foul air is to be found. We are thus led to the conclusion that our own breath is our greatest enemy." Miasma theory, coupled with the problem of overcrowded housing, led to the emergence of air as a dynamic design element in nineteenth-century efforts to mitigate the airborne transmission of disease, culminating in ventilation technologies. Hygiene manuals increasingly discussed natural and forced ventilation methods to alleviate the health hazards of expired air. Indoor air was cast as a dynamic, everchanging entity. Contemporary ventilation studies represented the void inside buildings as filled with air currents moving between inside and outside, and expired air and gases emitted by bodies that spread infectious diseases.

The perceived hazards of miasma and expired air in relation to infectious diseases led to experimental investigations of indoor air. In the

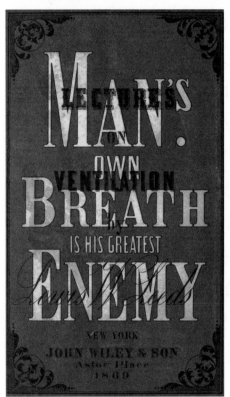

second half of the nineteenth century, German physician Max von Pettenkofer (1818–1901) made several seminal contributions to indoor air sciences. His studies quantified indoor air quality and turned the air into a tangible design criterion. He established how carbon dioxide could be used as the main indicator of indoor air quality when determining the required ventilation rate in a building for a person to remain healthy and comfortable. This indicator is still in use.

The agency of the miasma was dispelled after 1880 by bacteriologist and physician Robert Koch's germ theory of disease, which stated specific germs, not miasma, caused specific diseases. The miasma theory, however, persisted in popular imagination long after the scientific consensus behind it had crumbled. In the late 1800s, Pettenkofer and Koch were at the heart of the scientific debate over the causes of cholera. One of the most recalcitrant defenders of miasma theory, Pettenkofer incorrectly argued that the cholera germ became infectious only when it became cholera miasma after prolonged contact with the soil. To prove his thesis, in 1892, he drank a suspension of cholera bacteria and, remarkably, did not become seriously ill. This notorious episode aside, Pettenkofer's study of environmental factors had a significant influence on both public health and architecture. His scientific method of mapping everyday environments formed the basis of modern hygiene. By monitoring the exchange between the human body and built space, experimental hygiene rendered metabolic functions, such as breathing, architectural issues.

The requirement of consistent ventilation involved a rethinking of the spatial boundaries of buildings. Pettenkofer saw walls no longer as solid barriers that protected inhabitants from the elements but as a porous interface that mediated exchange between  the interior and the exterior. He equated walls with skin in their permeability. Porous external walls were necessary to facilitate fresh air access and to prevent humidity in the house. By advocating permeability, Pettenkofer challenged common views about the separation of the house's inside and outside. He believed that there was no such thing as self-contained architecture, and the house was inevitably part of the broader atmosphere.

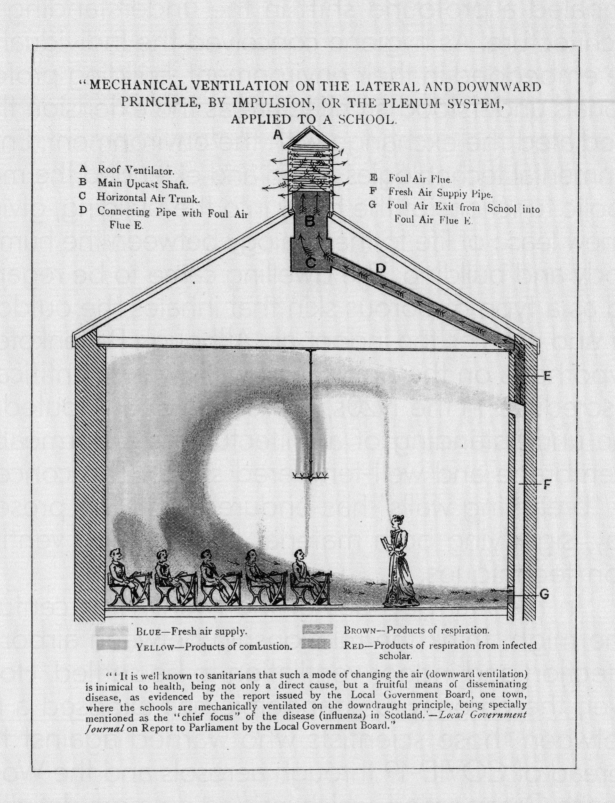

"MECHANICAL VENTILATION ON THE LATERAL AND DOWNWARD PRINCIPLE, BY IMPULSION, OR THE PLENUM SYSTEM, APPLIED TO A SCHOOL.

A Roof Ventilator.
B Main Upcast Shaft.
C Horizontal Air Trunk.
D Connecting Pipe with Foul Air Flue E.

E Foul Air Flue.
F Fresh Air Supply Pipe.
G Foul Air Exit from School into Foul Air Flue E.

BLUE—Fresh air supply.
YELLOW—Products of combustion.

BROWN—Products of respiration.
RED—Products of respiration from infected scholar.

"'It is well known to sanitarians that such a mode of changing the air (downward ventilation) is inimical to health, being not only a direct cause, but a fruitful means of disseminating disease, as evidenced by the report issued by the Local Government Board, one town, where the schools are mechanically ventilated on the downdraught principle, being specially mentioned as the "chief focus" of the disease (influenza) in Scotland.'—*Local Government Journal* on Report to Parliament by the Local Government Board."

HOW INFECTION IS SPREAD.

"The report on the influenza epidemic presented to Parliament by the Local Government Board indicates the extreme importance of proper ventilation—especially in schools—which is pronounced to be the only real safeguard against that disease.

"The statistics given point to one town, where the schools are mechanically ventilated on the downdraught principle, as being the 'chief focus' of the disease in Scotland. So far as the children in the schools are concerned this is easily accounted for, as the warm, infected air expelled from the lungs is returned by the descending current, and is not only reinhaled, but is also breathed by the other scholars. This is how infection is spread."—*Local Government Journal.*

This change in the status of the building's periphery signaled a profound shift in the understanding of architecture. As hygiene conceived the individual to be embedded in their environment, building professionals understood architecture as the extension that mediated the exchange with the environment. Environmental technologies aided and extended the metabolic functions of the body into the building, giving a new lease of life to the analogy between the human body and building. The dwelling came to be regarded as a type of porous skin that inhales the outdoor air and exhales the indoor air. Although Pettenkofer's hypothesis on the porosity of walls was scientifically discredited in the 1920s, it eventually contributed to the understanding of architecture as a permeable membrane and well-tempered space. The concept of "breathing walls" has endured until the present day, signifying both material qualities and ventilation techniques.

In the first decades of the twenty-first century, one might think the relationship between airborne infection and indoor ventilation to be settled. However, the coronavirus pandemic has exposed a rift between those scientists who warned against the spread of COVID-19 through aerosols and the World Health Organization, which insisted on more definitive proof of airborne transmission before it revised its guidelines. The World Health Organization's doctrine was that direct contact caused infection, not lingering airborne aerosols. Its initial skepticism regarding aerosol transmission goes back to the rejection of the miasma theory in the late nineteenth century. Modern medicine exorcized the ghosts of the miasma theory by requiring a very high level of proof to accept any disease as airborne. Critics have pointed out that the de-prioritization of aerosol transmission has resulted in the alarming lack of emphasis on indoor ventilation in official guidance early in the pandemic. Miasmas, it turns out, might not be meaningful on a molecular and biological level but are both real and, what is more, active from the perspective of public health.

Didem Ekici is an assistant professor at the University of Nottingham and a member of the Architecture, Culture and Tectonics Research Group.

fig. 1 Book cover from Lewis Leeds, *Lectures on Ventilation by Lewis Leeds: Man's Own Breath is His Greatest Enemy* (New York: Wiley, 1869), based on a course delivered at the Franklin Institute, Philadelphia (1866–1867)/Quotation from page 7

fig. 2 Illustration of air currents in a room, from Lewis Leeds, *Lectures on Ventilation*, facing p. 26
Source: Deutsches Museum Bibliothek, Munich

fig. 3 "Natural System of Ventilation ... applied to Schoolrooms," Plate VII, in Robert Boyle, *The Boyle System of Ventilation*, trade cat. (London: Robert Boyle & Son, ca. 1900), 174
Source: Cadbury Research Library, Special Collections, University of Birmingham

The Viral Balcony: Or the Vicissitudes of an Urban Element in Times of Pandemic

Tom Avermaete, Nicole de Lalouvière, Hamish Lonergan, Janina Gosseye, and Korinna Zinovia Weber

Tom Avermaete is Professor for History and Theory of Urban Design at the Institute for the History and Theory of Architecture (gta), ETH Zurich.

Nicole de Lalouvière is a doctoral fellow at the Institute of Landscape and Urban Studies (LUS) and Chair of the History and Theory of Urban Design, ETH Zurich.

Hamish Lonergan is a doctoral candidate at the Chair of the History and Theory of Urban Design of the Institute for the History and Theory of Architecture (gta), ETH Zurich.

Janina Gosseye is Associate Professor of Urban Architecture in the Department of Architecture, Faculty of Architecture and the Built Environment, TU Delft.

Korinna Zinovia Weber is a lecturer and research project manager at the Chair of the History and Theory of Urban Design of the Institute for the History and Theory of Architecture (gta), ETH Zurich.

1 For a historical introduction to this element, see Tom Avermaete, Rem Koolhaas and Irma Boom, *Balcony* (Venice: Marsilio, 2014).

2 Such an idea of the balcony emerging from a medieval military device, called the *hourd,* can for instance be found in Eugène-Emmanuel Viollet-le-Duc, "Bretèche," *Dictionnaire raisonné de l'architecture française du XIe au XVIe siècle,* vol. 2, (Paris: Morel, 1854), 244—49.

3 Publicist Paul Planat underlines that, as a result of the symbolic importance of the balcony, from the "fifteenth century, artistic experiments made themselves felt in the balconies more than in any other part of architectural ornamentation." Paul Amédée Planat, "Balcon," *Encyclopédie de l'architecture et de la construction,* vol. 2, (Paris: Aulanier et cie, 1892), 236.

4 The French architectural theoretician Quatremère de Quincy speaks of a *"mode des balcons"* during the nineteenth century. Quatremère de Quincy, "Balcon," *Dictionairre historique de l'architecture, contenant dans son plan les notions historiques, descriptives, archeologiques: Biographiques, theoriques, didactiques et pratiques de cet art,* vol. 1 (Paris: Librarie d'Adrien Le Clere, 1832), 148—49.

5 Jo Wheeler, "Stench in Sixteenth-Century Venice," in *The City and the Senses: Urban Culture Since 1500,* Alexander Cowan and Jill Steward, eds. (Aldershot: Ashgate, 2007), 25—38, here 27. See also Amanda Sciampacone, "'Epidemics in a Mist': Medical Climatology and Cholera in Victorian Visual Culture," *Journal of Victorian Culture* 25, no. 4 (2020), 492—511.

In the spring of 2020, as COVID-19 induced lockdowns across Europe, citizens searched for alternative ways to appear in public, new modes of meeting one another, and tactics to share, care, and support their communities; in short, for different ways of *commoning*. One urban element has played a key role in these efforts: the balcony.

The balcony is not a new urban element. **1** According to some accounts, it first appeared in medieval military architecture, where it took the form of a cantilevered platform from which to attack the enemy. **2** The balcony can also be understood as a symbolic urban element. Religious and secular leaders used the balcony as a platform from which to address crowds and, even in their physical absence, it remained a means to represent their power within the city's public space. **3** The many balconies on papal palaces, town halls, and belfries bear witness to the symbolic charge of the balcony. This capacity to symbolize authority in society can be seen in nineteenth-century paintings by French artists such as Gustave Caillebotte, Berthe Morisot, and Édouard Manet, in which the balcony became the visual expression of bourgeois culture. **4**

In the mid-nineteenth century, the balcony would receive an additional connotation, firmly linking it to viruses, bacteria, and disease. Architectural thinking about housing and the city became strongly influenced by a resurgence of interest in the atmospheric origin of epidemics, or "miasma theory." The belief that bad air directly caused disease can be traced back to the ancient world and is implicit in some of the oldest names of diseases such as malaria, but in the nineteenth century, thanks to discoveries in climatology and increasing problems with air pollution associated with early industrialization, the theory gained new currency in European metropoles. **5** Though miasma theory was soon replaced by germ theory, the preoccupation with clean air persisted well into the twentieth century, and many modern architects and urban designers emphasized the importance of providing balconies in urban settings. [6]

It was probably the Swiss architecture critic Sigfried Giedion who summarized the modern role of the balcony most clearly in his book *Befreites Wohnen* (Liberated Dwelling), which was published as a result of the first Congrès Internationaux d'Architecture Moderne. [7] This book identified the balcony as a universally applicable element that had the capacity to introduce light, air, and openness into the modern dwelling. Giedion explained: "the 'new architecture' has unconsciously used these projecting 'balconies' again and again. Why? Because there exists the need to live in buildings that strive to overcome the old sense of equilibrium that was based only on fortress-like incarceration." [8] Indeed, the spatial agency of the balcony is highly contingent on its tectonics, morphology, and materiality. Along with doorways and windows, the balcony is a threshold element: it mediates between the home and the street, the private and the public. The balcony has a particularly liminal quality, for it encloses private space while also projecting it into the city's public sphere.

The desire to overcome a state of incarceration also led to a rediscovery of the balcony's capacities in the twenty-first century. In the first weeks of March 2020, in many European countries the balcony emerged as a domestic space to exercise and socialize with neighbors, as a private platform to enjoy the outdoors and publicly support health workers, and as an individual stage for collective musical performances. New relationships have emerged from the productive friction of the individual and collective realms on the balcony. Spurred by the extraordinary conditions of COVID-19, we have witnessed poignant balcony exchanges to combat loneliness. From the individual balcony, collective practices have emerged. Images and videos that circulate online show balcony talks, lectures, dinners, concerts, dance parties, and DJ sets. The balcony was able to play these different roles thanks to its typical physical characteristics, but they were also (usually unwitting) recapitulations of the various historical functions alluded to above.

Cultural mores and climatic conditions inform the balcony's form and materiality which, in turn, regulate how the balcony is (or can be) used. In Islamic societies, for example, the *mashrabiya* or enclosed balcony that protrudes from the street-facing wall of the house is screened with near-opaque carved wooden latticework. Thus, in addition to providing much-needed shade and allowing for a breeze to pass through the home, it also protects residents' privacy and female modesty. [9] The balcony acts as a

6 Paul Overy, *Light, Air and Openness: Modern Architecture between the Wars* (London: Thames & Hudson, 2007) 83–97.

7 Sigfried Giedion, *Befreites Wohnen* (Zurich: Füssli Verlag, 1929).

8 Sigfried Giedion, *Building in France, Building in Iron, Building in Ferro-Concrete,* trans. J. Duncan Berry (Los Angeles: The Getty Center, 1995), 147.

9 Bechir Kenzari and Yasser Elsheshtawy, "The Ambiguous Veil: On Transparency, the Mashrabiy'ya, and Architecture," *Journal of Architectural Education* 56, no. 4 (May 2003), 17–25.

mediating screen between indoor and outdoor environmental conditions and between private and public realms.

In Ancient Rome, an early form of the balcony, known as a *maeniana*, resembled a loggia or stage-box, suggesting a close connection to the theater. The space of the balcony could accommodate spectators, thus bringing the experience of the amphitheater to the streets. [10] As an architectural element, it persisted into the Renaissance. It was widespread in cities like Venice, from the Doge's Palace to local artisans' residences. [11] Its formal and material omnipresence persists today across Italian cities, where its theatrical character was on full display during the early months of COVID-19 confinement. [12]

Balconies have enormous political potential. At a macro-level, they are often used as tools to exert and express power. Meanwhile, at a micro-level, they can not only facilitate and regulate citizens' access to the benefits of air and sun but also support their right to the city, and their ability to participate and appear in the public realm.

One of the earliest expressions of the balcony's macro-political capacities comes from the Mughal Empire, during which Akbar the Great (1542–1605) transformed the pre-Mughal Hindu ritual of sun greeting into a daily ritual of greeting the Islamic ruler. A balcony positioned the emperor closer to the heavens, thereby allowing his subjects to greet him with the sun. [13] Since then, examples of the use of balconies in expressions of power have multiplied, for instance from papal to royal to presidential power. Think, for instance, of the balcony of St. Peter's Basilica, where the pope periodically delivers his *"urbi et orbi"* blessing, or the prominent role that the balcony at Buckingham Palace plays during British royal ceremonies, such as Trooping the Colour, or the balcony at the Casa Rosada, the Argentinian Presidential Palace, from which Evita regularly addressed throngs of devoted followers.

The political agency of the balcony can also be observed on a smaller scale, in less explicit and more mundane ways. It is now evident that the COVID-19 pandemic has brought structural inequities in our society into the limelight. In one of the pandemic's earlier episodes, in February 2020, the *Diamond Princess* cruise ship was quarantined in Yokohama for a month, becoming one of the first spaces of contamination outside China. The narrative that quickly emerged was a tale of two types of passenger: one with a balcony, the other without. [14] Those in internal rooms — including families with young children and non-essential cruise ship workers — were confined to their mechanically ventilated quarters and allowed just an hour on deck each day for

10 Katherine E. Welch, *The Roman Amphitheatre: From Its Origins to the Colosseum* (Cambridge: Cambridge University Press, 2007), 32–35.

11 For an overview of this transformation, see Tom Avermaete, "Balcony," in Rem Koolhaas, ed., *Elements of Architecture* (Cologne: Taschen, 2018), 1078–1238.

12 See Matt Fidler, "Balcony Spirit: Hope in Face of Coronavirus," *Guardian*, March 19, 2020, https://www.theguardian.com/world/gallery/2020/mar/19/balconies-sites-hope-coronavirus-in-pictures (accessed January 29, 2021).

13 Catherine B. Asher, "Sub-Imperial Palaces: Power and Authority in Mughal India," *Ars Orientalis* 23 (1993), 281–302.

14 See Doug Bock Clark, "Inside the Nightmare Voyage of the *Diamond Princess*," *GQ*, April 30, 2020, https://www.gq.com/story/inside-diamond-princess-cruise-ship-nightmare-voyage (accessed January 29, 2021).

supervised exercise. In contrast, passengers who paid for larger, more expensive external cabins had regular access to air and sunlight on their personal balconies, with more room to roam without risking contact with potentially contagious passengers on deck. The balconies on the *Diamond Princess* proved a particularly vivid premonition of inequalities in balcony access following the global spread of COVID-19. Similar questions were raised in many cities, particularly in North America, where balconies remain relatively uncommon, and often attract higher rents. [15] For those without a balcony, going outside for fresh air and sunlight was accompanied by a risk of exposure to COVID-19.

The balcony also provides an ambiguous concurrence of the individual and collective urban realms, often becoming a site of tension. Since the twentieth century, for instance, architects seem to have prioritized the consistency of collective street appearance over the individual manifestation of the balcony. [16] Indeed, pioneering schemes like Sven Markelius's Collective House (Stockholm, 1932) used the careful modulation of balconies to provide the optimal healthy balance of privacy and sunlight to the individual but, even more importantly, acted as the public expression of progressive, collective living philosophies within. [17]

The field of tension between individual and collective realms also becomes apparent in the written and unwritten rules of the balcony. Practices such as nude sunbathing on a balcony elicit questions regarding the laws of decency in our cities. Often, firm regulations have been put in place to avoid individual transgressions of such collective norms. [18] In cities like Zurich, strict governmental noise legislation combines with local behavioral covenants in preventing residents from certain behaviors such as shaking out carpets on their balcony or limiting the use and storage of barbecues. [19]

When the first wave of lockdowns struck Zurich, the Chair of the History and Theory of Urban Design at ETH Zurich started to gather visual material related to these collective balcony practices on its Instagram account, catalogued under the hashtag #viralbalcony. Beginning with a call for followers to submit their own balcony experiences, this archive brought together widely shared photographs and videos alongside more intimate vignettes from the pandemic. Submissions covered a physically distanced Shabbat on the balconies of Zurich Wiedikon, clapping and cheering for first responders from Toronto's balconies, and white flags hung in honor of healthcare workers in the empty streets of Belgium. [20] Social media, in this way, became a means of assembling a crowd-sourced archive of the balcony in crisis, from global

15 See Linda Poon, "A Lesson from Social Distancing: Build Better Balconies," *CityLab*, April 20, 2020, https://www.citylab.com/life/2020/04/apartment-design-balcony-private-outdoor-space-zoning-laws/610162/ (accessed January 29, 2021).

16 "Balkone, Terrassen/ Balcons, terrasses/ Balconies, Terraces," special issue, *Werk, Bauen + Wohnen* 81, no. 6 (1994), 2–5.

17 Such progressive components included a communal kitchen, restaurant, child-care facility, and professional laundry service to relieve women of the burden of unpaid housework. See Lucy Creagh, "An Introduction to *acceptera*," in Uno Åhrén, Lucy Creagh, and Kenneth Frampton, eds., *Modern Swedish Design: Three Founding Texts* (New York: Museum of Modern Art, 2008), 126–39, here 135.

18 What is considered transparent varies greatly, even between similar cultures. In many places in the United States, it is illegal to be naked in any publicly visible place, even inside or on a balcony. In the UK, however, it is legal to be naked on a balcony, or indeed any public place, as long as the nudity is not deliberately provocative.

19 Regular online forum posts on balcony rules and expectations attest to the confusion felt by new arrivals to Zurich. See, for example, *glocals*, April 30, 2017, https://www.glocals.com/forums/general/BBQs-on-balconies-in-apartment-blocks---are-they-allowed--239732.htm (accessed January 29, 2021); *English Forum Switzerland*, October 14, 2011, https://www.englishforum.ch/other-general/128550-rules-balcony.html (accessed January 29, 2021).

20 These posts can be viewed on the Instagram account @ avermaete_gta_ethz (accessed January 29, 2021).

users in real time. Simultaneously, the hashtags allowed for a set of indirect and surprising analogies to emerge — including works of art, film stills, historical curiosities and cartoons — that revealed the changing role of the balcony in society.

The cases outlined below complicate an easy division between balcony haves and have-nots. In Hausmann's Paris, the fifth-floor poor were provided with balconies, even if only to ensure harmony. Rural Greeks were able to trade their private gardens for balconies in the *polykatoikies*. Expressions of support for health care workers on the balcony today continue a tradition of radi-

Maxime Zaugg is a doctoral candidate at the Chair of the History and Theory of Urban Design of the Institute for the History and Theory of Architecture (gta), ETH Zurich.

cal, political uses of the balcony in cities from Zurich to Mumbai. Across all these cases, the balcony reappears as a place to connect meaningfully with others.

Ultimately, the case studies presented here do not support abandoning the city, as some commentators have argued, but rather represent a call to think about its design more carefully. **21** Just as people are reconsidering the performativity, use, and access to parks, streets, and other public spaces in our cities, so, too, should we reconsider the balcony. The balcony has proven itself an adaptable tool in connecting people, maintaining relationships and mental health, providing us with sunlight and fresh air, and affording a political voice even in isolation. But the balcony is only a desirable urban feature if it provides access to safe and healthy environments, a civic-minded society, and an open public sphere.

The prominence of the balcony under COVID-19 represents a call for architects and planners to reengage with urban policies, real estate mechanisms, and building designs that would ensure that balconies are provided to more citizens and remain a core feature of cities in the future.

The Bourgeois Balcony in Paris
Maxime Zaugg

The transformation of Paris during the second half of the nineteenth century makes clear the intense relationship between the architecture of the balcony and discourses of disease control. **22**

Haussmann's widening of the streets provided greater distance between individual buildings, while extensive sewage systems allowed for the sanitary discharge of wastewater, and more and larger open spaces brought fresh air into the city. In addition to these large-scale urban interventions, more modest architectural elements also played an important role in this "hygienization" of Paris; one of them was the balcony. Introduced as an extension of the bourgeois apartment, it rapidly became a ubiquitous urban element in the city. From a sanitary point of view, it was commonly believed that disease could be avoided by maintaining

physical distance between people and the dirt in the street. [23] As a threshold space between interior and exterior, the balcony came to be understood as both a protective buffer and a means of access to clean air for the dwelling. However, the ideal and the real did not always coincide. Indeed, at the time, French newspapers such as *Le Figaro* and *Le Temps* reported that on warm days, it was frequently impossible to spend time on the balcony due to the smell of the streets. [24]

The balcony also contributed to the radical transformation of Paris into a coherent, urbanistic whole, and aided its conversion into a true bourgeois city. The balcony extended the interior salon into the urban realm, making it a stage for the *mise-en-scène* of bourgeois urban life. Haussmann's vision included the harmonization of building facades, demanding that balconies be aligned horizontally and face each other across the boulevards. These so-called *balcons filants* (continuous balconies) were usually situated on the second and fifth floors, following the strict class orders of the buildings. While the second floor (also called *bel étage* or *étage noble)* was reserved for the upper class, the fifth floor was intended for lower classes who may not have received balconies but for reasons of aesthetics and harmony. The resulting views and theatrical qualities of the balcony became a recurrent subject for painters at the time. Artists including Gustave Caillebotte and Édouard Manet captured the ways in which members of the bourgeoisie staged themselves to be objects of observation on their balconies while also actively

23 Aruna D'Souza, *The Invisible Flâneuse? Gender, Public Space, and Visual Culture in Nineteenth-Century Paris* (Manchester: Manchester University Press, 2008), 54.

24 David S. Barnes, *The Great Stink of Paris and the Nineteenth-Century Struggle against Filth and Germs* (Baltimore: Johns Hopkins University Press, 2018), 230–31.

observing urban life through the balustrades. Manet's painting of the self-confident Parisian bourgeoisie on the balcony was dryly interpreted, years later, by René Magritte. **fig.1**

The *Polykatoikia* Balcony in Greece
Marianna Charitonidou

Marianna Charitonidou is a postdoctoral fellow at the Chair of the History and Theory of Urban Design of the Institute for the History and Theory of Architecture (gta), ETH Zurich.

fig.5 Suzana and Dimitris Antonakakis, 118 Benaki Street apartment building, main elevation, Athens, 1975
Source: Suzana and Dimitris Antonakakis private archive

25 See Marjorie Housepian Dobkin, *Smyrna 1922: The Destruction of a City* (New York: Newmark Press, 1998).

26 See the introduction to this article above, 139.

27 See Marianna Charitonidou, "From the Research of a Modernity That Could Be Greek to a Multiplicity of the Present: 'Greek-ness' in Architecture or Architecture in Greece?" in Andreas Giacoumacatos, ed., *Greek Architecture in the Twentieth and Twenty-First Century* (Athens: Gutenberg, 2016), 166–76. See also David Leatherbarrow, *Uncommon Ground: Architecture, Technology and Topography* (Cambridge, MA: MIT Press, 2000).

The specificity of the Greek balcony during the second half of the twentieth century is set within a particular context: the emergence of the so-called *polykatoikia* typology (πολυκατοικία, from πολυ-, multiple, and -κατοικία, residence). The birth of the *polykatoikia* was, in part, a response to an increase in Athens' population. The defeat of the Greek army in August 1922, marking the end of the Greco-Turkish War, and the so-called Great Fire of Smyrna in September 1922, led to the arrival of refugees from Asia Minor. 25 In 1929, the "horizontal property" law emerged as a means to enable (and even promote) a system of *antiparochi*: a cashless contract between an entrepreneur, who would construct and sell the *polykatoikia*, and the owner of a building site, who would in return receive one or more flats in the newly built *polykatoikia*. Realized without any state support, the *antiparochi* system not only modernized Greek cities and turned large numbers of citizens into apartment owners but also helped to house the Greek citizens who migrated to Athens from decimated villages and towns after the civil war (1946–1949). The construction of *polykatoikies* intensified in the late 1950s and reached its peak during the 1960s and 1970s.

The *polykatoikia* soon became the symbol of Greek modernization, and its balconies contributed significantly to the optimization of passive heating and cooling strategies. Moreover, *polykatoikia* tenants also attributed symbolic value to their balconies. While northern European modernist debates placed emphasis on the technocratic aspects of the balcony, exemplified through slogans such as "light, air, and openness," 26 for Greeks the balcony also offered access to the spiritual aspects of natural light. In the 1960s, modernist Greek architects such as Aris Konstantinidis claimed that modern society had lost its connection with nature and, through a renewed engagement with light, aimed to reinvent the relationship between modern architecture and nature. 27

Being on the balcony of the *polykatoikia* thus came to be understood by many Greek citizens as a way of being in touch with the Mediterranean's light, spirit, and nature.

The practices taking place on *polykatoikia* balconies construct what Hannah Arendt calls a "common world," [28] which bridges public and private life and fosters the creation of common knowledge. Between the remembrance of a rural pattern of living, concerns for hygiene and climate, and the spiritual symbolism of light, the balconies of the *polykatoikies* represent a unique social and spatial physiognomy in the city of Athens.

28 Hannah Arendt, *The Human Condition* (Chicago: University of Chicago Press, 1958), 9.

The Micro-Politics of Mumbai's Balconies and the Right to the City
Fatina Abreek-Zubiedat

As the world grapples with the COVID-19 pandemic, the balcony's political capacities have gained new significance. Across the world, balconies have acted not as private spaces but as visible platforms for urban populations to connect and partake in social life by sending greetings, singing, clapping, and so on. In 2020 India, for instance, residents were encouraged by Prime Minister Narendra Modi to offer a collective applause for healthcare professionals and essential service providers from their balconies every day at five o'clock in the evening. Such activities were not directed at those in the streets below, as these were empty due to the containment restrictions, but at those around them. This raises the question: does the balcony have the potential to regulate entry to the public sphere and "the right to the city?" [29]

Fatina Abreek-Zubiedat is a postdoctoral fellow at the Chair of the History and Theory of Urban Design of the Institute for the History and Theory of Architecture (gta), ETH Zurich.

In Mumbai, the second most populous city in India (after Delhi), balconies have a long cultural tradition. [30] Balconies played a critical role in the chawls of Bombay from the second half

of the nineteenth century. The outbreak of a devastating plague epidemic in 1896 and the disorganization of economic and labor circuits triggered panic among the commercial elite, Bombay's mill owners, and the British colonial officials, and forced the latter to consider the issue of workers' housing. In response, the colonial state created the Bombay Improvement Trust to strengthen the commercial activities and to provide sanitary accommodations for the poor and working

29 Henri Lefebvre, *Writings on Cities* (Cambridge: Blackwell, 1996), 7–8.

30 Maura Finkelstein, "Ghosts in the Gallery: The Vitality of Anachronism in a Mumbai Chawl," *Anthropological Quarterly* 91, no. 3 (Summer 2018), 937–68, here 950.

fig. 2 Chawl galleries in Dadar, Mumbai Source: Maura Finkelstein classes. Two decades later, with the spread of 1918 Spanish Flu, the Bombay Development Department carried out far-reaching housing programs. [31] The development operations conflated power and control, and accelerated the rise of real estate speculation and class differentiations.

With the growth of the textile economy in the latter half of the twentieth century, Mumbai experienced a surge of migrants from the hinterland. As the city was unable to provide housing for all these migrant workers, mill owners responded by creating a new housing type — chawls. Chawls are typically four- to five-story high buildings with eight to sixteen single-occupancy rooms per floor. These rooms are commonly connected by exterior, gallery-like balconies. fig.2 Most chawls have an inner courtyard along which the floors are designed. Occupied by the "insurgent citizens" [32] of the working class, these balconies were historically used for political activities and became public platforms for political debate in the old Bombay. [33] Although these chawl balconies are still a prominent feature of Mumbai today, their political role has diminished following India's economic liberalization of the early 1990s, which has increasingly marginalized the urban poor. [34]

Zurich Balconies as Displays of Protest and Support
Irina Davidovici

During the weeks of lockdown, balconies throughout the world have broadcast messages of hope, solidarity, or grief on homemade banners. In Zurich, balcony banners represent an established, if low-key, political tradition which has its origins in the Swiss direct democracy system. Several times a year, as citizens prepare to vote on public issues with municipal or federal consequences — from the setting of minimum wages to the construction of a local by-pass — pre-printed canvas signs are hung from windows and balconies, announcing the inhabitants' voting intentions. In contrast to the official posters, which are aimed at undecided voters and urge Ja or Nein depending on which interested parties paid for them, the home banner tends to advertise where the vote is headed in the household. In November 2020, orange canvas banners were hung on balconies across the city in support of the initiative for corporate responsibility. They became a familiar sight in the weeks leading up to the vote, which, despite being rejected nationally, carried 52.8 percent of the Zurich vote. Rather than seeking to persuade, such banners confirm the implicit class solidarity of the kind of progressive, environmentally conscious, middle-class inhabitants who might occupy themselves with public ideological displays. Their concentration in a building

31 Caroline E. Arnold, "The Bombay Improvement Trust, Bombay Millowners and the Debate over Housing Bombay's Millworkers, 1896–1918," *Essays in Economic and Business History* 30, no. 1 (2012), 105–23; Vanessa Caru, "'A Powerful Weapon for the Employers'? Workers' Housing and Social Control in Interwar Bombay," in Prashant Kidambi, Manjiri Kamat, and Rachel Dwyer, eds., *Bombay Before Mumbai: Essays in Honour of Jim Masselos* (Oxford: Oxford University Press, 2019), 213–35, here 214.

32 James Holston, "Insurgent Citizenship in an Era of Global Urban Peripheries," *City & Society* 21, no. 2 (December 2009), 245–67, here 261.

33 Neera Adarkar, ed., *The Chawls of Mumbai 2011: Galleries of Life* (Bombay: ImprintOne, 2012); Manjiri Kamat, "The Palkhi as Plague Carrier: The Pandharpur Fair and the Sanitary Fixation of the Colonial State; British India, 1908–16," in Pati Biswamoy and Mark Harrison, eds., *Health, Medicine and Empire: Perspectives on Colonial India* (New Delhi: Orient Longman Limited, 2001), 299–316.

34 On the influence of liberalization on the urban development of Mumbai and the chawls, see for example Kidambi, Kamat, and Dwyer, eds., *Bombay Before Mumbai;* and Navtej Nainan, "Lakshmi Raj: Shaping Spaces in Postindustrial Mumbai: Urban Regimes, Planning Instruments and Splintering Communities" (PhD diss., University of Amsterdam, 2012).

Irina Davidovici directs the doctoral program of the Institute for the History and Theory of Architecture (gta) and is a senior researcher at the Chair of the History and Theory of Urban Design, ETH Zurich.

can be an informal indicator of its demographics, for example the collective ownership of a housing cooperative whose members are often politically active.

Among the balcony banners of Zurich, a few — larger, unrulier, ostensibly painted by hand — express the political views of the more radical Left. Depicting feminist and environmentalist messages, they tend to protest the neoliberal status quo independently of specific upcoming referendums. These banners also hang from old factory buildings or from improvised structures, signaling the existence of squatting communities or autonomous social centers. Given the nearly full occupancy of Zurich housing stock, however, squats and the homemade banner as its external manifestation are less likely to be observed in the city's residential quartiers. To see such hand-painted banners hanging from the elegant cast-iron railings of a nineteenth-century residential block would today be an exceptional occurrence. Such sights have been relegated to the archival records of the grassroots social movements that rocked Zurich in the 1980s, as the city transitioned from a predominantly manufacturing economy to its current status as a global center for financial services. fig.3 The organized building occupations and squats continued well into the 1990s and 2000s — from the protest occupation at Stauffacher Aussersihl (9–12 January 1983), to the established squats of Wohlgroth (1991–1993), Binz (2006–2013), and the soon-to-be-cleared autonomous cultural center at Koch Areal. Inherently precarious, in order to prolong their existence some of these temporary communities adopted the institutional format of housing cooperatives, within which they continued to implement a radical ideological program. While Karthago and Dreieck are the pioneers of this typical Zurich phenomenon, Kraftwerk1 and Kalkbreite remain to date the most visible examples, having since developed several new-build, large-scale estates in the city center and on the periphery. In the course of these transformations, the balcony as an architectural element has played an important representational role, going through a parallel trajectory of institutionalization.

The balconies of the Grunderzeit townhouse at Badenerstrasse 2, the focus of the Stauffacher occupation of 1983, served as the platform from which the protest became visible — and audible. Using the facade, the building's anarchist inner organization was projected further out unto the city. 35 Decorated with banners, flags, and balloons, masked squatters took over the small corner balconies during the protest. In their absence, grotesque cardboard masks adorned human-sized papier-mâché figures perched on the second-floor balcony, and the murals of squatting figures were depicted with white paint between the windows under

35 P. M. *Stauffacher, Aussersihl: Über die inventiven Kräfte der neuen Weltgesellschaft* (Zurich Verlag der Inventiven Kräfte, 1985).

the defiant slogan *Wir sind noch da (& dort)* (We are still here (and there)). A giant mobile, made of empty supermarket baskets, was suspended from the top floor. The banners hanging from balconies or between windows held a variety of anti-imperialist and anti-police messages, equally protesting against the United States' occupation of Grenada and the Swiss arms trade.

Easy to dismiss as attention-grabbing props, these decorations were, on the contrary, part of an established iconography consistent with the protesters' ideological agenda. Shortly after the police clearance, with the buildings once more boarded up,

fig. 3 Banners on Badenerstrase 2 in Stauffacher, Zurich, November 1983 Photographer: Gertrud Vogler/Source: Sozialarchiv Zurich

a Stauffacher activist published the pamphlet *Bolo'Bolo* (1983) under the pseudonym P. M., imagining an anti-capitalist utopia of autonomous communes (bolos), either built from scratch or taking over existing buildings. Intermediary spaces and elements were to be used as connective elements between distinct buildings, emphasizing their unity. Thus, houses could be "partially topped off with terraces for planting and provided with glass greenhouses to reduce energy loss" or "connected by arcades, intermediate buildings, communal halls, and workshops" — the common aim being that "different parts of the bolos should be reachable without exposure to the weather." **36** Some of these connective elements were represented as galleries or balconies stretching across the various facades, thus using architecture to transform the heterogeneous block into one autonomous entity. P. M.'s theoretical utopia was so closely attuned to Zurich's alternative culture as to anticipate features of its actual buildings. In the Wohlgroth squat, best known for its "Zu Reich" (Too Rich) mural

36 P. M., *Bolo'Bolo*, 3rd, Eng. ed. (New York: Autonomedia, 2011), 106–8.

that greeted trains into the main station, a number of occupied nineteenth-century speculative townhouses were connected with precarious, improvised bridges.

The squatting communities and neighborhood associations that later adopted the legal format of housing cooperatives also altered existing buildings and designed new ones according to a collective way of living. [37] Both the Karthago Cooperative, founded in 1991 by the original Stauffacher squatters, and the Cooperative Dreieck, formed by a neighborhood association in order to resist the demolition of an old perimeter block, added collective

spaces and used balconies and terraces as gathering places protected from the elements. In this process, the balcony emerged as a characteristic figure of cooperative life. In its tailor-made, designed reiterations, it is deep enough to contain large tables for communal dinners, benches for informal meetings, and even to store everyday items. In keeping with the cooperative's ecological credentials, balconies are extensively planted and roof terraces often equipped with solar energy panels. Kraftwerk1's Heizenholz development, designed by Adrian Streich, restored and extended two existing blocks through a connecting external circulation, integrating staircases and deep, covered verandas for collective use. The Kalkbreite development by Müller Sigrist (2009–2014) is organized around a connecting circular route that opens onto roof terraces with commanding views of the ensemble and the city, perfect for communal outdoor parties. And the blocks of Kraftwerk1's Zwicky Süd by Schneider Studer Primas (2009–2016) are connected with galleries and walkways, some opening onto suspended balconies. From these, as from other balconies in Zurich, pre-printed banners are hung at the time of upcoming referendums, confirming through their message the ideological leanings of residents. **fig. 4**

Since the 1980s street protests, Zurich balconies have been ritually colonized to act as billboards for ideological programs, vertical platforms for political protest. During the coronavirus crisis, they made public individual messages of solidarity and support, whether hung on homemade banners or expressed through applause. Their informal political role has been to canvass public opinion through the all-too-literal addition of words on canvas. These supplementary, improvised uses of the Zurich balcony

37 Developed in collaboration with the city, the programs of these developments were defined in consultation by work groups, then put into application by architects selected through competition. See for example Margrit Hugentobler et al., *More than Housing: Cooperative Planning; A Case Study in Zurich*, Edition Wohnen (Basel: Birkhäuser, 2016); Sabine Wolf et al., *Kalkbreite: Ein neues Stück Stadt* (Zurich: Genossenschaft Kalkbreite, 2015).

fig. 4 A balcony scene in today's Zurich Photographed by Irina Davidovici indicate how it transcends the condition of a bourgeois filter between private and public lives. It becomes itself a banner, a screen for the projection of the citizens' beliefs into the political realm — which is, after all, one manifestation of the thoroughly Swiss democratic procedure of raising your hand to be counted.

"We Have Enough Food—That Wasn't the Problem"
Lukas Stadelmann

One of the curious features of COVID-19 is its invisibility. It is not merely that contagion itself is invisible. The virus also produces no visible marks upon the body but rather is characterized by a sequence of withdrawals, from the sense of taste to the capacity to breathe. Attempts to represent the pandemic visually have therefore been obliged to focus on other aspects of our everyday life, on services and supplies normally taken for granted. And there, too, the visual impact has been characterized by absences. The first iconic representations to appear were everyday voids: photos of empty shelves where, before, pasta and toilet paper stood. They quickly moved on to ridicule. Memes online and newspaper editorials made sport out of the irrational and egoistic behavior of hoarders. Perhaps more than frail humanity, these voids revealed vulnerabilities of the logistics infrastructure that supplies goods, the "big boxes" and "architecture without content" that we so often overlook.

Take a single ordinary product—pasta, in this case, but it could easily be one of many others considered indispensable—under extraordinary circumstances. In Europe, the pasta market is both saturated and steady, met by a constant supply with almost no seasonal fluctuations. It is supplied by a highly optimized infrastructure with relatively few actors and a customer base across the whole of Europe. With supply and demand almost levelled, prices are low. The cost of transportation per unit makes up a large part of the overall cost—a truck voyage filled with pasta costs the same as one filled with consumer electronics—so there is an incentive for producers to keep these costs as low as possible. At the same time, storage close to consumers is expensive, as a high population density means high land prices. Conventional retailers usually hold the smallest possible volume of goods in their stores to accommodate as many customers as possible. If, due to higher demand, extra deliveries are completely filled with pasta and toilet paper, the entire shipment produces a financial loss. This explains why the shelves in the supermarkets emptied. It was not that production could not keep up but that the patterns of transportation were so optimized that they were particularly prone to disruption. "We have enough food—that wasn't the problem," as Thomas Gasser, head of logistics at Migros Suhr, told Benita Vogel and Michael West ("Migros-Logistik leistet Sondereffort," *Migros Magazine*, March 13, 2020).

But we did not start at the beginning: pasta is an end product, and while its manufacture could happen almost anywhere, the sourcing of its raw material does not. Wheat is grown in most European countries, but most of the durum wheat used in pasta is imported from Canada, while the main manufacturers of pasta within the European Union are located in Italy. The

biggest consumer, with the highest import quantities, is Germany, followed by France and the United Kingdom. Since the value of the grain is extremely low, it is not transported by airfreight, which explains the steady supply throughout the months of 2020. Arriving in the ports of Italy, the processed pasta leaves via the country's north, passing through Switzerland to reach the main consumer markets. And despite a Swiss public vote in 1994 (the Alpen Initiative) to transfer transit-traffic to rail, it took until 2020, when legal restrictions for road transportation came into force, for pasta manufacturers to use this form of transportation to reach the German market. The manufacturers themselves admit that train transportation is cheaper, more secure, and more reliable (aside from the obvious reduction in environmental impact). The reason for delay thus has another source. It is (again) a spatial problem: many producers and retailers no longer have access to the rail network. The low cost of road transportation has led to a logistics sprawl away from the rail infrastructure and human settlements, a consequence of the rocketing land prices close to consumers. In response to the pasta shortage, retailers told us that "the warehouses are full." Pasta storage is just not where the customers are. To make matters worse, the pandemic has also brought a surge in home delivery: more trucks are bringing pasta directly to the customer.

Ideally, rail transportation is used to transport the goods as close to the end-consumer as possible, but most inner-city rail infrastructure devoted to the relocation of goods has been rezoned for large-scale development. The cost of this is found in increased transportation volume and more emissions. An example is the SwissMill tower in Zurich. Extended in 2016 after a public vote, the silo provides grain for the Swiss market, in particular for the subcontractors of the retailer Coop. But while the tower represents the logistics heritage of the area, most manufacturers are no longer found in inner-city areas. This means that raw materials arrive in the city by train, are transported by truck to manufacturing facilities outside the city, and then brought back again to Zurich's consumers. This is a recent development. The Zurich Güterbahnhof (freight depot) was demolished in 2013 to make way for the police and justice department, and the Coop bakery moved from Zurich Nord in 2017 to Pratteln (Basel-Landschaft) one year after the SwissMill tower was finished. Coop's only pasta factory was closed in 2014. Since then, imports have mainly come from Italy and France.

The most visible consequence of these developments is the large, seemingly entranceless structures built in a region defined by an intersection where the east-west A1 highway and the north-south A2 axis merge the traffic for a couple of kilometers before the A2 departs south. The region does not have a single name. It includes Niederbipp in the Canton of Berne, Härkingen, and Oensingen, or the two towns called Wangen, one in Berne and one in Solothurn,

barely 20 kilometers apart. Today, it is easier to count the logistics providers that do not use this area for transshipment than the ones that do. The long-standing tradition among architects of describing the country as a continuous town has been fulfilled, but not as intended.

The simplicity of these structures appeals to architects. They trigger a fetish for clear shapes in a vast territory. "This is an architecture that nobody is prepared for," as Rem Koolhaas remarked. Koolhaas describes automated greenhouses and Tesla factories as "an intense piece of architecture without almost any need for inhabitation," leading to a "transformation of architecture" that he himself — at the Harvard Graduate School of Design Conference on the Countryside on October 28, 2015 — claimed he does not know how to relate to: "nobody could have thought of a building this extremely abstract, this codified, this uninflected by human need, this distant from us, and, nevertheless, kind of produced by us, and needed for us."

As The Invisible Committee declared in *To Our Friends* (Cambridge, MA, MIT Press: 2015), "Power is logistic. Block everything!" The romantic images of urban production, greenhouses and shady trees do not suffice for the challenges caused by a long-standing tradition of planning our cities by looking only at those aspects comfortable to us. The cracks in the cultivated stages that are our cities only show in times of disruption, but they show the complexities hidden behind. Cities originated around marketplaces and sites of transshipment: there is something inherently urban about the interaction with physical goods and the processes connected to them. The same potential can be found in today's infrastructure, but we require new images, and even a new imaginary, of the urban as we now encounter the clash between a lifestyle that consumers have grown accustomed to and the commitment to a sustainable future—an imaginary free of false romanticism that deals honestly with our dependence on infrastructure that extends far into what is sometimes called the hinterland. We need, in short, a vision of the city that includes its externalities.

Lukas Stadelmann is an architect and researcher with Malheur&Fortuna and Rapp in Basel, Switzerland.

fig.1 Malheur&Fortuna, Feasibility Study Zurich Hardfeld, 2020

fig.2 Bas Princen, *End of the Highway*, 2001

From the Bear Pit: On Architecture, Confinement, and Social Distancing
Stanislaus von Moos

Stanislaus von Moos is Professor Emeritus of Art History at the University of Zurich.

How to live in confinement while also obeying the imperative of social distancing? Logically, as in everyday life, the two conditions seem to be mutually exclusive: confinement implies forced intimacy with all its attendant risks; social distancing, the exact opposite. The last time Switzerland was forced into developing techniques for coping with this paradox was during the Second World War. The country had no choice but to negotiate its fear of being trapped within the prison of its own borders against its phobia of being overwhelmed by immigration. The price was paid by the tens of thousands who were stopped at the borders, [1] and within by those left behind by the wartime paralysis of civilian trade.

Prison

Architecture and architectural discourse have reflected these conditions no less than more obvious cultural seismographs like fiction writing and the theater. For Alfred Roth and other activist architects of his generation, the combination of the country's relative wealth and its political status of "neutrality" seemed like an excellent reason to claim a major role in future European reconstruction. In reality, the seemingly promising conditions came to narrow the margins of their actual field of action. [2] In a postcard of the Bärengraben (Bear Pit) in Berne adressed to Le Corbusier, Roth evoked the "prison"-like conditions suddenly imposed upon the country in the *Schicksalssommer* (fateful summer) of 1940. [3] fig.1 Perhaps it was a mere joke. Not so, to be sure, when half a century later at an event to honor Václav Havel in 1990, the playwright Friedrich Dürrenmatt, rather than castigating the prisons in the Eastern Bloc, spoke of Switzerland and its second nature as a "luxury prison": a ward built by its own residents in which the inmates served as their own guards. As was to be expected, the speech outraged the officials present at the ceremony. [4] It was easy for him to date his decision to become a writer, Dürrenmatt wrote on another occasion: it was January 5, 1945. The date coincides with the final weeks of the Second World War. Dürrenmatt, then a student, was serving as an auxiliary soldier in a border guard battalion near Geneva, killing time with "epic benders" on local farms with his buddies:

> *"The war had been decided; there was rubble all around us ... but one was just standing about in Switzerland, the country was entirely unscathed and there was no way of leaving. We were living as if in a prison. ... There I was, sitting in my vomit-filled*

1 See Alfred A. Häsler, *Das Boot ist voll: Die Schweiz und die Flüchtlinge, 1933–1945* (Zurich: Pendo, 1992). The subject matter of this essay is discussed in a broader context in Stanislaus von Moos, *Erste Hilfe: Architekturdiskurs nach 1940 — Eine Schweizer Spurensuche* (Zurich: gta Verlag, forthcoming 2021). An earlier version appeared in Irena Lehkozivova and Joan Ockman, eds., *Book for Mary: Sixty on Seventy* (New York: privately published, 2020), 398–403.

2 Roth's proposals for postwar reconstruction in Europe are discussed in detail in chapters 2 and 3 of von Moos, *Erste Hilfe*.

3 Herbert Lüthy, "Die Disteln von 1940," in Georg Kreis, ed., *Juli 1940: Die Aktion Trump* (Basel: Helbing & Lichtenhahn, 1973), 85–110, esp. 87.

4 Friedrich Dürrenmatt, "Die Schweiz, ein Gefängnis," speech delivered at the Gottlieb Duttweiler Institut, November 22, 1990.

fig.1 Postcard, *Bern. Der Bärengraben* (the Bear Pit)
Source: Fondation Le Corbusier, Paris

room; the rest of the world was full of corpses, but I had nothing to counter that with other than my vomit." [5]

5 Cited in Peter Rüedi, *Dürrenmatt oder die Ahnung vom Ganzen* (Zurich: Diogenes, 2011), 224.

In order not to let the matter simply rest, Dürrenmatt subsequently held a mirror to the epic comedy of "world events" by writing theater plays that that now form part of European postwar literature.

2020—1940—1915: "Discomfort in the Small State"

When, early in 2020, a sign appeared on Swiss freeways reading "(F)(D)(A)(I) *Ausfahrt erschwert*," [6] the situation was different to 1940 when sealed borders put the country in a state of confinement, lending Roth's postcard of the Bear Pit an immediate topicality. All the same, French President Emmanuel Macron's televised speech on March 17, 2020, was a declaration of war. What was new in this war was the invisibility of the enemy; as for the strategies of control, they were more familiar. Autarky through closing borders was the first step. Then, people hastened to declare their readiness to bury political rivalry in the interests of group survival, albeit just for the time being. This is to say nothing of the popular longing for powerful state intervention or of fantasies of expanding governmental power (the latter proliferating partly in response to the former and partly due to bureaucracy's innate anticipatory paternalism).

6 "(F) [France], (D) [Germany], (A) [Austria], (I) [Italy]: exit hindered," meaning that crossing the border was only possible in special cases.

For better or worse with respect to Switzerland around 1940, many of those fantasies were doomed, ultimately crushed between the "bumpers of the national buffer system." [7] Word had spread that after the fall of Paris, Le Corbusier had left the capital and taken up residence in the town of Ozon in the Pyrenees; the postcard was addressed to him there. The Bärengraben postcard was signed by the phalanx of the Swiss Congrès Internationaux d'Architecture Moderne (CIAM), which had apparently just ended a meeting in the Swiss capital of Berne and decided to let the absent *éminence grise*, Le Corbusier, know about it. [8] We do not know what was on the meeting's agenda, but given its date of October 21, 1940, the war was inevitably on people's minds. Both the image and the message suggest that the international situation had played a role in the discussions. For those present, the German occupation of large parts of France in July 1940 led to the complete closure of the border with France. Virtually overnight, Switzerland was a country entirely surrounded by Axis forces. The Zurich/Paris connection, vital to CIAM, was interrupted indefinitely. For some, the complications associated with that change must have weighed more heavily than the feeling of relief in early summer of the same year, perhaps already forgotten by then, that German troops had not skirted the Maginot Line at

7 Lüthy, "Die Disteln," 92.

8 The postcard is in the collection of the Fondation Le Corbusier, Paris. The complete list of signatories reads as follows: Francis Quétant, Geneva; René Schwertz, Geneva; Hans Brechbühler, Berne; Otto H. Senn, Basel; Ernst F. Burckhardt, Zurich; Hans Schmidt, Basel; Alfred Roth, Zurich; Max Bill, Zurich; Werner Krebs, Berne; Werner M. Moser, Zurich; Rudolf Steiger, Zurich; and Sigfried Giedion, Zurich.

France's largely unsecured southern flank (that is, via Switzerland, a fear that had been the source of considerable panic in May of that year). Rather they had broken through in the north, by way of the Netherlands and Belgium, with devastating consequences for both countries.

The postcard's somewhat jocular motif suggests that the group sought not to be overly destabilized by the circumstances. That said, the image of the bears trapped in their pit got right to the crux of a state of mind shared by just about everybody in the group (note, by the way, that the bear has always been Berne's heraldic animal). The text, written by Alfred Roth, himself of Bernese descent, reads "*chers amis, les CIAM suisses se réunissent dans leur prison pour l'embellir*" ("dear friends, the Swiss CIAM has come together in its prison in order to embellish it"). The message seems clear: as far as CIAM was concerned, the closing of the border meant nothing less than the end, for an indeterminate period, of international collaboration. Whatever *grands projets* were waiting to be tackled, [9] for those left behind in Europe's neutral backyard there were not many alternatives except to settle and isolate in local daily life.

Among the thousands of postcards stored at the Fondation Le Corbusier, there are quite a few from between 1940 and 1941 when the architect's notoriously ambiguous political entanglements entered a critical phase. [10] The Bärengraben postcard sits awkwardly within the universe of Le Corbusier's collection of postcard motifs, at least at first sight. Popular most of all as a destination for field trips of Swiss primary school students (surely including those from La Chaux-de-Fonds, Le Corbusier's birthplace), the *Bärengraben* may have resonated with the architect's own memories of claustrophobia in Switzerland. If it did, then these memories go back to the years of the First World War, when as the young Charles-Édouard Jeanneret he began to voice his frustration with the narrow-mindedness of clients and politicians and the limits imposed upon architectural endeavors that transcend the scope of the given budget, both recurring themes in the letters he exchanged with Auguste Perret between 1914 and 1915. More often than not, such limits were imposed in the name of "democracy." In hindsight, the decision to leave Switzerland for Paris during the First World War looks like an inevitable consequence of these local tribulations. On the other hand, the famous inscription added to the frontispiece of *La Ville Radieuse*, a book published sometime later, marks the point where the author's frustration with the constraints of life at home had definitely tilted into the fantasy of omnipotence that, by then, had already become his trademark—*dédie à l'autorité*. [11] Note

9 We know that Le Corbusier was desperate to get backing from Vichy for his extravagant plans for Algiers, whereas his cousin Pierre joined the politically opposed camp of the *résistance* in Grenoble.

10 Le Corbusier's enthusiastic commitment to Maréchal Pétain and his puppet government in Vichy, and the many nationalist and racist policies it decreed from 1940 onwards, have been discussed in great detail in François Chaslin, *Un Corbusier* (Paris: Seuil, 2015). For a comprehensive assessment of Le Corbusier's politics before and during the Second World War, see Jean-Louis Cohen, "Le Front Populaire De Le Corbusier," in Rémi Baudouï and Arnaud Dercelles, eds., *Le Corbusier 1930–2020: Polémiques, mémoires et histoire* (Paris: Tallandier, 2020), 83–96.

11 "Dedicated to authority." See Le Corbusier, *La ville radieuse* (Paris: Vincent Fréal & Cie., 1933 [1964]), frontispiece. The book's date of publication, 1933, adds an ominous ring to the inscription.

that when Karl Schmid wrote *Unbehagen im Kleinstaat* (Discomfort in the Small Nation), [12] the protagonists of this Swiss phenomenon were Jacob Burckhardt, Conrad Ferdinand Meyer, and Max Frisch. Had the survey included architects, Le Corbusier would have been the most conspicuous example.

The Temptation of the Archaic "Empiricism"

I do not know whether Dürrenmatt, who also came from a small town near Berne, ever wrote about the Bärengraben. For the Milanese architect Aldo Rossi, the Bear Pit was the epitome of an archaic era where there was no distinction between city and countryside. In connection with a project for the Klösterliareal, a site near the Bärengraben, he wrote in 1981:

"*The bears, as the symbol of the city, are not simply a promotional gag or a mini zoo for tourists. ... The bears represent the forest, the countryside, a pre-Roman civilization where the city and the countryside were not separated by walls; this mixture of city and countryside, in which the Gothic world behaves strangely analogously to the Greek world, is Bern's greatest asset.*"

Likewise, Berne's annual *Zibelimärit* (onion market) is "neither an urban nor a rural festival," Rossi argued; "it goes further back than this distinction." [13] Rossi's evocation of a primeval world populated by bears where people are busy cultivating onions seems like a late, pointed characterization of the Homeland Spirit, or *Landigeist*, that has so enduringly shaped everyday life in the era of the national *Anbauschlacht* (battle of the cultivators). [14] Is Rossi right, or is Jean-Jacques Rousseau's 1763 characterization of the country as "one big city," divided into thirteen neighborhoods more appropriate? [15] Both images may be read as characterizations of a process that has shaped the urban and suburban areas of life and work in the national ecology of modern Switzerland: the slow but steady neutralization of any clearly articulated difference between city and countryside in favor of a process ruled by the law of agglomeration; that is, avoiding, wherever possible, planning beyond the scale of a given construction project while also discouraging the formation of high-density urban clusters.

Compared to the rest of Europe, Switzerland experienced a veritable construction boom during the war years. The protagonists of "New Construction," as programed by the CIAM in the late 1920s, were now obliged to make peace with the *Heimatstil* and to reappropriate traditional methods of construction in wood and stone or else find themselves without commissions. In 1946, a large traveling exhibition summed up the results. [16] "When our misfortune began," Rudolf Schwarz wrote in the catalogue for the

12 Karl Schmid, "Unbehagen im Kleinstaat: Untersuchungen über Conrad-Ferdinand Meyer, Henri-Frédéric Amiel, Jakob Schaffner, Max Frisch, Jacob Burckhardt," in Judith Niederberger and Thomas Sprecher, eds., *Gesammelte Werke*, vol. 4 (Zurich: NZZ Verlag, 1963), 109–366.

13 Cited in Heinrich Helfenstein, "'Un revolver, c'est solide, c'est en acier': Zu einem wenig bekannten Entwurf Aldo Rossis für das Berner Klösterliareal," in Ákos Moravánszky and Judith Hopfengärtner, eds., *Aldo Rossi und die Schweiz: Architektonische Wechselwirkungen* (Zurich: gta Verlag, 2011), 107–17, here 114.

14 The term *Landigeist* is derived from the Swiss National Exhibition held in Zurich in 1939 and colloquially called the *Landi*. The *Anbauschlacht* refers to the battle for food self-sufficiency imposed by the government due to the massive reduction in imports after 1940. See Friedrich Traugott Wahlen, *Anbauschlacht* (Berne: A. Verlag and A.G. Francke, 1941), and Peter Maurer, "Landwirtschaftspolitik, Plan Wahlen, Schweizerisches Anbauwerk 1937–1943" (PhD thesis, University of Berne, 1984).

15 Jean-Jacques Rousseau to Maréchal de Luxembourg, January 20, 1763, in Bernard Gagnebin and Marcel Raymond, eds., *Œuvres complètes*, vol. 1 (Paris: Bibliothèque de la Pléiade, 1969), 1813–4.

16 *Switzerland Planning and Building Exhibition* (London: RIBA, 1946; Zurich: Orell Füssli, 1946).

exhibition's venue in Cologne, "the architecture of Switzerland was not very different from that of Germany ... in those years, freedom went into the mountains, and now it is returning to us from there." Today, he continued, the country can "show us what it would be like around us if all this had not happened."

Schwarz then went on to emphasize that what was perceived as Swiss was, after all, "the human decency of the buildings shown." [17] Given German architecture's saturation with the rhetoric of Speer, Schmitthenner, and Bonatz, one imagines what Schwarz might have had in mind. Nevertheless, to some Swiss ears the flattery may have had a different ring: what Schwarz praised as decency might equally be understood as his pinpointing of a modesty of ambition. No wonder, then, that being restricted to decorating the status quo, in 1940, resulted in a rather atypical kind of gallows humor from those unexpectedly trapped by the confinement imposed by the war, as if a profession entitled to practice surgery on the body of the city was now suddenly forced to restrict its efforts to palliative care. Note that Roth's barbs in the postcard ("the Swiss CIAM has come together in its prison in order to embellish it") cast light on a condition that was not specific to Switzerland — the twilight of an avant-garde in search of a role in a nation suddenly thrown back upon itself. After the war, Roth, now the editor of the architectural magazine *Werk*, grudgingly put up with the common-sense modernism that became the lingua franca of Swiss building for years to come; an Alpine variant of New Empiricism, even though, for him, much of it was a "mixture of Hollywood and Berchtesgaden." [18] Sigfried Giedion, by contrast, spoke of "New Escapism" instead of New Empiricism in referring to what he chastised as the era's ingratiating "handicrafts style." [19] Both Giedion and Roth knew well enough that significant parts of the Swiss CIAM, too, had by this point succumbed to the fever.

As to the effects of all this on the economy of sentiments, we lack the cavalier perspective needed to get the necessary overview. The March 2020 issue of Switzerland's leading architectural magazine declared "clay, chalk, wool, hemp, and straw" to be the heralds of today's building. [20] That would be considerably more down-to-earth than to retreat into the therapeutic mysteries of private or group wellness as prophetically proposed for the twenty-first century by the legendary Blur above Lake Neuchâtel at the 2002 Expo.

For the years around the Second World War, the return to craft traditions, and a restrained interest in folklore in general, were seen as necessary and healthy signs of cultural authenticity (as opposed to, say, a mere variant within a global spectrum

17 Rudolf Schwarz, "Helvetia docet," in *Schweizerische Architektur-Ausstellung Köln* (Cologne: DuMont Schauberg, 1948). For an assessment of the London venue of that exhibition, see John Summerson, "Swiss Architecture in London," *Listener*, September 26, 1946, 412–13.

18 Alfred Roth, "Zeitgemäße Architekturbetrachtungen," *Das Werk* 34, no. 6 (June 1947), 182–87, and 38, no. 3 (March 1951) 65–76, here 71.

19 Sigfried Giedion, "A Talk Given at a Joint Meeting of the MARS Group and the Institute of Contemporary Arts...," *Architects' Journal* 108, no. 26 (1948), 206–7. See also the preface in Sigfried Giedion, ed., *A Decade of New Architecture/ Dix ans d'architecture contemporaine* (Zurich: Editions Girsberger, 1951), 2–3.

20 Daniel Kurz and Roland Züger, "Authentisch konstruieren," *Werk, Bauen + Wohnen* 107, no. 3 (March 2020), 1–2.

21 Eidgenössische Justiz- und Polizeidepartement, ed., *Zivilverteidigung* (Aarau: Miles-Verlag, 1969), esp. 58–59, 76–77, and 110–11. Gerold Kunz sees the manual's strong tendency towards ranking low-density forms of cohabitation above high-density ones as a coded instruction by the Swiss military to the planning authorities. See Gerold Kunz, "Zieht Hinaus! Der Kalte Krieg und die Zersiedelung der Schweiz," *Heimatschutz/Patrimoine* 4 (2010), 14–16, here 15.

of administered ethno-centric traditionalism). More intriguing, perhaps, is the long-lasting appeal of ruralism amongst planners. Around 1940, this was regarded as a prophylactic against bombs even though, as a dogma, it may not have been officially formalized until 1969, when the Federal Department of Justice and Police distributed its curious civil defense manual among Swiss households. [21] However, the pendulum has swung back and architects have begun to crusade in favor of densification. To what degree they may be able to shatter the collective confidence in the single family home and the private car remains to be seen. The current stigmatization of public space and public transportation as hazard zones is unlikely to help them. As for the possible postcard that sums up this contradictory condition, it may already be floating unrecognized in the ether as an Instagram post. One hopes it will soon land in an appropriate archive.

Syncytium
Caroline A. Jones

Let us praise the *syncytium*—syn + cyte = "together cell," a single cytoplasmic mass with many nuclei—for the syncytium makes the placenta, and us mammals, possible. 1 **fig.1** Why is the syncytium not the most theorized part of the body's architecture? 2 Although philosopher Peter Sloterdijk comes close to asking this question, when he acknowledges his fantasized *ur-architektur* as "not so much a mother/child but a child/placenta relationship," 3 he nonetheless reverts to the more familiar womb or uterus as the privileged "shell" that colonizes his architectural imaginary: "The construction of shells for life creates a series of uterus repetitions in outdoor milieus. Architects must understand that they stand in the middle between biology and philosophy. Biology deals with the environment, philosophy with the world." 4

Likewise, Buckminster Fuller conjured notions of a telepathic "worldaround Wombland" of chatty, protesting fetuses refusing to come out of their shells, since "Wombland" protected them from a polluted world, circa 1970. 5 These metaphors of original architectures—indeed, the entire genre of biological just-so stories about mimesis or the New Swarmism 6 —miss the most useful lessons architecture might draw from contemporary genomics about how life actually works.

This essay is not in pursuit of a new "primitive hut." The syncytium instead teaches the ongoing, future-facing lesson of viruses: you do not have to live anywhere in particular (you do not even have to be "alive") to affect how things get built. You do not need a shell, or the fiction of "individuals," to perform certain evolutionarily significant *functions* in life systems. The virally propelled syncytium teaches that mediating the exchanges across boundaries may be the defining role of "architectures" in life.

Dear readers: we do not need to be feminists or equipped with ovaries to understand the stakes here. Let's start with the basics. The uterus or womb is a stretchy, muscular cavity (Indo-European *udero*, belly or stomach; Germanic *wamb*, belly) possessed by female mammals. It begins in the embryo as an

Caroline A. Jones teaches art history, runs the Transmedia Storytelling Initiative, and serves as Associate Dean for the School of Architecture and Planning at the Massachusetts Institute of Technology.

1 I am grateful for the lively (and nourishing) feedback from the editors of *gta papers*. Jeffrey Fraser Landman helped with the Sloterdijk, and his sourdough starter is still keeping me going in the pandemic. Publications by biologist of symbiosis Scott Gilbert, and our conversations, have been inspiring; Stefan Helmreich is also a treasured interlocutor.

2 In addition to the mammalian placenta, syncytia are also found in mammalian cardiac muscle cells and certain smooth muscle cells that have the capacity to be synchronized electrically (as in the heart muscle). The term can broadly refer to tissues showing many nuclei but no cell walls, the result of fusions from uninuclear cells, a process often propelled by viral proteins whose remnant DNA can be identified in the biotic material. We will explore in this essay the intriguing electrical potential for signaling that syncytia make possible, even in a syncytial deep ocean sponge.

3 Peter Sloterdijk, "Talking to Myself about the Poetics of Space," *Harvard Design Review* 30 (Spring/Summer 2009), n.p., http://www.harvard-designmagazine.org/issues/30/talking-to-myself-about-the-poetics-of-space (accessed December 15, 2020). There is also this astonishing pronouncement: "Women's bodies are apartments!"

4 Sloterdijk, "Talking to Myself."

5 Buckminster Fuller, introduction to *Expanded Cinema*, by Gene Youngblood, 50th, Anniversary ed. (New York: Fordham University Press, 2020), 16–17.

6 For "Swarmism" en route to "Tectonism," see Patrik Schumacher, "The 'Digital' in Architecture and Design," *Architectural Association Files* 76 (Summer 2019), n.p.

7 Mark A. Hill, "Embryology: Uterus Development," *University of New South Wales Embryology*, April 5, 2020, https://embryology.med.unsw.edu.au/embryology/index.php/Uterus_Development%2523Uterine_Development_Movie (accessed December 15, 2020).

fig.1 Syncytium of fused cellular tissue, formed through the virus HSV-1 (herpes simplex) interacting with the artificial cell line known as "Vero" Source: Wikimedia commons

invagination (a folding of tissue to enclose a space) that comes with gonadal differentiation (in the gestational stage of nine weeks), when the female-hormone-cued fetus begins to develop future eggs (protected in an ovary) along with a place to put them once they are fertilized (the uterus). [7] The uterus thus already exists at the earliest stage of the anatomy of the embryonic mammalian female. Yet the placenta is generated by any mammalian fetus before it even has a sex. What the fetal cells build is a flat, spongy, layer-cake (Greek *plakuos*, Latinized as "placenta") connected on the one side to the uterine wall and on the oth-

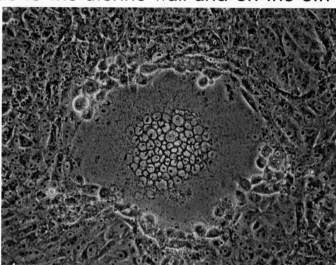

er to the embryo—soon linked by a busy umbilicus constantly pulsing with fluids going in both directions. The placenta begins to develop immediately upon fertilization, as the outer layer (called the "trophoblast") of the fertilized egg differentiates itself from the inner layer, which will become an embryo. That outer layer gets busy producing an organ outside the fetus that will mediate between developing embryo and maternal life support; the developing placental membrane allows the rapidly dividing egg cells to "implant" themselves into the wall of the uterus before the umbilicus forms. The trophopart of the blastula is what expands into the "flat cake" that will provide "nutrition, gas exchange, waste removal, a source of hematopoietic stem cells, endocrine, and immune support for the developing fetus." [8] The placenta "belongs" to the developing embryo, and will be expelled from the uterus as soon as the fetus is. If we were to construct architectural metaphors, the uterus is framing, the placenta, temporary plumbing.

Plumbing, waste, nutrition, and gas exchange are the onerous parts of architectural design, but their management inside the maternal body, rather than in an extruded egg, was an essential precondition for mammalian evolution and clearly a driver for mammalian reproductive success. That the uterine, in both Fuller's and Sloterdijk's imaginary, presents the ideal manifestation of the (Leon Battista) Albertian ideal of *commoditas*, suggests a placental hauntology—its lowly functions of maintenance and care sublimated into elevated notions of comfort. Most likely these architecturally minded types think of the flexible uterus as commodious because the mechanics of life support (heating, ventilation, and

8 Mark A. Hill, "Embryology: Placenta Development," *University of New South Wales Embryology*, September 13, 2020, https://embryology.med.unsw.edu.au/embryology/index.php/Placenta_Development (accessed December 15, 2020).

air conditioning; electricity; and plumbing) are both sub-contracted and automated in bodies, as they are in modern architectural practice. [9]

9 Namely in building information modeling and the "autonomic" nervous system.

Sloterdijk's conversion of the uterus into a shell (an invagination transformed into an extrusion) needs some comment. We could wonder whether Sloterdijk is at least historically accurate—did architects become obsessed with shells? Is the uterine-as-shell appealing because of its paradoxical combination of stasis and portability? The shell gives us a metaphor that is clean and inert, seemingly permanent, growing ever whiter in the sun. Is Sloterdijk's strange inversion of the folded (uterine) into the deposited (shell) a privileged "shell-imagining" that allows technology to conceive a tidy, separable, indeed discardable box-like unit under the command and control of its maker? A shell that survives beyond the death of its occupant? Or, finally, were Sloterdijk and Fuller simply inheriting that epistemology of Western science that relies on dead specimens and skeletons, making it difficult even to conceive of the pulsations of syncytia (such as the myocardial tissues that propel the action potentials of our own hearts)?

Thinking about how syncytia come to be in biological assemblages through viral agents might help architects move beyond the limits of shells as animal "property," not to mention that domain of the *tektōn* (carpenter), "tectonics." Doing so would allow us to engage the functional tangles of actual life systems—as in the placental *villi* that Leonardo da Vinci drew in the corner of his drawing dominated by a violently opened womb. fig.2 In this telling detail, the artist seeks to understand, by pulling apart, the entwined intra-active surfaces of placenta and uterus to enable the classic view in which there is an "invasion" of the maternal uterine wall, now penetrated by placental "fingers" (*villi*). [10]

In place of the static, portable, and no longer biotic "architectural members" of tectonics and shells, let us think of the enmeshment of membership. This demands that we conceive the with-living entities that participate in the ubiquitous condition of symbiosis, a polemic I have begun to call symbiontics. [11] It is biologist Lynn Margulis who inaugurated this

10 The language of "invasion" is still operative in embryology: "[fetal] cytotrophoblastic cells proliferate and differentiate into an *invasive phenotype* that *invade* ... the maternal decidual stroma," Hill, "Embryology," my emphasis. Note that da Vinci had difficulties obtaining gravid but dead female bodies, and made do in some instances with the uterus of a domestic animal: "one of the most significant errors of the studies of the walls of the human uterus is Leonardo's inclusion there of cotyledons that are present in ungulates such as the cow ... but not in humans," Kenneth David Keele and Jane Roberts, *Leonardo Da Vinci: Anatomical Drawings from the Royal Library, Windsor Castle* (New York: Metropolitan Museum of Art, 1983), 57. The drawing illustrated here is numbered 19A in this monograph; the cow "cotyledon" is visible in the detail to the right of the opened womb.

11 Symbiontics is a portmanteau developed to incorporate notions of symbiosis found in Lynn Margulis's work with the "ontics" of technical philosophy (that which is): symbiosis-as-that-which-is. So far, the sites in which "symbiontics" has been seeded include *Olafur Eliasson, Symbiotic Seeing*, exhibition at Kunsthalle Zurich (2020); Jenna Sutela, *NO/NO/NSE/NSE*, exhibition at Kunsthall Trondheim, Norway (2020); Caroline A. Jones, "Virions: Thinking Through the Scale of Aggregation," *Artforum* 58, no. 9 (May/June 2020), 98–101, notes on 196; Caroline A. Jones, "Symbiontics: A View of Present Conditions from a Place of Entanglement," *Brooklyn Rail* (July/August 2020), n. p.; Stefanie Hessler and Jenny Jaskey, eds., *Agnieszka Kurant: Collective Intelligence* (Berlin: Sternberg Press, forthcoming 2021), and various online forums. My polemic deeply respects and joins forces with concepts already in circulation, such as Donna Haraway's "sympoiesis," which in turn draws on Scott Gilbert's "symbiopoiesis." For my part, because I am after broad cultural change, I want to lodge my polemic directly inside ontology (the study of what it is to exist) rather than theoretical biology. See Donna J. Haraway, *Staying with the Trouble: Making Kin in the Chthulucene* (Durham, NC: Duke University Press, 2016), and Scott F. Gilbert et al., "Symbiosis as a Source of Selectable Epigenetic Variation: Taking the Heat for the Big Guy," *Philosophical Transactions of the Royal Society B: Biological Sciences* 365, no. 1540 (February 2010), 671–78.

fig. 2 a, b Above: placental villi from *Studies of the Foetus in the Womb,* Leonardo da Vinci, ca. 1510. Recto: Red chalk and traces of black chalk, pen and ink, wash. Right: full sheet
Source: Royal Collection Trust

12 Will the ubiquitous novel coronavirus jumping out of bats transform the human genome? The "long-haulers" may be experiencing profound disruptions to their immune systems, but the virus would have to be passed on with ova or sperm to be truly endo-symbiotic.

13 Lynn Sagan, "On the Origins of Mitosing Cells," *Journal of Theoretical Biology* 14, no. 3 (March 1967), 225–74. After her divorce from Carl Sagan, Lynn Margulis (née Alexander) made common cause with James Lovelock in launching the Gaia theory, for which see James E. Lovelock and Lynn Margulis, "Atmospheric Homeostasis by and for the Biosphere: The Gaia Hypothesis," *Tellus* 26, nos. 1–2 (February 1974), 2–10.

revolution, recognizing in 1967 what could only be confirmed by genomics decades later: we are symbionts all the way down, into deep time when "endosymbiosis" (the incorporation of symbiotic others into a single cell) created the first mitosing cells and bequeathed us multi-cellular beings with cellular "power plants" (mitochondria) derived from engulfed cyanobacteria. 12 The presence of bacterial DNA in our mitochondria reveal a presumably random coupling that turned out to convey explosive evolutionary advantage (the benefits of symbiosis).

A long time later, these enhanced cells merged into multi-cellular organisms, and later still they incorporated the clever trick of viral proteins in dissolving (*lysing*) those very cell walls and/or membranes for yet further evolutionary twists and turns. 13 Triggered for the highly successful family of mammals by lysogenic viruses long since incorporated into our cell lines, the syncytium is made of those fused cells (many nuclei, no membranes) that comprise the flat cake of the placenta. To restate: the ability to form the flat cake of the placenta can be traced back to DNA appropriated from a lysogenic virus. That virus was capable of creating syncytia (many nuclei, no membranes), but that ability is now entirely enlisted in our reproductive lives. (The viral trace is only a fragment; it can no longer escape to move freely.)

The incorporation of this viral DNA into our cell lines is a defining moment in the differentiation of the class of mammals from other vertebrates. But it is not the "cake" that nourishes the fetus, rather this temporary organ induces the body of the host to provide what is needed. The placenta produces flows of chemicals such as oxytocin that make its host happy to have it. Flows of gonadotropin thicken the uterus with increased blood vessels, enabling the nourishment of the guest. Flows of lactogen make sure the host body correctly prepares further nourishing secretions, to feed the helpless infant animal upon exit. We know, as da Vinci did not, that the placenta begins as a few alien cells that the host might otherwise expel. Crucially, the cells are disguised, because that two-week-old fertilized blastula uses its lysogenic tools to generate an outer layer whose cell walls have fused (via those viral genes)—first gluing themselves to themselves, and then gluing to the nearby tissues of the mammalian host (with the right chemical supplementation and invaginated space, it could be a male or female body doing the hosting). The new organ is characterized by these undifferentiated, fused cells that then defend the new occupant against annihilation by the host's immune system, which literally cannot "recognize" the alien-cells-without-walls.

Some have characterized the fetal occupier as a parasite, shielded by its virally camouflaged "cake" so that it can summon

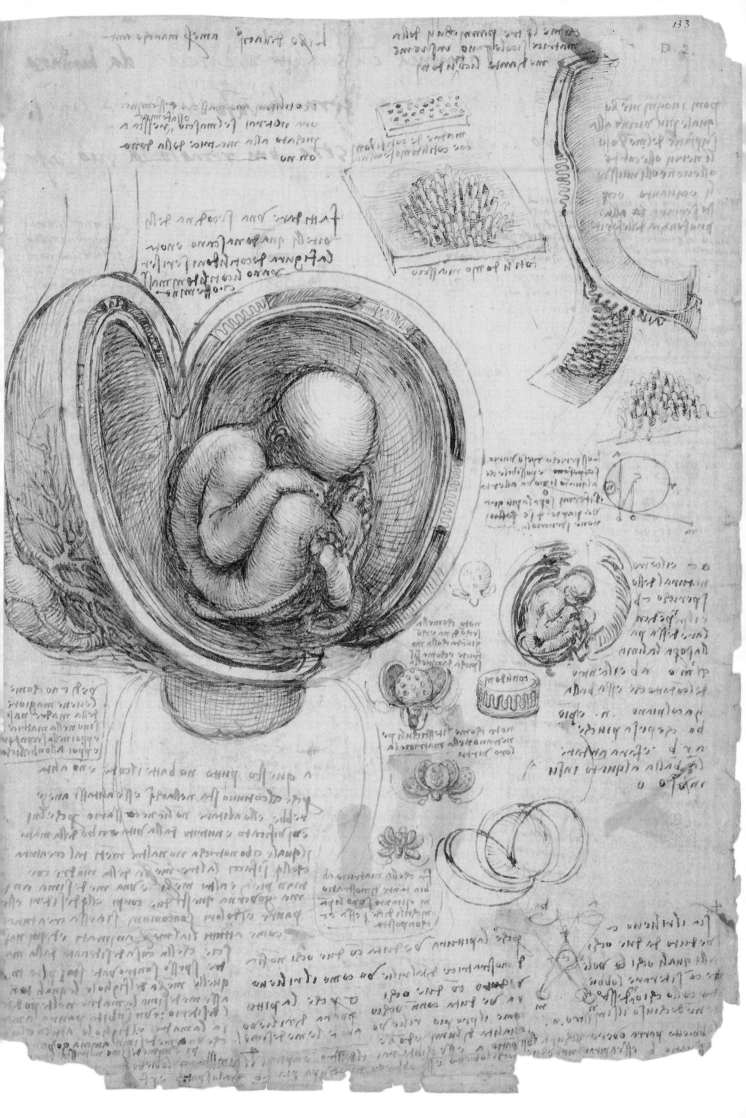

14 The politics around pregnancy discourses are intense, woven into choice/abortion debates. "Guests" might indicate my position, for guests can be politely shown the door. For an early medical view, see Donald J. Naismith, "The Foetus as a Parasite," *Proceedings of the Nutrition Society* 28, no. 1 (March 1969), 25–31.

15 See Bruce Clarke and Mark Hansen, eds., "Introduction," in *Emergence and Embodiment: New Essays on Second-Order Systems Theory* (Durham, NC: Duke University Press, 2009), 1–25, esp. 9–12, in which they explore these issues. (The phrasing is by Evan Thompson, cited on page 10). The concept of life systems and semiotic systems are further explored by sociologist/media theorist Niklas Luhmann in "Self-Organization and Autopoiesis" (from Niklas Luhmann, *Einführung in die Systemtheorie* (1991), trans. Hans-Georg Moeller and Bruce Clarke), in Clarke and Hansen, *Emergence and Embodiment*, 143–56.

16 See Irigaray's reading of Plato's *Hystera* in *Speculum of the Other Woman*, trans. Gillian C. Gill (Ithaca, NY: Cornell University Press, 1985), 243–364. On the matrixial as a force within art, see Catherine de Zegher, *Inside the Visible: An Elliptical Traverse of 20th Century Art in, of, and from the Feminine* (Cambridge, MA: MIT Press, 1996). This materializes important thinking by psychoanalyst Bracha Ettinger regarding "matrixial borderspace," for which see Bracha Ettinger, *Matrixial Borderspace* (Minneapolis: University of Minnesota Press, 2006). This is further developed in Irina Aristarkhova, *Hospitality of the Matrix: Philosophy, Biomedicine, Culture* (New York: Columbia University Press, 2012).

17 "Volume-Fluidity," in Irigaray, *Speculum*, 227–42.

nutrients and recruit support from the unwitting host. I choose to describe the embryo and its organ as "guests" of the hosting body. **14** No doubt, these guests are demanding. But the systems they install do much of the work during their visit. Bringing in oxygen and carrying away waste CO_2 from the rapidly multiplying cells of the embryo, the mammalian placenta is the ultimate "machine for living," but in place of that industrial engineering metaphor, let us instead imagine the chemical flows, interdependencies, endocrine affects, and epigenetic responses characteristic of the with-living flux of symbiosis.

Are we merely substituting for the sheltering hut, cave, shell, or muscled uterus a membranous tent or "tympanum" whose stretchy layer is all about communication, food logistics, and a kind of camouflage? There is indeed a kind of biosemiosis in symbiontics, but it is not the tidy signaling of Jakob von Uexküll's separated creaturely *Umwelten*. It is rather the second-order cybernetics in which "the operational closure of autopoiesis demands that the organism be an open system." **15** In symbiontics, the "organism" is never the fictive individual but always contains multitudes. An architecture aware of this would have to enter a space of permanent and ongoing cooperation, finding different metaphors for the production of symbiotic flourishing.

It is this surfing on intra-active conviviality that might productively inspire architecture. Nesting networks of vivid interdependency replace the bony carapaces of mollusks or the inert materials of the builder. I do not absolve my feminist heroes from architectural obsessions with the structure or the shell rather than the all-important flow. But at least when Luce Irigaray theorizes the primordial architecture of our philosophies, she knows that the cave and the womb are also sites of *functions* she identifies as "matrixial." Irigaray celebrates how *la matrice* — the matrix — translates an ancient Greek word for womb, and traces this "metra" into material and matter. **16** I am tempted to find, in the inexhaustible Irigaray, an explanation for the ubiquitous celebration of tectonics as the scattered "parts" that must always remain separated for picking up by "others" (*tektōns*) to build with, a process of "assembling" revealed by her to be a "dissembling" of the primordial force that is the matrixial:

"[Woman] is not uprooted from matter, from the earth, but yet, but still, she is already scattered into x number of places that are never gathered together into anything she knows of herself, and these remain the basis of (re)production — particularly of discourse — in all its forms." **17**

We should not romanticize this originary force of procreation, least of all through masculinist views of primordia (invariably,

fig. 3 Sketches of various *Hexactinellid* sponges, Franz Eilhard Schulze Source: *Brockhaus' Konversations-Lexikon*, vol. 8. (Leipzig: F.A. Brockhaus, 1892)

women lose out in that rumination). Science of the syncytium helps release us from the rigidities of human ontogenies and their tectonic discourses (*homo faber* needs to navigate towards a bit of other-than-human thinking). Mind you, we need to pick and choose our syncytial science. Ernst Haeckel's "recapitulation" theories of embryology managed to erase both fetal agency and that of the maternal host, creating developmental sequences out of doctored photographs that erased not only the placenta but different embryos' membranous shrouds, tails, and other creaturely flourishes. **fig. 3** Such prevarication allowed Haeckel to insist on a grand evolution of forms (a tectonic parade fueling a teleological Great Chain of Being.) [18] Cleaning up the ragged edges of embryos rather than dealing with the bewildering variations in placentation (mammalian placentas vary more than any other single organ), [19] Haeckel ignored what I am here insisting upon: the syncytial encourages us to think of architectures pulsing within, not abstracted from, living systems.

Sciences of the syncytium are not without their tectonic beauties. (Without mammalian skeletons to hold them, symbionts seek other structuring relations.) Think of the elegant and mysterious deepwater Glasschwämme or *Hexactinellida* family of "glass" sponges. These looked redoubtably tectonic to the nineteenth-century biologist F. E. Schulze, who made them more so by combining the soggy individual specimens he received into a cluster of pert structures dwelling together. Their chimneys, swirls, cups, and pipes appear in his work as a fantastic metropolis, stretching up from the ocean floor. Writing from Berlin for the British expedition publishing these specimens in 1887, Dr. Schulze characterized the rare sponges' "fine central canal ... [as] surrounded by numerous concentrically arranged layers of a solid substance [resembling] glass so closely that it has been ... spoken of as *vitreous fibre.*" [20] Contemporary chemists reveal these to be, indeed, silicon dioxide — glass formed throughout the sponge body by a continuous mass of cytoplasm with many

18 Many thanks to Adam Jasper for insisting that the gorgeous and faked images by Haeckel be part of this tirade. On Haeckel's telos-obsessed cheating, see Nick Hopgood, *Haeckel's Embryos — Images, Evolution, and Fraud* (Chicago: University of Chicago Press, 2015).

19 See the online atlas *Comparative Placentation* by medical pathologist Kurt Benirschke, maintained by the University of California at San Diego, http://placentation.ucsd.edu/homefs.html, last updated January 19, 2012 (accessed January 31, 2021)

20 F. E. Schulze, "Report on the Hexactinellida Collected by H.M.S. Challenger during the Years 1873–76," *H.M.S. Challenger Reports*, vol. 21 (Edinburgh: Adam & Charles Black and Douglas & Foulis, 1887), 27, http://www.19thcenturyscience.org/HMSC/HMSC-Reports/Zool-53/htm/doc.html (accessed January 29, 2020). In his section on the skeletal, Schulze recognizes that little is known of the development of these remarkable silica structures and the soft mass that connects them in the center of the sponge.

fig. 4 Scanning
electron microscopy,
in Cristina Bayer et al.,
"Microbial Strategies
for Survival in the
Glass Sponge *Vazella
pourtalesii*," *Msystems*
5, no. 4 (August 2020),
fig. 2. Original caption
describing the complex
symbioses found within
a glass sponge reads:
"Microscopy of *Vazella
pourtalesii* tissue. (A)
Scanning electron
microscopy overview
of spicule scaffolds
(scale bar, 75 _m). (B)
SEM closeup image of
a biomass patch (scale
bar, 3 _m). (C and
D) Light microscopy
image (scale bar, 5 _m)
(C), and TEM image
of the same biomass
patch (scale bar, 1 _m)
(D). (E) SEM closeup
presumably showing
smaller microbes
attached to larger ones
by stalk- or filament-like
structures (scale bar, 1
_m). (F) TEM images of
adjacent microbial cells
(scale bars, 500 nm)."

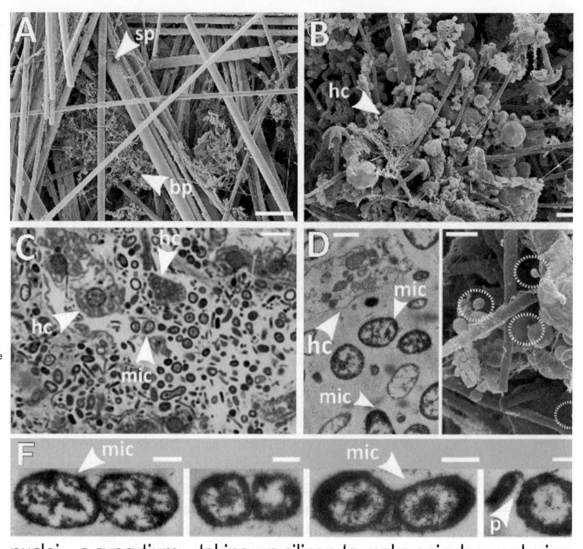

21 Eleanor Lawrence,
"Nervous Sponge,"
Nature Briefing,
April 15, 1999, https://
www.nature.com/
news/1999/990415/
full/news990415-5.html
(accessed December 15,
2020).

22 Nicole S. Webster
and Torsten Thomas,
"The Sponge
Hologenome," *mBio*
7, no. 2 (March/April
2016), e00135-16. The
authors write of a
"paradigm shift" in
biology as symbiotic
relationships appear
active in all living
organisms, now
understood to be part
of a "hologenome"
comprising the genome
of host and all its
symbionts.

23 Kristina Bayer et al.,
"Microbial Strategies
for Survival in the
Glass Sponge *Vazella
pourtalesii*," *mSystems*
5, no. 4 (July/August
2020), e00473-20.

nuclei — a syncytium — taking up silicon to make spicules, replacing the normal epidermal cells that other kinds of sponges possess. In place of those conventional, contractive spongey cells with their tidy membranes, these silica builders craft a rigid syncytial net of amoebocytes (doubtless propelled by lysogenes taken from viruses) supported by glass spicules. Uniquely, the glassy fretwork of the *Hexactinellida* allow these deep ocean dwellers to conduct electricity rapidly throughout their bodies, a signal system "used by the sponge to shut down its food-filtering system [via flagellar arrest] ... when conditions outside risk the system becoming damaged." **21** This syncytial dynamic also collaborates with the sponge's numerous microbial companions (a "consortium of bacteria, archaea, unicellular algae, fungi, and viruses" **22**) to form one of the most ancient structural testaments to symbiosis.

Contemporary microbiologists have the tools to probe the interior of Glasschwämme to see these "microbial strategies" in action. **23** In the 2020 scanning electron microscopy images published by Kristina Bayer and her collaborators, "bp" indicates syncytial biomass patches in which the sponge cells lose their membranous walls (that evolutionary lysing program that viruses are so good at), becoming dedifferentiated platforms nesting in scaffolds of silica and hosting bacterial partners who do the work of secreting the amino acids that keep the sponge alive in its deep, low-oxygen, lightless environment. **fig.4**

This digression into an alien species' syncytium concludes the more-than-human polemic I have launched here. Astonishing forms are possible from the symbiotic engagement of cell and not-cell, working together in a synchrony of productive guests and adaptive hosts: not spheres and shells but syncytia and systems, not husks or rinds but interdependent matrices and meshworks, not tectonics but symbiontics. [24] Architecture can flourish like the adaptive, hospitable systems featured here, recognizing that it is already suffused by flows and linked by interrelations at every scale.

[24] The editors ask, "does symbiontics cause us to reimagine housing, or airports, or mortgages?" Obviously, I hope it can—and welcome the collective needed for this reimagining. Keller Easterling, *Medium Design: Knowing How to Work on the World* (London: Verso, forthcoming 2021), has some suggestive outlines of one kind of adaptive, flexing, collaborative, guesting and hosting—in which architectural systems (mortgages no less than airports) must acknowledge aspects like the waste, nutrition, and gas exchange that support their emergence. "Solutions" for Easterling are often counter-intuitive and indirect, depending on attending to feedback loops of care and maintenance rather than driven by black boxes, debt loads, or shell construction.

Cathelijne Nuijsink is a postdoctoral fellow at the Chair of the History and Theory of Urban Design of the Institute for the History and Theory of Architecture (gta), ETH Zurich.

Some Inflated Expectations
Cathelijne Nuijsink

In the 1960s, the creation of indoor environments took on an entirely new meaning. Inspired by new materials, technologies, and the recent romance of space-travel, young architects with a countercultural sensibility started to explore a novel type of micro-environment that was minimal, lightweight, and portable, and that paid special attention to the qualities of the building envelope and the level of comfort of the human body within the "skin." Originally invented by the US military in the aftermath of the Second World War as easily deployable radar domes, inflatables were adopted by architects in the 1960s and 1970s to build mobile spaces for dissent. Incorporating the technique in polemical lightweight "wearable" structures, progressive architects such as Archigram, Utopie, UFO, Coop Himmelb(l)au, Ant Farm,

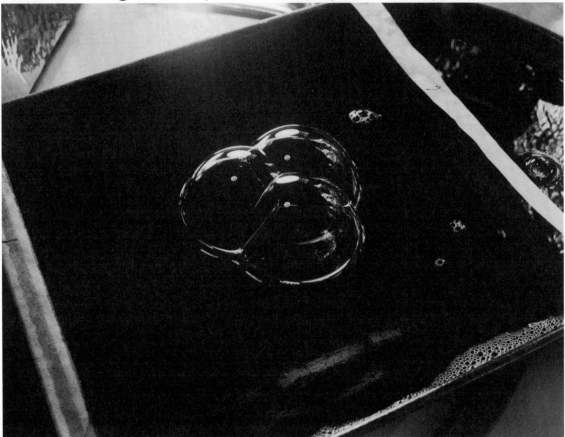

fig.1 Frei Otto, Soap Bubble Experiment (n. d.)
Source: Archiv für Architektur und Ingenieurbau, Karlsruher Institut für Technologie (KIT)

Haus-Rucker-Co, Superstudio, and Hans Hollein provided a bodily experience with which they could roam the streets and stage a protest. Situating architectural inflatables in today's debates around personal protective measures and home-office working, bubbles represent a critique of societal participation equally valid in situations of enforced and voluntary quarantine.

Indoor ecology as a bubble was explored in the 1950s by visionaries who actively promoted climatic envelopes for human enclosure. Inspired by soap bubbles, engineer Frei Otto was among the first to experiment with thin membranes of synthetic

fig. 2 Buckminster
Fuller, *Geodesic
Dome over Midtown
Manhattan*, 1961
Source: courtesy of the
estate of R. Buckminster
Fuller

fabric in the way that layers of soap stick together. His Domed
Hall (1959), fig.1 Offshore Storage Facility (1958/1959), and Large-
Scale Envelope for Agricultural Use (1959) propose minimalist
pneumatic structures for human settlements to survive in extreme
climates. A soap bubble, according to Otto, was the ideal pneumatic form to produce urban-scale climatic envelopes "skinning
over whole cities." 1 The resulting indoor climates were paradisal
spaces set in extreme environments. Buckminster Fuller's take
on the indoor ecology was the two-mile Geodesic Dome over
Midtown Manhattan (1962), a huge protective skin covering an
entire neighborhood. fig.2 The bubble here was a semi-perma-
nent inflatable structure supported by pressurized air that reg-
ulated weather conditions and reduced air pollution within the
dome. Archigram member Peter Cook retrospectively recognized
in Fuller's design "the powerful idea that a building does not have
to cope with exterior weather conditions." 2

        The cover of the November 11, 1957, issue of *Life Magazine*
prominently featured Walter Bird's Air-Supported Dome for All-
Year Swimming (1957), a plastic bubble sheltering a private swimming pool. 3 fig.3 The corresponding article's section "The New
Technology Already has Samples of Changes it Made in Everyday
World" situated Bird's invention amid those of jet-engine autos,
nylon air houses, and one-man aircraft as examples of recent
inventions that were not mere theoretical experiments but had
been developed for domestic settings or commercial purposes.
For a mere two thousand dollars, one could not only dream of,

1 Cited in Peter
Cook, *Experimental
Architecture* (New York:
Universe Books, 1970),
50.

2 Cook, *Experimental
Architecture*, 50.

3 "Tomorrow's Life
Today: Man's New
World, Part II," *Life
Magazine*, November
11, 1957, 132—47, here
132, https://books.
google.de/books?id=t-
VYEAAAAMBAJ&lp-
g=PA132&hl=de&p-
g=PA132#v=one-
page&q&f=true
(accessed February 1,
2021).

but own, an all-season outdoor swimming pool. fig.4 In 1948, the designer of this pool dome had already made significant advances in air-inflated structures with his invention of the radome, a pneumatic shelter for radar devices. Bird's shelters had long served as prototypes to protect military radars from harsh climatic conditions. He was quick to recognize the lightweight, mobile, and easily deployable qualities of radomes, and started experimenting with the application of the same technique to spaces for human shelter.

Architectural bubbles started to take on an entirely new meaning in the countercultural climate of the 1960s. For architects, the free forms associated with bubbles aligned with avant-garde ways of thinking. New materials and technologies, such as plastics and pneumatics, made possible forms that were diametrically opposite to the rectangles of modernism, a viewpoint that historian Reyner Banham readily embraced:

"What is new is the confluence between changing taste and advances in plastic technologies. The taste that has been turned off by the regular rectangular format of the official modern architecture and Bauhaus-revival modern-antique furniture, is turned right on by the apparent do-it-yourself potentialities of low-pressure inflatable technologies." 4

In his 1965 essay "A Home Is Not a House," Banham went so far as to propose an "environment-bubble" of a domesticated utopia equipped with modern amenities. Interested in both the formal and spatial possibilities of comfort provided by mechanical services, Banham used textual form to introduce the idea of the house as a minimal membrane of enclosure, wondering "when it [your house] contains so many services that the hardware could stand up by itself without any assistance from the house, why have a house to hold up?" 5 With this "unhouse," 6 Banham set the tone for "a radical and anti-monumental prototype for rethinking architecture's relationship to technology, humans, and the environment." 7 The media were actively deployed to promote Banham's environmental bubble. In a 1967 BBC television show, Banham made a performance by living naked for a full day in a mockup of his bubble. Being in this inflatable, in reference to philosopher Peter Sloterdijk, was made possible by a climatic control system located in the bubble's skin that could condition the indoor environment to a comfortable level.

fig.3 Walter Bird, "Air-Supported Dome for All-Year Swimming," *Life*, November 11, 1957, cover
Source: Life Magazine Archive, Google Books

4 Reyner Banham "Monumental Windbags," *New Society* 11, (April 1968), 569–70.

5 Reyner Banham, "A Home is Not a House," *Art in America* 2, (1965), 70–79, here 70.

6 Joan Ockman, ed., "1960–1968," in *Architecture Culture 1943–1968: A Documentary Anthology* (New York: Rizzoli 1993; repr. 2007), 317–463, here 370.

7 Whitney Moon, "Environmental Wind-Baggery," in Daniel A. Barber and Eduardo Rega, eds., *Structural Instability, a collaboration between e-flux Architecture and PennDesign*, August 1, 2018, https://www.e-flux.com/architecture/structural-instability/208703/environmental-wind-baggery/ (accessed February 1, 2021).

In line with Banham's ideas laid out in "A Home Is Not a House," performative avant-garde architectural groups that shared the contemporary interest in nomadism increasingly turned to inflatables in the 1960s as a quick and inexpensive means to create a lightweight space for dissent and experimentation. Their ideal bubble was transparent, superlight, and as portable as a suit "in which the boundary between inside and outside was as thin as possible." [8]

NYLON AIRHOUSES pop up on a university campus in Kentucky. Made of U.S. Rubber Company's Fiberthin, a vinyl-covered nylon fabric that forms a strong as waterproof cotton yet 50% lighter in weight, dome-like houses are kept up by air, pumped in by small blowers. They are anchored at base by ballast rings of sand or water. Already catching on for industrial and military use, they are being developed as vacation houses for around $1,000 for a 20-foot-diameter unit.

At both the scale of the family dwelling and at an urban level, Archigram members Michael Webb, Peter Cook, Ron Herron, and David Greene readily experimented throughout the 1960s—alone or in collaboration—with prefabricated capsule dwellings, plastic living capsules, and portable environments. Greene's Living Pod (1966), a womb-like mobile home with integrated machinery, could exist independently or be plugged into larger structures as a capsule-dwelling module. On an urban scale, Herron's Sea Bubbles (1966) or Cook's Instant City (1968—1970) were emblematic in their use of inflatables to capture the notion of mobile architecture. The first was a speculative project for inflatable housing units suspended from a mast structure, dangling over and under the sea. The latter was a "traveling metropolis" that, using trucks and especially air inflatables for transportation, injected a metropolitan dynamic in the form of cultural events, mobile facilities, and information technology into what were otherwise sleepy towns.

Webb's Cushicle was a preliminary proposal for a nomadic shelter-cum-clothing that incorporated a small vehicle. *Suitaloon*, the successor to the Cushicle, was the built prototype of a wearable suit that covered all the basic needs of living, which could inflate into a comfortable personalized environment. Or as David Greene would later write, "Suit and Balloon collide to make Suitaloon. Cushion and Vehicle make Cushicle." [9] Designing pneumatic living cells for nomadic lifestyles was one of the key strategies of the architectural collective Archigram to move past the stagnation of the British architectural scene.

With the Cushicle, Webb started to advance Banham's idea of a house with the ultimate minimal skin. First introduced in 1966 in the eighth edition of *Archigram* as an example of comfort-giving architecture, the Cushicle envisioned a living envelope for the human body "that enables a man to carry a complete environment

fig. 4 Frank Lloyd Wright, "Nylon Air Houses," *Life*, November 11, 1957, 134 Photographer: Andreas Feininger/Source: Life Magazine Archive, Google Books

8 Hadas A. Steiner, *Beyond Archigram: The Structure of Circulation* (New York: Routledge, 2013), 157.

9 David Greene and Samantha Hardingham, *L.A.W.U.N. Project #19: A Dictionary for De-Urbanised Man* (London: Architectural Association, 2008), 152—57, here 153.

fig. 5 David Greene in Michael Webb's Suitaloon, garment made by Pat Haines and photographed by Dennis Crompton at the Milan Triennale XIV, 1968 Source: Archigram archives, with thanks to David Greene and Michael Webb
→ 180/181

10 Michael Webb, "The Cushicle," in Peter Cook et al, eds., *Archigram: The Book* (London: Circa Press, 1972), 64–65.

11 Webb, "The Cushicle".

on his back," according to Webb. **10** The project consists of two main components: a spinal system that forms the chassis and provides support for the appliances, and an inflatable membrane that serves as the house's skin. With the chassis and the envelope both fully opened, the Cushicle turns into a fully serviced air cushion vehicle carrying food, water, a radio, a miniature projection television, and a heating apparatus. **11** As Cook explained, Webb's bubble very much relied on its own mechanism:

"In the Cushicle Mark II a portable membrane is arranged in such a way that when the carrier has decided to set up home, he places it in the ground and by walking into part of the membrane can push the structure out. This structure consists of a series of veins, of fabric and electrical supply and lighting wires. We can get to something very like a man-as-a-bat where the skin of the enclosure is dependent upon a system of vertebrae that responds very directly to the nervous system of the person within." **12**

12 Cook, *Experimental Architecture*, 55.

13 Cook, *Experimental Architecture*, 116.

The new architectural idea embedded in this project was that "man can have its own container," suggesting that "each person, on arriving at a state of relative emancipation, should receive a degree of personal support that he cannot get from the collective artifact (house, family car, the village)." **13** Webb's Cushicle is about using the military industrial complex against itself: turning the bubble into a liberatory vehicle.

Webb's Suitaloon further refined the idea of the *Cushicle* "down into a system of pipes worn around the body that heat and

fig. 6 Coop Himmelb(l)au, Restless Sphere, Basel, Switzerland, 1971 Photographer: Peter Schnetz/Source: courtesy of Wolf Prix and Coop Himmelb(l)au

14 Cook, *Experimental Architecture*, 117.

protect it, while additional facilities can be clipped on." **14** **fig. 5** While *Cushicle* was an indoor environment, the size of a small living room, the plastic suit of Suitaloon represented an absolute minimal habitat tightly wrapped around the human body. Webb himself likened Suitaloon to "clothing for living in," arguing that "if it wasn't for my Suitaloon I would have to buy a house." **15** Responsive technology incorporated in the shell

15 Michael Webb, "Suitaloon," in Cook et al., *Archigram*, 80.

expanded the functions of the human skin, as much as it created the feeling of a personal cocoon, a haven in the metropolis.

In contrast to architectural bubbles that limited themselves to strictly private individual indoor ecologies, Cushicle and Suitaloon contained a novel sociable aspect. Webb envisioned that the autonomous Cushicle "could become part of a more widespread urban system of personalized enclosures" once invested with service nodes and additional apparatus. [16] Comfort for Two (1967) illustrated that multiple suitaloons were able to join together in a single enclosure. One person wearing a suitaloon was able to merge with another suitaloon utilizing a plug, a feature that Webb demonstrated with an illustration showing a male–female couple joining suits:

"You can plug into your friend and you will both be in one envelope, or you can plug into any envelope, stepping out of your suit, the suit being left clipped onto the outside ready to step into when you leave. The plug also serves as a means of connecting envelopes together to form larger spaces." [17]

Webb further imagined that Cushicles and Suitaloons could cater to different kinds of individuals and family configurations.

Together, Cushicle and Suitaloon illustrate Archigram's search for an efficient alternative to conventional architecture, one that is light, portable, and transformable. Its skin-like envelope contained environmental qualities that question architecture as a solid enclosure. [18] As scholar Stamatina" Kousidi has argued, Cushicle/Suitaloon also presented a conceptual shift from wearable clothes to a portable space. This in-between space is a comfortable living room that houses the human body (*"Einen Raum, der den menschlichen Korper beherbergt umschliest"*). [19] More than functional attire that keeps its wearer comfortable, one could also argue that Cushicle/Suitaloon is a form of protective clothing, "shielding the human body from physical, social, emotional and spiritual threats, real and imagined" outside the personal—in other words, a shell. [20]

Cushicle/Suitaloon is a self-sufficient bubble that proposes a lifestyle independent from social structures, reflecting pleasure and fun, as much as the liberation of the individual. It represents, in a way both provocative and earnest, a kind of architectural autonomy. As such, it sits in contrast to the anti-architectural inflatables by the San Francisco group Antfarm, for example, who were a reaction to America's heavy consumerism and stereotyped suburban lifestyle. Antfarm members Chip Lord and Doug Michels toured America with inexpensive, portable bubbles to promote an alternative, low-key, and nomadic lifestyle. [21] The Parisian Utopie group turned to mobile architecture to counter the existing power structures in the fields of architecture and town planning. [22] They used inflatables as a form of agitative practice, analyzing what happens in reality and acting in accordance. [23] Webb's stance was not as explicitly political. Instead, he employed inflatables as a form of architectural action, staging architecture as both media and event.

16 Webb, "The Cushicle," 64.

17 Cook, Experimental Architecture, 116.

18 Cook, Experimental Architecture, 54–55.

19 Stamatina Kousidi situates Webb's Cushicle/Suitaloon in the body discourses of the 1960s and 1970s and uses "dress" and "clothing" as theoretical tools to discuss the project. See Stamatina Kousidi, "The Skins We Live in: Zu Archigrams Cushicle and Suitaloon (1966–1968)," in Karl R. Kegler, Anna Minta, and Nicklas Naehrig, eds., RaumKleider: Verbindungen zwischen Architekturraum, Körper und Kleid, (Bielefeld: Transcript Verlag, 2018), 179–94, here 180.

20 Susan Watkins, "Protective Clothing," in Valerie Steele, ed., Encyclopedia of Clothing and Fashion, vol. 3 (New York: Scribner/Thomson Gale, 2005), 58.

21 Spatial Agency, https://www.spatiala-gency.net/database/ant.farm (accessed October 16, 2020).

22 Hubert Tonka, Jean-Paul Jungmann, and Jean Aubert, "Architecture as a Theoretical Problem," Architectural Design 6 (May 1968), 255.

23 Marc Dessauce, ed., The Inflatable Moment: Pneumatics and Protest in ,68 (New York: Princeton Architectural Press, 1999).

Contrary to Archigram's utopian proposals, which nevertheless contained possibilities for future living, the "Vienna Scene" of Haus-Rucker-Co, Coop Himmelblau, Zuend-up, Nalbach, and Hans Hollein opted for more dystopian postures. **fig.6** Thanks to the support of cultural institutions such as Galerie St. Stephan in Vienna under the auspices of Otto Mauer, the Austrian avant-garde had a platform to meet and experiment with new forms. They particularly embraced the opportunity to develop an alternative to the standard "narrative" mode of exhibiting into one of architectural action. **24** Haus-Rucker-Co, founded in Vienna in 1967 by Laurids Ortner, Günther Zamp Kelp, and Klaus Pinte, explored the performative potential of architecture through installations and happenings using pneumatic structures that aimed at altering the perception of space. **fig.7** As part of what they called their "Mind-Expanding Program," Ortner, Zamp Kelp, and Pinte developed a series of

24 For the important role of Galerie St. Stephan in the development of the Viennese avant-garde scene of the 1960s, see Eva Branscome, *Hans Hollein and Postmodernism: Art and Architecture in Austria, 1958–1985* (London: Routledge, 2016), 161.

fig.7 Laurids Ortner, Günter Zamp Kelp, and Klaus Pinter (Haus-Rucker-Co), *Environment Transformers: Flyhead, Viewatomizer, and Drizzler*, 1968 Photographer: Gert Winkler/Source: courtesy of Gerald Zugmann

25 "Mind Expander", https://www.artbrain.org/haus-rucker-co-mind-expander-project/ (accessed August 31, 2020).

26 "The Mind Expander Chair & Other Inventions from the Far-Out World of 60s Architects Haus-Rucker-Co," https://dangerous-minds.net/comments/the_mind_expander_chair_other_inventions_from_the_far-out (accessed August 30, 2020).

27 Branscome, *Hans Hollein*, 215.

futuristic helmets that intended to provide the wearer with a psychedelic experience. With small "bubbles" placed onto the head, one experienced the environment through a completely different lens. The bee-like eyes affirm the privilege of subjectivity and perception over mobility. **25** Yellow Heart, to name another of their emblematic projects, was a pulsating pneumatic space capsule for two. Inside the bubble, one experienced the surrounding space expanding and flowing out, again in response to the rhythmic swelling of the soft, air-filled chambers. **26**

Architect Hans Hollein is a key figure in the emergence of conceptual architecture amongst the Austrian avant-garde. **27** Educated at the Academy of Fine Arts in Vienna, Hollein had

fig. 8 Hans Hollein *Just Landed: Hans Hollein in His Mobile Office* (1969) Copyright: Private Archive Hollein/Source: courtesy of the Generali Foundation Collection, permanent loan to the Museum der Moderne Salzburg

the opportunity to continue his studies in architecture at the Illinois Institute of Technology in Chicago and the University of California, and to meet and work with some of the American masters, such as Mies van der Rohe, Frank Lloyd Wright, and Richard Neutra. However, as his subsequent career shows, his contact with the counterculture in the United States proved decisive. In his master's thesis, entitled *Plastic Space* (1960), Hollein advocated architecture as a corporeal experience, claiming that "there is no difference between outside and inside space. There is only space." [28]

Hollein's preoccupation with the limits of the human body stemmed from a fascination with space travel. Inspired by the architecture of the spacesuit, "the very best house because you have everything you need," Hollein imagined a human shelter with climate-regulating capacities. According to Marshall McLuhan's definition, dwelling is a means to control body temperature, and, for thousands of years, we have tried to perfect this through means of construction. [29] Today, the most advanced architecture of this kind is the space suit, an architecture that liberates us from the built context and that creates completely new possible relationships between humans and their enviroment. [30]

Hollein's sensibility for irony became visible in his 1967 manifesto *Alles ist Architektur* (Everything is Architecture), [31] a work in which Hollein, according to historian Joseph Rykwert, developed a truly original intuition. [32] Here, Hollein extended the concept

28 Hans Hollein, "Plastic Space" (MA thesis, University of California, Berkeley, 1960).

29 Marshall McLuhan, "Housing: New Look and New Outlook," in *Understanding Media: The Extensions of Man* (New York: McGraw Hill, 1964), 123–130, here 123.

30 "Vorstoss und Rückstoss," editorial in *Bau: Schrift für Architektur und Städtebau* 4 (1966), 65. Quoted from English translation in Branscome, *Hans Hollein*, 194.

31 "Alles ist Architektur (1967)," *Bau: Schrift für Architektur und Städtebau*, 23, no. 1 of 2 (1968), 1–35.

32 Joseph Rykwert, "Irony: Hollein's General Approach," *A + U* special issue on Hans Hollein (February 1985), 194–196, here 194.

33 Branscome, *Hans Hollein*, 161.

34 Hans Hollein, in part of a longer Austrian portrait on Austrian television, as quoted in Andreas Rumpfhuber "Architecture of Immaterial Labour," lecture, December 2013, Volos, Greece, https://www.youtube.com/watch?v=RKSWEW7vYak (accessed January 29, 2021).

35 For an extensive explanation of this argument, see Andreas Rumpfhuber, "The Architect as Entrepreneurial Self: Hans Hollein's TV Performance 'Mobile Office' (1969)," in Peggy Deamer, ed., *The Architect as Worker: Immaterial Labor, the Creative Class, and the Politics of Design* (London: Bloomsbury, 2015), 44–57.

of architecture to include the environment as a whole, proclaiming that "architects have to stop thinking in terms of *building*," urging them instead to focus on non-buildings, invisible architecture, and media environments. In 1969, Hollein designed Mobile Office, an installation made of a PVC membrane that, blown up, created a workspace-on-the-go. **fig.8** **33** "A modern man who changes from place to place does not want to stay in one box, but prefers to carry his home with him," Hollein argued. **34** Hollein envisioned his Mobile Office as an extreme version of an inflatable object, which can easily be packed and inflated with any kind of hoover or source of compressed air. Once inflated, one crawled into the small bubble, entering a personal shell. Compared to Webb's inflatables, Hollein's Mobile Office is more socially critical, as it turns the bubble into a metaphor for the subjectivity of an office worker.

Mobile Office was, above all, a self-conscious media production in which Hollein confidently presented himself as a "creative entrepreneur." **35** Commissioned by an Austrian television company that wanted to promote national intellectuals among the public, the two-minute performance was filmed by a professional film crew. In the movie, we see Hollein arriving at the airport in a small propeller airplane. Upon arrival, he takes out a PVC package, hooks it onto a vacuum cleaner to inflate it, and wriggles himself into the bubble to begin working, as if a routine event. Once confined to the office, Hollein starts drawing a plan of a house before taking a telephone call from a client, in which Hollein confirms that the design is progressing well and agrees to a meeting with the client. Archetypical architectural tools—such as a pencil, ruler, drawing board, eraser, and telephone—are used to evoke the now-redundant work of the architectural office. Hollein's performance both declared the immediate realization of the utopian promises of other bubble inflators and deflated them by showing the architect trapped in a professional routine, much harder to escape than the office itself.

Reconstruction and Redistribution: A Transatlantic Conversation on Architecture, Politics, and Pandemic
Anne Kockelkorn and Reinhold Martin

Between July and August 2020 — several months after the global lockdown due to the COVID-19 pandemic — Anne Kockelkorn and Reinhold Martin engaged in a transatlantic email conversation, focusing on how the inequalities revealed by the pandemic have impacted American society and how this, in turn, impacts the conceptualization of architectural history. The conversation begins with the situation in New York in early July. It investigates

Anne Kockelkorn is Assistant Professor of Architecture and Dwelling at the Architecture Department at TU Delft.

Reinhold Martin is Professor of Architecture at Columbia University's Graduate School of Architecture, Planning and Preservation (GSAPP), founder of the journal *Grey Room*, and director of the Temple Hoyne Buell Center for the Study of American Architecture.

fig.1 Photograph Reinhold Martin July 2020

the modalities of biopolitical infrastructures of care and violence, traces histories of inequality in the United States back to the Reconstruction era, and, finally, reflects on the need for common histories of redistribution.

July 6, 2020
Anne Kockelkorn: New York, one of the most densely populated cities in the world, was an epicenter of the pandemic and an epicenter of the protests against racial killings in the United States. As an architectural historian living close to the Columbia University campus, what did you observe, and live, during the last months of imposed social isolation?

July 10, 2020
Reinhold Martin: Given the speed of change, I should begin by noting that I am writing in early July 2020. At Columbia, we

began moving online to remote instruction on March 9; New York City public schools closed on March 16, and New York State began "sheltering in place" on March 20. Confirmed COVID-19 case numbers in the city's five boroughs (Brooklyn, The Bronx, Manhattan, Queens, Staten Island) peaked on April 6; deaths peaked the following day. As elsewhere, data were and remain imprecise but plentiful, and the trends were clear. In the United States, most of the response has been guided at the state level rather than at the federal or municipal level. As is well known, the White House has combined barbaric bravado with calculated indifference. Consistent with neoliberal doctrine, the plan was not to have a plan.

State-level responses have varied widely. Daily press briefings from New York State Governor Andrew Cuomo became a counter-theater of technocratic "competence" that masked several disastrous early decisions, like the initial hesitation to close and the later decision to return thousands of elderly COVID patients to nursing homes, which by many accounts dramatically increased deaths in these facilities. To date, total confirmed and probable deaths from COVID-19 in New York City are over twenty-three thousand. Even so, the numbers could have been much higher.

Sometime in mid-March, the New York City soundscape changed. Ambulance sirens became nearly constant. Working from home, several blocks from the Columbia campus and near a hospital, has therefore entailed a mix of privilege — as so many others have lost their jobs or risked exposure to keep the city running — and dread. At some point individual ambulances seemed to blend into a single scream. Each announced a life in the balance, another statistic but also another story. In the immediate aftermath of the brutal police killing of George Floyd on May 25 in Minneapolis, helicopters took over. Many Black Lives Matter protest marches and demonstrations passed near or through our neighborhood. Those in which we participated were peaceful, but the helicopters hovering loudly overhead registered the constant threat of state-sanctioned violence against which protesters assembled. These were not separate events. In New York, as in the rest of the United States, the most devastating effects of COVID-19 by far have been on Black and Latinx communities. Each event, however, has had its hardware. The pandemic: ambulances, personal protective equipment, ventilators, and a surreal heterotopia of hospital tents in Central Park set up by a homophobic religious group. The protests: helicopters, guns, batons, riot shields, masks, microphones, tear gas canisters, and statues. In the middle of it all, on June 23, New York State held a primary election in which an unusual number of left-progressive local Democrat candidates — including several democratic socialists — ran strong campaigns. The ballots are still being counted.

July 13, 2020
AK: You have often emphasized how biopolitics, modern economic rationality, and the interests of those who profit from it more than others are interrelated. The calculated indifference of the "plan to not have a plan," however, seems to entirely revoke the biopolitics of hygiene underlying the birth of the modern institution and modern infrastructure. How would you characterize the fragile infrastructures in New York (and the United States) today and their mode of functioning — and what could be strategies for their reappropriation given the increasing collective refusal to put so many lives at risk?

July 17, 2020
RM: This is a complex question. Let me begin again with electoral politics, and then go to biopolitics and governmentality. In New York City, virtually all the left-progressive local campaigns emphasized racial and class discrepancies that led to highly divergent risks associated with COVID-19, and expressed the intersectional nature of these risks with slogans like "Housing is Healthcare." The Black Lives Matter protests have further emphasized the role of the police in maintaining and propagating the social order of the carceral state on a magnitude well beyond that of the reformist, Benthamite "discipline" addressed by Foucault, even as prisons, including New York's notorious Riker's Island, became sites of major COVID outbreaks. Among the most consistent demands made by protesters was to "Abolish the Police," or more modestly, to "Defund the Police," both of which recognized the centrality of specific police techniques to the neoliberal urban order, such as "stop and frisk" practices or the "broken windows"-policing of petty crimes, which imposes harsh penalties for minor offenses (like a broken window) based on the theory that offenders are entrepreneurs making cost-benefit calculations and can be deterred by raising the material costs of committing more serious crimes. This policy is among those that have led to outrageously disproportionate incarceration rates, especially among Black and Hispanic populations.

Unlike Minneapolis, which took more dramatic steps toward police reform, most of the discussion in New York centered on a proposal to cut one billion dollars from the New York Police Department's six-billion-dollar annual budget. After a long, rancorous debate, the New York City Council voted to reallocate an amount close to that (depending on what you count) but in a manner that did not match the goals of substantial defunding. All of this took place amid a budget crisis stemming from the huge economic losses related to the pandemic and the federal government's project of forcing much of the cost onto states and municipalities.

Institutions of biopolitical governmentality, most notably hospitals, bent under the stress. It is worth remembering that the principal object of Foucault's critique was the European welfare state—a form quite different from that in the United States. On one level, with mounting "caseloads" and insufficient "surveillance testing," New York healthcare workers have essentially demanded more (or more competent) governmentality, not less. Or rather, to adapt Foucault's language, they have demanded "not to be governed" in a manner that grants near-absolute sovereignty to market dynamics expressed, for example, as supply chains, procurement, and pricing of personal protective equipment. The plan not to plan is in itself a way of governing. Early on it became clear that, despite decades of prior warning, federal preparedness and stockpiles of necessary medical equipment like personal protective equipment or ventilators were woefully inadequate. This was not accidental; rather, it was the purposeful result of off-loading (over these same decades) what remained of planning onto the anti-planning "dynamism" of markets—most pathetically expressed by the spectacle of individual US states competing with each other for access to price-gouged equipment from third-party suppliers in a microcosmic replay of the neo-Darwinian competition among nation-states for the same supplies and treatments and eventually, perhaps, for a vaccine.

Importantly for the US context, most states, unlike the federal government, are unable to engage in significant deficit spending due to balanced budget requirements. For a state like New York and its hardest-hit municipality, New York City, this has meant that, even with low interest rates, debt has to be offset with income. Thus, with an estimated nine billion dollars in losses due to the pandemic, municipal institutions of biopolitical care like public education, housing, and transportation, and not institutions of state violence like police or prisons, have faced the most severe budget cuts. So in terms of strategies of reappropriation, one possible step for popular movements (like Black Lives Matter, the climate movement, the movement for universal healthcare, and others) is, through left-progressive allies in government, to gain control of budgets from the municipal to the national level and redirect funds from the military and the police toward what we can call "systems of care" like housing, education, and healthcare. Each of these systems has a hardware: a technical infrastructure and an architecture. Reimagining and redesigning that hardware to save lives and improve them, rather than to shorten or end them, is the first task for professionals, educators, and activists working on the built environment.

July 23, 2020
AK: The pandemic renders the need for what you call "institutions of biopolitical care" — schools, hospitals, housing — more visible and more urgent. You state two possible access strategies: first, redirect budgets to those institutions of care — and with it, the empowerment for local governments to resist neoliberal state rescaling and austerity; and, second, reimagine the institution, possibly via the power and skill of the architectural imaginary. Something similar appears in your recent essay "Abolish Oil," when you relate a drinking fountain of the public facility of the New Deal institution being reserved for "WHITES" to the way the New Deal legislation silently facilitated Jim Crow laws—the state and local laws that maintained racial segregation in the Southern states of the United States. I wish to pause a little on that relation between the drinking fountain and infrastructure politics, law, and architecture. Contemporary professional practice tends to neatly separate legal frameworks from their architectural materialization. How to relate the manifestations of biopolitical governing and "architecture" — as in "design of the built environment" for professional practice? Does your understanding of "architecture" as a technological medium of organization and distribution facilitate this rapprochement?

July 25, 2020
RM: In the United States, as in most capitalist countries, law and law enforcement are fundamentally tied to property. As I write, heavily equipped and armed anonymous federal police units — storm troopers by any other name — have deliberately initiated violent confrontations with unarmed protesters on a nightly basis in Portland, Oregon. The most widely reported clashes have taken place in and around Chapman Square, Terry Schrunk Plaza, and Lownsdale Square, a sequence of adjacent plazas in downtown Portland, opposite the Mark O. Hatfield United States Courthouse. Among the most common public excuses made for this provocation, after weeks of mostly peaceful civilian protests, has been the defense of federal property, in this case the Hatfield Courthouse. The backdrop is the toppling or attempted toppling of statues and other monuments to white supremacy in cities across the country, including in Washington, D.C., where

such cultural artifacts are counted among federal property, and their defacement, like that of federal courthouses, is considered a crime. The decision to provoke crimes against property and then enforce laws protecting that property is thus at the heart of this armed assault on legal, constitutionally protected civilian protest in Portland. Wherever it goes from here, this is clearly an electoral strategy on behalf of a beleaguered sovereign, and, should conditions deteriorate, a made-for-TV advertisement for governing by paramilitary force.

This law-and-order project is related to the Jim Crow laws in a manner that compares with New York's notorious "poor doors," some of which are still visible on the facades of new apartment buildings. Like the "separate but equal" drinking fountains, bathrooms, and library entrances of Jim Crow, these contemporary "poor doors" are separate entrances for the mostly Black and Hispanic working-class residents of the "affordable housing" that the city's laws require real estate developers to include as a supplement to market rate speculative units.

Beyond its occasional appearance on television and now, in citizen-journalist videos of the protests, how does architecture-as-medium figure here? Insofar as the police are instruments of an explicitly racist biopolitical order, their extensions into the built environment are equally so. Since the 1970s, architects and urbanists have incorporated police functions like "defensible space" and "eyes on the street" into instruments of biopolitical care like public housing; these functions have, in turn, been taken up by the very police discourse that was, directly or indirectly, responsible for the death of George Floyd. I am referring to the "broken windows" policing I mentioned earlier. Translated into the language we are speaking, the window, like the "poor door," is therefore an order-producing medium; its breaking signals the onset of disorder, which, according to the theory, can be deterred by one of two things: watchful "eyes on the street" or asymmetrical police violence.

July 30, 2020
AK: Aiming to understand the increased inequality caused by COVID-19, you bring three objects of scrutiny to the fore: property (understood as the political DNA of the United States), television shows and their infrastructure, and the racist policing of public institutions. Architecture, then, is what mediates a social order of what you have called dispossession along the axes of race and class, which can be traced back to the plantations of the North American colonies. If we, as architectural historians, are to construct a usable past relevant to confront future challenges,

how can we provide the grounds to conceive of measures that refund biopolitical institutions of care and to conceptualize their architectural articulations?

August 7, 2020

RM: There are indeed histories that may prove "usable" not only in opposing an authoritarian project but also in replacing it with a genuine left-progressive vision. The New Deal, and in particular, those New Deal policies and programs that recognized the strength of an organized working class and the necessity of large-scale economic and ecological planning, have provided historical support to ambitious proposals like the Green New Deal. In the article on oil abolition, I argue that the historical imagination should reach further back, toward the abortive, incomplete project of post-Civil War Reconstruction — the massive effort among Southern Black workers, a Black intelligentsia, and Northern white abolitionists to build what W. E. B. Du Bois called an "abolition democracy."

Thinking this way that every negation must also be an affirmation — that abolition must not only negate oppression but affirm democracy — means in a sense that for every "de-" word (decolonize, decarceral, defund, etc.) we need a "re-" word that does not restore but reconstruct. In the neoliberal US context, systems of care have been built upon inequalities, instabilities, and precarities that have been revealed and exacerbated by the current crisis and by the longer, slower crisis of planetary warming, the effects of which are no less racialized. Reconstruction, then, means redistribution. In solidarity with activists, architects and urbanists might therefore ask: What principles, practices, and histories of redistribution can assist in reimagining new systems of education, healthcare, and housing, particularly as the climate crisis looms?

August 16, 2020

AK: As neoliberal ideologies are in full operation within the discursive framework of architecture, redistribution has become increasingly unthinkable. I wonder how it may become intelligible to architects that the impact (or absence) of these histories is intertwined with the impact and aftermath of the pandemic; how it may become intelligible that architecture — discourse and materialization — mediates dispossession to the one or access to resources to the other, depending on which body or subjectivity they cater to.

During the short twentieth century, modern architecture and urban planning played a crucial role in implementing a governmental attempt towards redistribution. At the same time, their histories are tainted with their uncanny other, be it colonial exploitation, racism, state terror, or capitalist complicity. Revisiting those stories to construct a usable past could mean expanding the picture within which they are set and acknowledging their modes of exclusion and amnesia; or reconstructing role models by setting them within the purview of their adversaries, such as the urban policies of Red Vienna during the 1920s that provided the backdrop against which early Austrian neoliberal theorists, Friedrich von Hayek and Ludwig von Mises, established their doctrines to protect an immaculate world market. Yet I have no answer to the need for both nuanced histories that acknowledge this contradictory heritage and the (re-)construction of operational programs that feed into discourse and build on the economic disposition that sustains them. I return the question: If we accept that a singular story, no matter how relevant, cannot change the power of discourse, what could be today the economic and technological grounds on which architectural histories of redistribution can take hold?

August 23, 2020

RM: One place to begin if not to end is familiar, since architecture does have a radical historiographical tradition, albeit a minor one. Take an example from the history of liberal capitalism that is strangely close to what we have been discussing yet also astonishingly far: the collaborative work by the group of historians known as the Venice School, the book *The American City: From the Civil War to the New Deal*, edited by Giorgio Ciucci, Francesco Dal Co, Mario Manieri-Elia, and Manfredo Tafuri. You could say that the whole book attempts to answer the question famously posed in 1906 by another economist of relevance to us, Werner Sombart: *Why is there no socialism in the United States?* Given that book's publication date (1973, neoliberalism's *annus mirabilis*), a lack of engagement with the contradictions of post-Civil War Reconstruction in the South—perhaps the greatest doomed experiment in material redistribution in US history—is understandable. However, a failure to recognize the role played by race as well as capital in shaping the American cities, and indeed in shaping imperial capitals like London, Paris, or Berlin, is less understandable.

Reconstruction entailed, among other things, a monumental program of land reform that was thwarted by racial capitalism. To understand its importance, and perhaps to recover the project of reparations for slavery to which those reforms were dedicated, historians of architecture must look at the land underneath their buildings. Looking skyward in the immediately following Gilded

Age (considered in detail in *The American City*), wealth was massively redistributed in the other direction: upwards. This redistribution is literalized in the Chicago School skyscrapers with which Tafuri begins his contribution to the volume: the skyscraper as an instrument of upward redistribution. Reading these buildings as reified testaments to architecture's alleged helplessness, Tafuri is unable to see in them the primitive accumulation of slavery and its aftermath—and of course, the expropriation of Indigenous lands—on which they were built.

The later developments in neoliberal thought in reaction to social democratic reforms in Europe that you mention (Red Vienna was another preoccupation for Tafuri and his colleagues) are related to this earlier history. Important revisionist architectural history has been written on both subjects since then (think, for example, of Joanna Merwood Salisbury's work on the Chicago School and Eve Blau's on Red Vienna); but much remains to be done. Tafuri's negativity was realistic, but it was also that of a bourgeois, white intelligentsia: architects and their theorists. The legacy of W. E. B. Du Bois, whose *Black Reconstruction in America* (1935) radically transformed the historiography, was to recognize anti-racist, anti-capitalist struggle everywhere and to expose more about the oppressors than the oppressors knew about themselves.

A related crisis looms behind all that we are discussing. As I write, fires burn again in California's forests, and the Sahara's edges grow drier daily. Tafuri was skeptical of the ecological turn of the 1970s and, in particular, of the technocratic pretensions of environmental design, very little of which could be construed as truly anti-capitalist. But when we put climate change and capitalism together, and when we learn to see race and gender as well as class as both the preconditions and the products of the latter—racial capitalist patriarchy—then the battle lines for historians are redrawn. Because if, as Walter Benjamin said so well, history is a backward-facing angel, that angel's rear-view mirror looks toward the future.

To return then to where we began: A submicroscopic virus continues to rewrite human history as the fragile interdependence of society and nature. Masked, we now fear inhaling one another's breath. Social distancing is not spatial; it is pulmonary. The upcoming US election will likely be a referendum on the viral threat. Meanwhile, uncounted molecules of carbon dioxide emitted by our buildings and by our machines across the modern era have trapped heat in our atmosphere, differentially warming the air we breathe. It may seem unrelated that, pinned to the Minneapolis pavement by the police, George Floyd's last words were "I can't breathe." But what modernity called space we must now call air. And there will be no redistribution, no justice, no peace, and indeed no change until we learn to see the complex of forces at work in that air, which, like the land underneath a building, can be life-sustaining and deadly at once.

November 26, 2020

AK: It is difficult to fathom that if not for the pandemic, Democrats would not have won the US presidential race. In the meantime, Europe and the United States seem to be separated by more than just another lockdown: by different calculation modes of "affordable" deaths. Not that this is news, but it has become more visible. How would you describe architecture's implication in the amalgam of racial and environmental justice, the art of governing, biopolitical care, and a viral threat during these last weeks? Are these all simply mediatic events that will be quickly forgotten, or do they represent an epistemic shift that allows for different formations of truth?

December 6, 2020

RM: It has now been about a month since the US election. The fact that a majority of Republican voters do not yet appear to accept the results is striking less as evidence of misinformation or denialism than of an underlying power struggle among classes, races, and other social groupings. No less striking is the assault on left-progressive movements now being waged in the Democratic Party on behalf of neoliberal suburban "moderates" who, rather than being held responsible for the electoral setbacks incurred by the Democrats in the congressional races, are openly celebrated as a substitute for the party's former working-class base. Radical posturing aside, architecture as a cultural form and as a profession, and architects as exemplary members of the professional-managerial class, stand firmly on the side of the neoliberals. With some notable exceptions, there have been few calls from the professional-managerial class for material redistribution, few concrete proposals that respond to those voices coming from the streets asserting that "Housing is Healthcare" and demanding to "Defund the Police."

Now too, after months of deliberate failure to manage the pandemic, economic crisis looms. As I write, a path to recovery that does not intensify existing inequalities is all but blocked. Most ominously, the neoliberal hegemony has responded to the widely popular Green New Deal with the open admission that the plan for climate change is the same as for COVID-19: distribute casualties and collateral damage according to a sliding scale of power rather than redistribute resources to prevent those casualties in the first place. Still, we appear to have avoided—or at least delayed—the worst. Now, as the sense of relief slowly passes, begins the hard work of reconstruction.

Scientific Board
Tom Avermaete
Eve Blau
Mario Carpo
Maarten Delbeke
Mari Hvattum
Caroline Jones
Laurent Stalder
Philip Ursprung

Editorial Committee
Irina Davidovici
Erik Wegerhoff
Matthew Wells
Nina Zschocke

Academic Editor
Adam Jasper

Copy-editing
Jennifer Bartmess

Proofreading
Thomas Skelton-Robinson

Graphic concept and design
büro uebele visuelle kommunikation, Stuttgart
Dominik Bissem, Adrian Dickhoff, Christian Lindermann, and Andreas Uebele

Production
Offsetdruckerei Karl Grammlich GmbH

Typeface
GT Eesti

Paper
MaxiScript 90 g/sm
MaxiScript 170 g/sm

Cover illustration
Hans Hollein *Just landed. Hans Hollein in his mobile office* (1969)
Copyright: Private Archive Hollein. Courtesy Generali Foundation Collection—Permanent Loan to the Museum der Moderne Salzburg.

Bibliographic information published by the Deutsche Nationalbibliothek
The Deutsche Nationalbibliothek lists this publication in the Deutsche Nationalbibliografie; detailed bibliographic data are available on the Internet under http://portal.dnb.de.

ISBN 978-3-85676-415-9
ISSN 2504-2068

gta Verlag

ETHzürich